Crime Control and Community

Crime Control and Community
The new politics of public safety

edited by

Gordon Hughes
Adam Edwards

WILLAN
PUBLISHING

Published by

Willan Publishing
Culmcott House
Mill Street, Uffculme
Cullompton, Devon
EX15 3AT, UK
Tel: +44(0)1884 840337
Fax: +44(0)1884 840251
e-mail: info@willanpublishing.co.uk
website: www.willanpublishing.co.uk

Published simultaneously in the USA and Canada by

Willan Publishing
c/o ISBS, 5824 N.E. Hassalo St,
Portland, Oregon 97213-3644, USA
Tel: +001(0)503 287 3093
Fax: +001(0)503 280 8832
e-mail: info@isbs.com
website: www.isbs.com

First published 2002

ISBN 1-903240-54-9 (cased)

British Library Cataloguing-in-Publication Data
A catalogue record for this book is available from the British Library

Printed and bound by T.J. International, Padstow, Cornwall
Typeset by GCS, Leighton Buzzard, Beds.

For Priya and colleagues in the
Highfields Community Association
(Adam Edwards)

For my sister Sylv
(Gordon Hughes)

Contents

Notes on contributors

Adam Edwards is Senior Lecturer in Criminology at Nottingham Trent University. His principal research interest is in the politics and ethics of policy responses to crime and disorder. He was Director of the UK Economic and Social Research Council's (ESRC) research seminar series on *Policy Responses to Transnational Organised Crime*, and participated in the ESRC's *Local Governance Research Programme* by conducting a comparative analysis of local crime prevention strategies in the East Midlands. Findings from this research have been published in a number of international journals.

Gordon Hughes is Senior Lecturer in Social Policy at the Open University. Recent publications include *Understanding Crime Prevention: social control, risk and late modernity* (Open University Press 1998), *Crime Prevention and Community Safety: new directions* (Sage 2002, co-edited with John Muncie and Eugene McLaughlin), and *Youth Justice: critical readings* (Sage 2002, co-edited with Muncie and McLaughlin). His current interests lie in the comparative field of local community safety partnerships and the local politics of urban security, and communitarianism and the contested politics of community. He is currently a member of the Milton Keynes Crime and Community Safety Partnership.

Eugene McLaughlin is Senior Lecturer in Criminology and Social Policy at the Open University. His primary research interest is police governance and he is currently researching the future of police complaints in the UK. He has written extensively on policing and criminology, his most recent book being the *Sage Dictionary of Criminology* (Sage 2001), edited with John Muncie.

Nick Tilley is Professor of Sociology at Nottingham Trent University and a Visiting Professor at the Jill Dando Institute of Crime Science, University College London. He is also a consultant to the Research, Development and Statistics Directorate at the Home Office, and has published extensively in the areas of policing, crime prevention and programme evaluation methodology.

Roy Coleman lectures in criminal justice at Liverpool John Moores University. He is currently completing a PhD thesis entitled 'Surveillance and Social Order: a case study of closed circuit television'. He has published articles (with Joe Sim) in *the British Journal of Sociology* and the *International Review of Law, Computers and Technology*.

Joe Sim is Professor of Criminology, School of Law, Liverpool John Moores University. His publications include *Medical Power in Prisons, British Prisons* (with Mike Fitzgerald), and *Prisons Under Protest* (with Phil Scraton and Paula Skidmore).

Dave Whyte is a Lecturer in Criminology at Manchester Metropolitan University. He has published widely in criminology and the crimes of the powerful. Recent publications include articles in *Studies in Political Economy* and *Policy and Politics*.

Kevin Stenson is Professor of Social Policy and Criminology, and Director of the Social Policy Research Group at Buckinghamshire Chilterns University College. His interests lie in the fields of criminological theory, and governance, and has carried out research on social work practice, the social organisation and control of youth, community policing and safety, social deprivation and regeneration strategies, inter-ethnic conflict, parent support programmes and early years crime prevention strategies. Recent publications include (edited with Robert R. Sullivan) *Crime, Risk and Justice: the politics of crime control in liberal democracies* (Willan 2000).

Janet Foster has recently joined the Sociology Department at the London School of Economics. She has had extensive experience as a qualitative researcher on crime, community and policing issues. Her most recent book, *Docklands: cultures in conflict, world in collisions* (UCL Press 1999), based on a two-year ethnographic study of urban change and conflict, documents the competing visions of urban change, and the social exclusion and racism which emanated from it.

Simon Hallsworth is Deputy Director of the Centre for Social Evaluation Research at London Guildhall University. His research interests include examining penal trends in late modernity, and contemporary changes in local crime prevention. He is currently completing a research project examining street crime in south-east London and is working with community safety providers in Lambeth to develop a youth justice strategy for the borough.

Preface

The genesis of this book can be traced back to a conversation between the editors and one of the contributors, Kevin Stenson, at that splendid Liverpool institution, the Adelphi Hotel, in 1999. The context was the biannual conference of the British Society of Criminology during which, for the first time, a specific stream was set aside for local studies of community safety and community-based crime control. For the three of us, the debates in this stream represented a long overdue recognition by mainstream British criminology of the salience of community safety strategies for the future direction of crime control policy and its relationship to the 'discipline' of criminology. In the course of this conversation we discussed the need for a longer-term project considering the lessons that can be drawn from the practice of community-based crime control in different localities. Over the past decade there has been an accumulation of detailed, qualitative case studies of this practice in different English localities, which both justifies and enables lesson-drawing through *intra*national comparisons. Taken collectively, these local case studies suggest that what is most insightful about the conduct of community-based crime control is its diversity. Whereas the predominant trend in official discourse has been to generalise particular instances of 'best' practice in the search for universal models of 'what works', our preference is to reverse this logic of policy change and learning to recognise particularity and distinguish the locally specific from the genuinely universal. The discovery of what practices are genuinely universal and are, therefore, robust enough to stand translation from one locality to others with often very diverse social, economic and political histories is a key objective of policy-oriented learning and not its simple, unproblematic, starting point. Discovering what, if any, crime control practices are universal is a key contribution that social science can make to the process of policy-oriented learning and provides the core rationale of this edited collection and the broader project of crime control policy analysis of which it is a part.

In shifting the terms of debate away from the assertion of universal models of what works towards recognition of the particular contexts and practices of crime control, this project challenges policymakers to question the possibility of learning from and transferring practices among diverse localities. How transferable are these practices? What are the potential consequences of their transfer? Who is actually involved in decisions about what works, for whom and in what contexts? Questioning the possibility of learning in this way reveals the political and ethical content of governmental processes like crime control. While there is a strong tradition in Anglo-American official discourse of divorcing 'policy' from 'politics', defining the latter as the provenance of legislatures and regarding the former as the apolitical administration of their laws, studies of the implementation of public policy have consistently demonstrated the omnipresence of political agency throughout the entire process of policy formulation, implementation and evaluation. The other core theme of our approach to policy change and learning is, therefore, to understand the exercise of political power inherent in the conduct, not just the formulation, of crime control policy.

In turn, community-based strategies provide an acid test of policy-oriented learning about contemporary crime control. The appeal to community is at the epicentre of major changes in the relationship of citizens to political authorities in Britain and other advanced liberal democracies. The perceived failure of attempts to govern through public bureaucracies and through quasi-markets has provoked increasing interest in the 'third way' of governing through partnerships of public, private and voluntary organisations. Whether public-private partnerships are regarded as a genuinely alternative method of governing or just as another forum in which advocates of public service and private interest struggle to define the ends of public policy, their establishment raises important questions over the legitimacy of directly involving private interests in public government. This is especially the case in the emotionally charged field of crime control where the direct participation of communities in their own government can, conceivably, mean anything from attending a cursory public meeting through to vigilante action and the exacting of 'street justice' from suspected offenders. The unintended, as well as intended, consequences of introducing universal models of 'what works' into very diverse social contexts is thus of immediate practical as well as policy and theoretical interest. Indeed one of the distinguishing qualities of the contributions to this edited volume is the finding that issues of legitimacy, equity and justice, far from being the preserve of 'ivory tower' theorising that is a distraction from the immediate, practical concerns of crime reduction, are actually part of the everyday dilemmas encountered by crime control practitioners sent out into 'the community' to foster partnership work.

This collection presents a point of departure for an approach to policy-oriented learning that affirms the practical adequacy of political and normative theories of crime control, recognises the effect of the particular local contexts in which crime control policies are implemented and, in doing so, builds a more determinate understanding of control by distinguishing locally specific practices from those that are genuinely universal. The focus of this text is primarily on the processes of community-based crime control, rather than on its outcomes for rates of crime and disorder, which reflects the orientation of qualitative case study research in English localities. We hope, however, that this volume can contribute to a broader programme of intranational and trans-national comparative research into the conduct and outcomes of local crime control in Britain and in other advanced liberal societies.

We wish to acknowledge the contributors for their commitment to this project and for their patience in putting up with our demands as editors. Special thanks also go to our publisher Brian Willan for his support and continuing enthusiasm for our collective project.

Chapter 1

Introduction: the community governance of crime control

Adam Edwards and Gordon Hughes

In December 2001, as we were finalising this edited volume, a story broke in the British media about the murder of a suspected sex offender on the Kirkholt housing estate in Rochdale, Greater Manchester, in the North of England (BBC 2001a). George Crawford, who was due to face trial on ten charges of child sexual abuse, had been beaten to death in an attack which both his brother and local police thought was connected to these charges. Students of the recent history of crime control in England may note the irony of vigilante 'street justice' on an estate made famous by Home Office action research into the virtues of situational crime prevention and, in particular, the prevention of repeat victimisation (Forrester *et al* 1990). It is, however, precisely in the vacuum of political authority generated by the perceived failure of government strategies to control crime that vigilante action thrives.

In England it is reported that such action has intensified in recent years, especially in relation to attacks on actual or suspected sex offenders (BBC 2000a). It is also thought that a particular catalyst for these attacks has been the media campaign to 'name and shame' paedophiles conducted by one tabloid newspaper, the *News of the World*, in July and August 2000 in the wake of the sexual assault and murder of the infant Sarah Payne (*News of the World*, 23 and 24 July, 6 August 2000). Following this campaign, in which names, residential details and in some instances the pictures of sex offenders were published, one male bearing the same name as a sex offender 'outed' by the *News of the World* had to be given police protection after letters accusing him of child abuse were circulated to 500 residents around his south London home by an organisation claiming to provide 'a service to the community' (BBC

2000b). In another incident an innocent male who resembled one of the sex offenders pictured in the *News of the World* campaign was attacked in Bradford (BBC 2000c). Both of these incidents were, however, over-shadowed by five nights of rioting on the Paulsgrove estate in Portsmouth when over 100 people carrying the picture of an alleged sex offender, as it appeared in the *News of the World*, besieged and ransacked his home, fire-bombed his sister's car and then assaulted the police who were protecting the suspect (BBC 2000d). While the editor of the *News of the World* condemned the violence and called for 'vigilance not vigilantism', she defended the campaign, arguing that 'every parent has an absolute right to know if they have a convicted child offender living in their neighbourhood' and that the newspaper had a mandate for the campaign expressed through 'overwhelming public support' and given 'the disturbing truth that the authorities are failing to properly monitor the activities of paedophiles in the community' (BBC 2000c).

The trend towards vigilante groups exacting their own justice from suspected offenders is not restricted to the highly emotive issue of child sexual abuse but relates to a more general lack of faith in the ability of statutory authorities to deliver public safety. Following the conviction of the Norfolk farmer, Tony Martin, in April 2000 for shooting and killing a young burglar on his premises, Members of Parliament representing rural constituencies claimed there was strong support among their electorates for 'defending themselves if the police were unable to help them' in the context of severe reductions in service from rural police forces (BBC 2000e). Vigilante action was also feared by local councillors in Bangor, North Wales, when residents on the Maesgeirchen estate responded to an upsurge in vandalism and attacks on the homes of pensioners in August 2001 by patrolling the estate. One local councillor sympathised with the frustration of local residents at the paucity of not only policing but general statutory services on the estate, while another actually expressed tacit support arguing that, 'As a home care worker on the estate, I have seen youngsters climbing over roofs and banging on doors. There are residents who are 70, 80 and 90 years old who do not want this; they are frightened to open their doors … These men who have been going out on patrol have been doing more than the police and if they are not doing any harm, good luck to them' (BBC 2001b).

Community governance and the crisis of legitimate crime control

These stories of vigilante 'service to the community' exemplify a broader crisis of legitimacy facing statutory authorities in advanced liberal democracies. The willingness of citizens to take the law into their own hands forms part of a more general disenchantment with political authorities and, more dangerously, with the process of liberal democracy itself (Pharr and Putnam 2000). In the context of this crisis, the appeal to 'community' in crime control and across the spectrum of public policy can be understood in terms of the struggle by political authorities to relegitimate their powers. Yet, whereas the active participation of local communities in their own government has been promoted by successive administrations in Britain over the past two decades as an unqualified 'good' thing, both for the democratic accountability and economic efficiency of liberal government, experiments in what has become known as 'community governance' have provoked major controversies among social scientific commentators (Hughes and Mooney 1998).

The recent intensification of vigilante action in British localities has a broader salience beyond the immediate exigencies of controlling sex offenders, burglars and the incivilities of youth gangs etc., precisely because it exemplifies the extent to which the legitimacy of political authorities has been eroded and popular consent to be governed withdrawn. From this perspective, the real significance of experiments in 'community governance', beyond official platitudes on increasing the economy of 'joined-up' government, reducing duplication of effort and bureaucratic waste, 'empowering' citizens to take greater responsibility for their own security and well-being etc., is the reformulation of sovereignty for *social* modes of governing (Stenson 1999, and in this volume). What distinguishes this social mode of governing from that of the welfare state is the replacement of universally provided services, whether healthcare, education, housing, public safety etc. by inter-ventions that are targeted on those cohorts of the population in which problems of chronic illness, poor educational attainment, housing blight and crime etc. are thought to be concentrated. This use of community, to signify 'hot-spots' of trouble, is one way of interpreting the distinctive 'third way' approach to governing adopted by the administrations of New Labour since their election in May 1997 (Stenson and Edwards 2001; Stenson in this volume; Edwards in this volume). Neo-Marxist studies have also interpreted community governance as a means of reasserting sovereign authority, but with a particular focus on the political-economic rationale of this authority in advancing the interests of capital (Coleman and Sim 1998; Coleman, Sim and Whyte in this volume; Jessop 2000).

Alternatively exercises in community governance, in which responsibility for governing is shared between 'partnerships' of statutory, voluntary and commercial organisations, have been interpreted as the means by which responsibility for goods, such as security, is being genuinely devolved from statutory authorities to private citizens and organisations (Stoker 2000). One influential analysis in criminology describes this process under the heading of 'responsibilisation'. It is claimed that over the past two decades, private citizens and commercial firms have been encouraged to assume greater responsibility for their own security and well-being (Garland 2001). This signifies the erosion, even 'death', of public, 'social' modes of government, characteristic of the welfare state, which aim to promote collective solidarity and shared security. These have been replaced increasingly by a Darwinian, competitive struggle for survival, which favours the strongest and most resourceful. In this climate, those individuals and population groups least fitted for the struggle suffer from, at best, 'benign neglect' by state agencies. In crime control, as in other spheres of policy, this approach to government seeks to manage the risks presented by poor and disaffected populations. It also seeks to 'liberate' wealth creators from the burden of redistributing resources to the poor and weak, in the belief that public authorities cannot, and should not, intervene to correct the inequalities of free market economies (Rose 1996; O'Malley 1992; Taylor 1999).

Yet others have interpreted community governance as a genuine attempt to formulate a new model of 'associative', 'participatory' and 'cosmopolitan' liberal democracy, in which the interests and needs of diverse communities of interest and identity can be recognised and addressed (Hirst 2000; Held 1995). Here the deficiencies of representative democracy and government through public bureaucracies are contrasted with the potential of public-private partnerships and networks to give voice to the real pluralism of social relations in advanced liberal societies (Hughes 1998 and this volume; Foster in this volume). In place of the 'one size fits all' model of the welfare state and the 'Darwinianism' of the neoliberal state, critical pluralists advocate the cultivation of 'self-governing communities' allowed to regulate the affairs of their own members according to the values shared by those members. So, for example, cities could be divided into 'permissive' and 'restrictive' zones with regard to the use of various sexual and narcotic services (Hirst 2000). It is argued that far from exacerbating conflict between communities of interest and identity with divergent norms, such a system of self-governing communities would reduce inter-community friction and restore public faith in, and consent to, political authority, 'People would not be criminalized for matters of value choice – remember when homosexuality was a crime in the UK? In consequence they would not come to hold the whole apparatus of law in contempt. For that core of common offences, agreed by all, the police would enjoy greater cooperation and respect' (Hirst 2000: 142).

The community governance of crime control

These competing interpretations of the real meaning and salience of appeals for community governance are indicative of the capacious way in which notions of community have been used in relation to crime control policy. The elusiveness of what 'community' actually means in relation to crime control, the absence of any clear consensus over what constitutes 'community-based crime control', 'community safety', 'community crime prevention' and 'community policing' etc., is a product not of intellectual vacuity but of the political struggles to define the responsibilities for, and strategies of, crime control. Rather than reducing an explanation of community governance to *either* the reformulation of sovereign authority *or* making private citizens more responsible for their self-government *or* the search for a new model of associative democracy *or* a more economical government of crime etc., it is better to see these objectives as coterminous. They are being advanced by different policy actors who each regard the capacious character of community governance as an opportunity for advancing their particular agenda for policy change. Whether a particular governing strategy wins out and defines the uses of community or whether crime control policy drifts chaotically along, vacillating between equally matched coalitions of policy advocates is a contingent outcome of broader political struggles and not the unfolding of some inevitable and inexorable logic of social change (see Hallsworth in this volume).

The reassertion of sovereign authority

The changing uses of 'community' in crime control can be illustrated through reference to discernible periods of law and order politics in postwar Britain. The reassertion of a 'paternalistic' sovereign authority can be discerned in the establishment of the Community Development Projects (CDP) by the Wilson and Callaghan administrations of the 1970s. Significantly, the CDPs were the brainchild of a Home Office civil servant, Derek Morrell, and were implemented in the context of concerns over the consequences of urban deprivation and racial tension for serious public disorder, as had been experienced in the US during the 'hot summers' of the mid- to late-1960s (Higgins *et al* 1983). Morrell's paternalism was premised on a 'pathological' view of 'individual, family and community malfunctioning' (Higgins *et al* 1983: 25) and was challenged by the Marxist-inspired coordinators of the Coventry CDP for concentrating on the consequences of poverty in the rising crime rate rather than its causes in the structural inequalities produced by capital accumulation (Higgins *et al* 1983: 33). The consequence of this political struggle over the rationale of the CDPs was their termination by Callaghan's administration following the publication of a report on the CDPs, *Gilding the Ghetto*. This was produced by local policy actors who had participated in this scheme and who were highly critical of Morrell's vision (CDP, 1977).

Responsibilisation

A decade later, in the aftermath of major urban rioting in English cities, Lord Scarman offered a more structural interpretation of the root causes of crime and disorder by identifying the failures of social policy to ameliorate inequality and disadvantage and the role of the police themselves in undermining relations with local communities in Brixton, Toxteth and other multicultural inner-city neighbourhoods in which disorders had occurred (Scarman 1981). In the seismic change to the national political context marked by the election of Margaret Thatcher's 'New Right' administration in 1979, however, the redistributive aspects of Lord Scarman's Report, along with the wider lessons drawn from the failure of the CDPs, were ignored in favour of a vision of limited government intervention for social welfare. This was combined with an expanded capacity for maintaining public order and exercising social control through investment in the police and criminal justice system (Downes and Morgan 1994). Given the political pressures of rapid increases in recorded crime, further instances of major urban disorder throughout the 1980s and Treasury resistance to further public expenditure on policing and criminal justice, the Thatcher administrations switched tack by arguing, in the Home Office Circular 8/84, that crime prevention cannot be left to the police alone but, 'is a task for the whole community' (Home Office 1984). This appeal to community, for private citizens to assume greater responsibility for their own security, is described by criminologists as a 'responsibilisation' strategy and was ideal for a Conservative national administration wishing to distance itself from crime control policy failures while maintaining its rejection of the welfare state (Benyon and Edwards 1997). It is in this context that the vision of community governance as a 'responsibilisation' strategy prevailed against alternative conceptions of community-based crime control.

The reformulation of sovereign authority

As we have argued elsewhere, however, an unintended consequence of this vision was the devolution of significant decisionmaking powers to local policy actors, especially Labour Party-led municipal authorities, who used their involvement in experiments in local crime prevention partnerships, funded in particular by the Conservative national administration's 'Safer Cities' programme, to redefine crime control in terms of 'community safety' (Hughes 1998 and this volume; Edwards and Benyon 2000). Through the concept of community safety Labour municipal authorities and their national policymaking bodies, the Association of Metropolitan Authorities (AMA 1990) and Association of District Councils (ADC 1990), broadened crime control strategies beyond the narrow concern with situational crime prevention to encompass measures focusing on the social and economic causes of crime.

This philosophy was articulated in the landmark report of a Home Office sponsored working group, headed by the independent consultant James Morgan, into *Safer Communities: The Local Delivery of Crime Prevention Through the Partnership Approach* (Home Office 1991). In addition to measures for reducing the opportunities for crime to be committed, the Morgan Report advocated 'employment and training programmes, youth programmes, community development programmes and neighbourhood initiatives' among a raft of other policies for 'tackling the causes of crime' through social and economic regeneration (Home Office 1991: 32). Although sponsored by the Home Office's 'Standing Conference on Crime Prevention' the Morgan Report was produced by an independent working group and its recommendations to shift more resources towards the poor were rejected by the Conservative government that claimed it did not wish to burden local authorities and local taxpayers with a statutory duty in this area of policy (Home Office 1992).

Notwithstanding this political setback, the Morgan Report marked the start of a rapid expansion in local community safety strategies fuelled by resources from national grant aid programmes such as the Single Regeneration Budget. It also influenced the reformulation of the national Labour Party opposition's crime control policies prior to the election of 'New Labour' in May 1997. Subsequently recommendations from the Morgan Report informed the provision of a statutory duty placed on all district local authorities and constabularies to form partnerships for the reduction of crime and disorder. The election of New Labour marked the emergence of another vision of community governance influenced by the 'communitarian' philosophy of the American sociologist Amitai Etzioni (1995) whose views on balancing the rights of private citizens with their responsibilities to the wider public interest have found favour with Prime Minister Blair and Chancellor Brown (Crawford 2001; Hughes 1996). It is with reference to this communitarian philosophy that some distinguish the community governance of crime control under New Labour as not just an exercise in shifting responsibility for security onto private citizens but also the means by which the national state seeks to reassert its sovereign authority over the 'hard to reach', 'socially excluded' populations that were 'benignly neglected' under successive Conservative administrations post-1979 (Stenson and Edwards 2001). In these terms community governance is seen as a means of 'joining-up' local strategies for the reduction of crime and disorder with other programmes aimed at the social and economic regeneration of excluded populations, such as the New Deal for Communities, Neighbourhood Renewal Programme, Surestart and Connexions etc. (Social Exclusion Unit 1998; Neighbourhood Renewal Unit 2001).

It could, however, be argued that there is an irony in the effect of New Labour's project of reasserting sovereign authority over socially excluded populations. Precisely because the post-1979 Conservative administrations had a greater interest in blocking social investment in these populations rather than directing the implementation of what residual interventions were made through competitive grant aid, greater discretion was actually given to local partnerships to define the scope and content of community governance. Conversely, New Labour's interest in the minutiae of policy implementation, its enthusiastic adoption of performance management etc., has constrained local crime control policymaking around the relatively narrow notions of crime and disorder reduction and, in the process, undermined the imaginative links that local partnerships were making between crime, housing, education and labour markets and other areas of social policy while their community safety strategies were being ignored by the Conservatives (Hughes, Stenson and Edwards in this volume).

Sovereignty, citizenship and the paradox of community governance

These political struggles, to define the scope and content of the community governance of crime control in relatively narrow (reducing the opportunities for 'crime' and 'disorder') or expansive (enhancing public safety and reducing the 'harms' associated with local social and economic change) terms, are one way of interpreting appeals to community during New Labour's first term of office (1997–2001). Recent events have, however, added further complexity to the uses of community in this area of policymaking.

The series of major disturbances in the northern cities of Oldham, Burnley and Bradford following the re-election of New Labour in the summer of 2001 and the subsequent review of 'Community Cohesion' headed by Ted Cantle placed the relationship of pluralism and citizenship at the epicentre of debates over community governance (Home Office, 2001). Echoing the Scarman Report produced two decades earlier, the Cantle Report identified social policy failures as a significant cause of the riots. Where, however, the Scarman Report spoke in general terms about the need for better coordinated and more accountable social policy, the Cantle Report details the failure of national and local government decisionmakers to address the problem of governing heterogeneous populations. National government policies for urban regeneration are criticised for forcing communities of interest to compete against each other for limited grant aid, necessarily producing high-profile winners and losers in the regeneration game. Local government policies are criticised for failing to communicate clear criteria for the targeting of certain neighbourhoods rather than others leading, certainly in the case of Bradford, to the perception that 'black' communities were being favoured over disadvantaged white communities, a perception that was subsequently exploited for political advantage by extreme right-wing organisations such as the British National Party (BNP).

The significance of the Cantle Report for current debates over the community governance of crime control in Britain cannot be underestimated as it provides official recognition of a problematic paradox at the heart of all appeals to community governance. If this appeal is seen as a means of relegitimating sovereign authority in the future, by enabling the direct participation of private interests, it nonetheless opens public government out to existing conflicts between competing communities of interest and identity in the here and now. The advocacy of community governance therefore has the liability of *affirming* rather than *transforming* these tensions (Young 2001; and see Hughes, Foster, Edwards and Stenson in this volume).

If the institutionalisation of conflict is a liability of community governance *per se*, it is especially the case in the highly emotive and value-laden policy field of crime control. In his conception of 'self-governing communities', Hirst (2000: 141ff.) argues that we should accept the reality of social fragmentation into 'communities of choice' and that political authority should be devolved to these communities who would then be charged with governing themselves, rather than a particular community imposing its interests and values on everyone else under the guise of universal sovereign law and *the* public interest. The problem, indeed utopianism, of this vision of community governance and the allied notion of 'multiple public orders' (Johnston 2000), is that it presumes a neat fit between a community of interest and a geographical territory. Indeed Hirst makes this point explicit in his invitation to 'imagine cities clearly divided into permissive and restrictive zones' (2000: 43). Conversely, the withdrawal of political consent, from the riots of the Paulsgrove estate to the eruption of inner-city Bradford, is precisely about the clash of interests and values among communities living cheek-by-jowl.

In essence, this paradox is about the meaning of citizenship, and thus consent to sovereign authority, in increasingly plural social orders. It clarifies the mixed messages of the debate over citizenship in Britain provoked by the Cantle Report. For example, in so far as the New Labour administration supports the growth of single-faith schools in public education they concur with a 'cosmopolitan' model of government. Yet, the key lesson drawn from the Cantle Report by Home Secretary Blunkett is the recommendation for a 'sense of civic identity' that transcends the values of different communities of choice, that could be reinforced through a mandatory 'oath of alliegance' that sets out a 'clear primary loyalty to this nation' (BBC 2001). This vacillation between models of liberal democracy that seek to recognise, and give 'voice' to, diverse communities of interest and identity on the one hand and, on the other, reassert the sovereign authority of the nation-state, is our preferred way of understanding the anomalies of contemporary crime control in Britain. It underpins the ambiguities and political struggles around such acid tests of community governance as the control of sex offenders, street prostitution, illicit drug use and 'anti-social' behaviour.

The local politics of community governance

Having made the argument for treating appeals to the community for crime control as irreducibly political in nature, it is important to recognise the spatial character of this politics. While it is possible to discern distinctive periods in the focus of national political debates on the uses of community governance, to reassert or reformulate sovereign authority and to shift responsibility onto private citizens or self-governing communities, a second key theme of this edited collection is the locally particular expression of this politics.

A crucial limitation of commentaries on the national politics of crime control in 'Britain' is that they are innately forgetful. They forget the effect that the diverse social, economic and political histories and the consequent cultural milieu of particular localities have on the generation of social problems such as crime and disorder and on the governmental responses to these problems (but see Keith 1993; Girling *et al* 2000; Taylor *et al* 1996; Hope and Sparks 2000a). As a consequence they provide relatively indeterminate accounts of the actual conduct of crime control 'on the ground', for, as political scientists have demonstrated, all centres of political authority, whether supranational, national, regional or local, encounter an 'implementation gap' between their legislative and policy commands and the practice of government (Marsh and Rhodes 1992; Ryan *et al* 2001). Central authorities are dependent on subordinate policy actors or 'street-level bureaucrats' to enact their commands and it is in the interstices of this interdependent relationship that local actors can resist, contest and manipulate central commands to fit their own agendas.

Given the accumulation of qualitative case studies into community-based crime control in a diversity of English localities over the past decade, there are now greater opportunities to draw more determinate and less speculative lessons about the 'localities effect' in this area of public policy. While neither this, nor any, edited collection could provide a comprehensive review of this body of case study research, we have selected contributions from scholars working in a diversity of localities, from the de-industrialised cities of the North (Coleman, Sim and Whyte; Foster) and Midlands (Hughes; Edwards) through the affluent counties of the Thames Valley (Stenson) to the extreme social polarities of life in the capital (Foster; Hallsworth).

Taken together, these local case studies suggest that what is most insightful about the actual conduct of community governance is its diversity. In their study of the Safer Merseyside Partnership, Coleman *et al* (Chapter 5) document its role in reasserting the sovereign authority of commercial interests in the regeneration of Liverpool City Centre through the coercive policing and surveillance of those disenfranchised populations that are believed to threaten capital accumulation. This coercion is bought at the cost of public investment in services for the socially excluded and neglects the social harms perpetrated by corporations through, for example, the toxic waste associated with chemical production in the Mersey Basin. Stenson (Chapter 6) notes the use of community governance as a means of reformulating sovereign authority in advanced liberal polities. Through his study of the Thames Valley, he documents the consequences of the shift from a universal provision of public services to their targeting of 'hot-spots' of crime and social disadvantage. The use which departments in Whitehall make of various audits of crime and social exclusion in deciding the allocation of grant aid and other sources of public investment disadvantages partnerships located in affluent regions. For, while High Wycombe is ranked as the fifteenth wealthiest local authority district in the UK, it nonetheless has pockets of high crime, victimisation and poverty that are visible only through audits conducted at the level of enumeration districts (the smallest unit for compiling Census data). Given their consequent exclusion from access to government funding programmes through these processes of audit, local agencies in the Thames Valley region have had to lever in resources through pioneering crime control programmes on, for example, restorative justice, problem-oriented policing and domestic violence. Notwithstanding its location in a region dominated by Conservative Party politics, the Thames Valley Police, for example, have, as a result, acquired a considerable reputation for their liberal and innovative ethos.

In his comparative analysis of community governance in the cities of Leicester and Nottingham in the East Midlands of England, Edwards (Chapter 7) examines the strategic dilemmas of the partnership approach to crime control. While there are formal similarities in the recent political economy of these localities, there have been significant differences in their apprehension of these dilemmas. They emphasise the analytical and practical importance of political agency in understanding the powers of partnerships to reintegrate socially excluded populations, and dangers in fostering bigoted and exclusionary constructions of crime control. In her ethnographic study of partnership practice in London Docklands and the (anonymous) estate of 'Bladon' in a Northern English city, Foster (Chapter 8) examines this 'neglected but essential element' of political agency, or the 'people pieces', in community governance. Both of the partnerships considered paid lip-service to the importance of 'empowering' communities to better govern themselves while effectively subordinating the interests and priorities of local citizens to the 'self-serving professional interests' of professional participants in 'cynically' meeting the performance targets placed upon them by national administrations obsessed with managerial efficiency. Evidence from these ethnographies suggests that New Labour's enthusiasm for performance management is further undermining the power of local partnerships to enable effective citizen participation.

Hallsworth (Chapter 9) draws upon his research into responses to street crime in South East London to further explore the rhetorical nature of community governance and challenge the tendency, in both administrative and critical criminological research, to misrepresent the practice of crime control partnerships. 'Liberal' conceptions of partnership as a potentially democratic means of controlling crime (cf. Hughes, Stenson and Edwards in this volume) and 'critical' conceptions of partnerships as a vehicle for the coercive reassertion of sovereign authority (cf. Coleman *et al* in this volume) overestimate the rationality of policymaking and implementation. In reality partnership practice is more chaotic and 'labyrinthine' because it is characterised by a 'deficit' of the political resources that would be needed to deliver either the empowerment or coercion of local communities.

Comparing the community governance of crime control

Taken at face value, a comparison of the findings from these case studies corroborates our interest in a more anthropological approach to drawing lessons about public policy that distinguishes what is particular about a certain practice in a specific place and time from that which can, consequently, be seen as genuinely universal. Notions of 'what works' in administrative criminology (Sherman *et al* 1997) can be criticised for their 'false universality' in generalising crime control practices in one locality as 'best practice' for other localities, irrespective of the effect their particular social, economic and political histories may have. However, anthropological approaches risk producing 'falsely particular' accounts that reflect the subjective observations of researchers rather than any objective, 'real' diversity of experience. Is it, for example, 'really' the case that community governance in Liverpool is about the coercive policing of threats to the commercial interests of the urban elite whereas in Nottingham it provides a genuine means of community empowerment? Were other researchers, with other theoretical orientations, to examine the conduct of partnerships in these localities would they observe the same patterns of community governance?

Confronting the challenge of false particularity has an importance beyond the production of more determinate explanations of how community governance is actually conducted. Distinguishing the possibilities for how community governance could be conducted in future is of immediate practical importance for drawing lessons for policy change and learning about the processes of crime control through partnerships. Understanding the importance of localities is central to debates over the transferability of crime control policies across diverse social contexts. An appreciation of this effect is also necessary if policy-makers are to anticipate and minimise any unintended consequences of emulating crime control practices that are implemented in very different circumstances elsewhere. This concern over the consequences of policy transfer has, for example, been at the heart of controversies over the adoption of so-called 'zero tolerance' policing strategies initially developed in New York in English cities with a history of violent community reactions to aggressive street policing (Pollard 1997; Stenson 2000).

The chapters by McLaughlin, Tilley and Edwards examine this conundrum in greater detail. McLaughlin (Chapter 3) presents an anti-realist argument through his 'postmodern reflections on crime prevention and community safety'. Through a consideration of the anomalies in New Labour's promotion of 'evidenced-based' policy on 'what works' and its simultaneous use of crude, 'tough on crime' initiatives to curry favour with the electorate, McLaughlin questions the possibility of discerning any coherent patterns in the actual conduct of crime control. Rather, his argument shares an affinity with Hallsworth's (Chapter 9) vision of community governance in South East London, where the capacity to distinguish the universal from locally particular attributes of crime control is precluded by its haphazard character. Conversely, Tilley (Chapter 4) argues for the possibility of learning about 'what works' in local crime control through reference to a 'scientific realist' observation of regular patterns in the conduct and outcomes of situational measures for the reduction of crime and disorder. Drawing upon Karl Popper's philosophy of scientific discovery, Tilley argues that the observation of regular patterns of behaviour, albeit 'triggered' in diverse social contexts, enables policymakers to identify universal qualities of crime control that can inform exercises in 'piecemeal social engineering'.

The contributions of McLaughlin and Tilley correspond to debates over the total transferability or total blockage of public policies (cf. Rose 1993: 34–40). Comparative policy analysts have argued that claims that there is a total blockage of learning presented by trying to move the cultural and institutional features of one community to another are as implausible as the argument that *anything* can be learnt and transferred between any community (Rose 1993: 40–2). Rather, the challenge is to develop comparative conceptual frameworks that at the very least generate better, if provisional, statements about that which is particular and that which is universal. Edwards (Chapter 7) suggests that the debate over 'learning from diversity' has been hampered by a preoccupation with 'formal relations of regularity and difference' that is theoretically and practically less important than identifying substantive relations of 'necessity'. The latter, by definition, will be universal. These must be distinguished from those aspects that are 'contingent' between policy actors and their objects of intervention; they will be specific to the contexts they inhabit. For example, the interdependence of actors at different supranational, national and subnational tiers of government is a necessity of exercising political power that grants all policy actors (albeit unequal) resources to advance their cause. How certain actors inhabiting particular contexts apprehend these resources and exploit them for their own advantage is a contingent quality of their political acumen.

From this perspective theoretical and practical lessons are drawn by questioning what the 'contingent necessities' of community governance are. Is it, for example, necessarily the case that local partnerships exercise crime control through the coercive policing of 'threatening' populations or is this a contingent quality of how certain partnerships acted in certain instances at certain moments? Is it necessarily the case that local partnerships target their interventions on 'hot spots' of victimisation when elsewhere it has been possible to provide universal security? By questioning what is necessary, what must be the case, for the community governance of crime control to occur, it is possible to build more determinate accounts of its powers and liabilities and, therefore, draw lessons about how local crime control could be conducted.

Implications for policy change and learning

Hughes (Chapter 2) draws upon his own experience of action research on community safety in Northamptonshire over the past decade to question the implications of community governance for contemporary crime control practice and the direction of policy-oriented research. He identifies a broadening of the policy and research agenda beyond the uses of community in criminal justice to crime prevention and through to notions of community safety and, more recently, the politics of 'public safety'. In turn, this entails an intellectual movement beyond the disciplinary boundaries of criminology to sociology, political economy and social policy (cf. Matthews and Pitts 2001). Simultaneously, he notes a narrowing of focus from criminal justice to principles of 'crime reduction' and then to the situational reduction of opportunities for specific types and instances of crime and disorder. Intellectually this reorientation of crime control policy is associated with the rise of a 'pragmatic' criminology (cf. Hope and Sparks 2000b) and even a sub- or post-criminological discipline of 'crime science' (Hughes *et al* 2002; Tilley in this volume). This history of the present demonstrates the future directions which policy change and learning about community governance could take.

References

ADC (Association of District Councils) (1990) *Promoting Safer Communities: A District Council Perspective*. London: ADC.

AMA (Association of Metropolitan Authorities) (1990) *Crime Reduction: A Framework for the Nineties?* London: AMA.

BBC (British Broadcasting Corporation) (2000a) *Vigilantes target innocent people*. http://news.bbc.co.uk/hi/english/uk/newsid_882000/882188.stm.

BBC (2000b) *Innocent man branded child abuser*. http://news.bbc.co.uk/hi/english/uk/newsid_864000/864693.stm.

BBC (2000c) *Vigilante attack on innocent man*. http://news.bbc.co.uk/hi/english/uk/newsid_848000/848737.stm.

BBC (2000d) *Fifth night of 'paedophile' protests*. http://news.bbc.co.uk/hi/english/uk/newsid_870000/870837.stm.

BBC (2000e) *Tories warn of rural vigilantes*. http://news.bbc.co.uk/hi/english/uk/newsid_724000/724702.stm.

BBC (2001a) *Police appeal over 'vigilante' death*. http://news.bbc.co.uk/hi/english/uk/newsid_1728000/1728151.stm.

BBC (2001b) *Vigilante concern on estate*. http://news.bbc.co.uk/hi/english/uk/newsid_1503000/1503939.stm.

Benyon, J. and Edwards, A. (1997) 'Crime and Public Order', in P. Dunleavy, A. Gamble, I. Holliday and G. Peele (eds), *Developments in British Politics 5*. London: Macmillan.

Coleman, R. and Sim, J. (1998) 'From the Docklands to the Disney Store: Surveillance, Risk and Security in Liverpool City Centre', *International Review of Law, Computers and Technology*, 12 (1), 27–45.

Crawford, A. (2001) 'Joined-up but Fragmented: Contradiction, Ambiguity and Ambivalence at the Heart of New Labour's "Third Way"', in R. Matthews and J. Pitts (eds), *Crime, Disorder and Community Safety: A New Agenda?* London: Routledge.

Downes, D. and Morgan, R. (1994) ' "Hostages to Fortune"? The Politics of Law and Order in Post-War Britain', in M. Maguire, R. Morgan and R. Reiner (eds), *The Oxford Handbook of Criminology*. Oxford: Oxford University Press.

Edwards, A. and Benyon, J. (2000) 'Community Governance, Crime Control and Local Diversity', *Crime Prevention and Community Safety: An International Journal*, 2 (3), 35–54.

Etzioni, A. (1995) *The Spirit of Community: Rights, Responsibilities and the Communitarian Agenda*. London: Fontana Press.

Forrester, D., Frenz, S., O'Connell, M. and Pease, K. (1990) *The Kirkholt Burglary Project: Phase Two*, Crime Prevention Unit Paper 23. London: Home Office.

Garland, D. (2001) *The Culture of Control: Crime and Social Order in Contemporary Society*. Oxford: Oxford University Press.

Girling, E., Loader, I. and Sparks, R. (2000) *Crime and Social Change in Middle England: Questions of Order in an English Town*. London: Routledge.

Held, D. (1995) *Democracy and the Global Order: From the Modern State to Cosmopolitan Governance*. Stanford, CA: Stanford University Press.

Higgins, J., Deakin, N., Edwards, J. and Wicks, M. (1983) *Government and Urban Poverty*. Blackwell, Oxford.

Hirst, P. (2000) 'Statism, Pluralism and Social Control', in D. Garland and R. Sparks (eds), *Criminology and Social Theory*. Oxford: Oxford University Press.

Home Office (1984) *Circular 8/84: Crime Prevention*. London: Home Office.

Home Office (1991) *Standing Conference on Crime Prevention: Safer Communities – The Local Delivery of Crime Prevention Through the Partnership Approach*. London: Home Office.

Home Office (1992) *Home Office Response to the Report: 'Safer Communities – The Local Delivery of Crime Prevention Through the Partnership Approach'*. London: Home Office.

Home Office (2001) *Community Cohesion: A Report of the Independent Review Chaired by Ted Chantle*. London: Home Office.

Hope, T. and Sparks, R. (2000a) 'Introduction: Risk, Insecurity and the Politics of Law and Order', in T. Hope and R. Sparks (eds), *Crime, Risk and Insecurity: Law and Order in Everyday Life and Political Discourse*. London: Routledge.

Hope, T. and Sparks, R. (2000b) 'For a Sociological Theory of Situations (or How Useful is Pragmatic Criminology?)', in A. von Hirsch, D. Garland and A. Wakefield (eds), *Ethical and Social Perspectives on Situational Crime Prevention*. London: Hart.

Hughes, G. (1996) 'Communitarianism and Law and Order', *Critical Social Policy*, 49, 17–41.

Hughes, G. (1998) *Understanding Crime Prevention: Social Control, Risk and Late Modernity*. Buckingham: Open University Press.

Hughes, G. (2002) 'The Shifting Sands of Crime Prevention and Community Safety', in G. Hughes, E. McLaughlin and J. Muncie (eds), *Crime Prevention and Community Safety: New Directions*. London: Sage.

Hughes, G. and Mooney, G. (1998) 'Community', in G. Hughes (ed.), *Imagining Welfare Futures*. London: Routledge.

Jessop, B. (2000) 'Governance Failure', in G. Stoker (ed.), *The New Politics of British Local Governance*. London: Macmillan.

Johnston, L. (2000) *Policing Britain: Risk, Security and Governance*. London: Longman.

Keith, M. (1993) *Race, Riots and Policing: Lore and Disorder in a Multi-Racist Society*. London: UCL Press.

Marsh, D. and Rhodes, R.A.W. (eds) (1992) *Policy Networks in British Government*. Oxford: Oxford University Press.

Matthews, R. and Pitts, J. (2001) 'Introduction: Beyond criminology?', in R. Matthews and J. Pitts (eds), *Crime, Disorder and Community Safety*. London: Routledge.

Neighbourhood Renewal Unit (2001) *Community Empowerment Fund: Preliminary Guidance*. London: Department for Transport, Local Government and the Regions.

O'Malley, P. (1992) 'Risk, Power and Crime Prevention', *Economy and Society*, 21 (2), 252–75.

Pharr, S. and Putnam, D. (eds) (2000) *Disaffected Democracies*. Princeton, NJ: Princeton University Press.

Pollard, C. (1997) 'Zero Tolerance: Short-term Fix, Long-Term Liability?', in N. Dennis (ed.), *Zero Tolerance: Policing a Free Society*. London: Institute for Economic Affairs.

Rose, N. (1996) 'Governing "Advanced" Liberal Democracies', in A. Barry, T. Osborne and N. Rose (eds) *Foucault and Political Reason: Liberalism, Neo-liberalism and Rationalities of Government*. London: UCL Press.

Rose, R. (1993) *Lesson-Drawing in Public Policy: A Guide to Learning Across Time and Space*. Chatham, NJ: Chatham House.

Ryan, M., Savage, S. and Wall, D. (eds) (2001) *Policy Networks in Criminal Justice*. London: Palgrave.

Scarman, Lord (1981) *The Brixton Disorders 10–12 April 1981: Report of an Inquiry by the Rt. Hon. the Lord Scarman, OBE*. London: HMSO.

Sherman, L., Gottfredson, D., Mackenzie, D., Eck, J., Reuter, P. and Bushway, S. (1997) *Preventing Crime: What Works, What Doesn't and What's Promising*, Research in Brief, National Institute of Justice. Washington, DC: US Department of Justice.

Social Exclusion Unit (1998) *Bringing Britain Together: A National Strategy for Neighbourhood Renewal*. London: Cabinet Office.

Stenson, K. (1999) 'Crime Control, Governmentality and Sovereignty', in R. Smandych (ed.), *Governable Places: Readings on Governmentality and Crime Control*. Dartmouth: Ashgate.

Stenson, K. (2000) 'Some Day Our Prince Will Come: Zero-Tolerance Policing and Liberal Government', in T. Hope and R. Sparks (eds), *Crime, Risk and Insecurity: Law and Order in Everyday Life and Political Discourse*. London: Routledge.

Stenson, K. and Edwards, A. (2001) 'Rethinking Crime Control in Advanced Liberal Government: the "Third Way" and the Return of the Local', in K. Stenson and R. Sullivan (eds), *Crime, Risk and Justice: The Politics of Crime Control in Liberal Democracies*. Cullompton: Willan Publishing.

Stoker, G. (ed.) (2000) *The New Politics of British Local Governance*. London: Macmillan.

Taylor, I. (1999) *Crime in Context: A Critical Criminology of Market Societies*. Cambridge: Polity Press.

Taylor, I., Evans, K. and Frazer, P. (1996) *A Tale of Two Cities: Global Change, Local Feeling and Everyday Life in the North of England. A Study of Manchester and Sheffield*. London: Routledge.

Young, J. (2001) 'Identity, Community and Social Exclusion', in R. Matthews and J. Pitts (eds), *Crime, Disorder and Community Safety*. London: Routledge.

Chapter 2

Plotting the rise of community safety: critical reflections on research, theory and politics

Gordon Hughes

In the beginning ... an autobiographical note

My initial interest and active involvement in the field of community safety began in modest circumstances in Northampton, England in 1989. At that time I was a lecturer in sociology, somewhat unusually specialising in the teaching of both the classical theorists of modernity and the microscopic studies of deviancy, conformity and social order. It was the latter interest which no doubt led to my first skirmishes in the tangled undergrowth of community-based crime prevention and its messy policies, practices and politics. However, my intellectual debt to, and fascination with , the so-called 'classical tradition' of such thinkers as Marx, Durkheim, Weber and Elias and more latterly Giddens would also come to play a vital role in my subsequent research and theorising of the nascent field of community safety specifically and crime prevention more generally. To return to the encounter in 1989 which led me into a new 'career' as researcher and commentator on crime prevention and community safety, the HE institution where I was then employed was approached by a leading police manager and the chair of the Northamptonshire Police Authority to undertake an evaluation of the 'new' arrangements for police/community consultative arrangements in the Northampton town centre police sector as compared to the structures and processes of consultation in the other police sector areas across the county. As the nearest thing to a bone fide criminologist in the institution, I was asked to consider undertaking what would now be termed a 'quick and dirty' evaluation. Little did I know that this initial encounter with the barely researched and seemingly sociologically 'unsexy' area of police/community consultative arrangements for crime prevention would lead to an intellectual preoccupation with 'all things crime prevention and community safety' over the next ten years and lasting to this day.

The 'successful' completion of this initial evaluation led to four other funded projects for both the Police Authority and the County Council between 1991 and 1995 in Northamptonshire. Increasingly the research evaluations became focused on multi-agency partnerships in crime prevention and 'diversion' and the implementation of a community safety strategy across the county. It was a piece of good fortune for me as a researcher that the county of Northamptonshire had gained a reputation by the 1980s as an innovative pioneer of both multi-agency working and 'new managerialist' policy and practice in policing and community safety in the post-Morgan Report era. Indeed, in retrospect much of the discourse of the Morgan Report was influenced by the 'solutions' already tested out in Northamptonshire. This series of projects on the 'post-Morgan' developments in community safety and crime prevention would generate a number of published academic research papers (see Hughes 1994, 1996b, 1997a; Hughes *et al* 1998) as well as more practical, policy-relevant public reports (Hughes 1992, 1995; Hughes *et al* 1996). Throughout my research work during this period in the early to mid-1990s, I was concerned to try and juggle, if not merge, the concerns of the sponsors of the evaluations with practical outcomes and policy recommendations with a sociologically driven interest in exploring the social relationships and processes at play in this, to me, 'new' field of policy and practice. Throughout my work on the funded evaluation projects, I therefore quite explicitly sought to combine the practical concerns of the research sponsors ('what works well', 'how can improvements be made', etc.) with my own interests as an ethnographic researcher in a new terrain of social relations. As it turned out, I learnt much about the 'late modern' condition of our times from my encounters with the research participants (ranging from 'active' citizens, practitioners, policy-makers, politicians, etc.) in what is often dismissed as 'contract culture' research. Of course there are many dangers and limitations associated with the production of 'policy-relevant' research knowledge in the social sciences (Hughes 2000d). Nonetheless the engagement of the sociologist as public intellectual with local policy developments should not be underestimated in providing opportunities for the generation of new ideas and discourses which may challenge existing orthodoxies around what constitutes *governmental savoir* (Stenson 1998a).

Since 1995 and my taking up of a new post at the Open University, my research has engaged with broader developments at the national and international dimensions of crime control and community safety (Hughes 1998a, 2000a, 2000b, 2000c; Hughes *et al* 2002a; Hughes and McLaughlin 2002) as well as changes in the post-welfare, managerial state (Hughes 1998b; Hughes and Lewis 1998; Hughes *et al* 1998; McLaughlin *et al* 2001). Alongside these efforts, my work has continued to concentrate on the complexly negotiated realities of local community safety practices, policies and politics. In particular, my focus has turned to the developing 'professional' and 'managerial' careers and experiences of *arriviste* community safety experts in the post-Crime and Disorder Act local partnerships across Britain (Gilling and Hughes 2000; Hughes 2002).

'A moving target'? Mapping the construction of the field of policy study

This section begins by placing my work in the context of the existing field of crime prevention studies as constituted when my research 'journey' began at the beginning of the 1990s through to the end of that decade. This critical reflection will attempt to capture and summarise the dominant 'domain assumptions' of crime prevention studies throughout the 1980s and 1990s. I then examine the increasingly significant place accorded to community crime prevention *qua* community safety in this hybridised body of knowledge, expertise and practices associated with criminological and to a lesser extent social policy analysis. In particular, I argue that the 1990s witnessed a paradigmatic shift from 'crime prevention' to 'community safety' (see also Gilling 1997) . Put simply, the field of crime prevention and community safety may be described as a 'moving target'. Attempting to isolate crime prevention and community safety as one or two distinct fields of policy study produces some conceptual grief and may necessitate on occasions some awkward linguistic slippages. In reality much of the important work in this so-called 'third sector' of prevention (Garland 2001) exists on the borderlands of several academic disciplines and so is difficult to pin down. Furthermore, the notion of contributing to existing field(s) of knowledge does carry connotations of an unchanging and somewhat monolithic body of work which is hardly appropriate for understanding the 'states' of knowledge and research in the social sciences generally. Indeed, I am by no means convinced that the naming of the specialist field as 'crime prevention and community safety' is entirely adequate.

Rivals in the nomenclature could include 'strategies of crime control', 'crime and disorder reduction' and such like.

Crime prevention studies: from Cinderella to the technicist belle of the ball?

Much of the impetus for research into crime prevention has come traditionally from both central and local governments' desire to find out 'what works' in terms of measurable techniques together with other agencies' wish to prove that their preferred options have succeeded in preventing certain crimes and forms of victimisation. Until the late 1970s, the academic study of crime prevention was virtually non-existent.[1] Since the late 1970s, crime prevention has emerged as a major strategy of crime control across a number of 'advanced liberal' societies. Its two key faces have been that of situational techniques of target hardening and risk reduction, and 'community'-based social pro-grammes and initiatives.

There has clearly been a rise to prominence of crime prevention in political and policy circles in the 1980s and 1990s when compared to its obscurity in the 1950s and 1960s in the UK (Gilling 1997: 69). However, at the risk of overgeneralising, crime prevention studies in the 1980s and 1990s nevertheless gained a reputation for being criminology's own 'dismal science', generally perceived to be a specialist technical and pragmatic field of policy-relevant research which was largely untouched by the broader intellectual currents associated with debates in modern social theory. This unfortunate reputation is in some important respects deserved during this period.[2] Much of the mainstream literature in the field of crime prevention studies over the last three decades in the UK has traditionally been focused on which types of crime prevention techniques and strategies can be shown to 'work' most effectively. One of the world's leading researchers-cum-policy commentators on crime prevention is Ken Pease. In the first edition of the highly influential student criminology text in the UK, *The Oxford Handbook of Criminology*, Pease (1994: 659) makes the following telling comment about – and dismissal of – the place of sociologically informed work in his overview of the field of crime prevention studies:

Throughout the history of their discipline, many criminologists trained in sociological traditions have been interested primarily in how the demands of the capitalist state have shaped the scope of the criminal law and the apparatus established to enforce it. Such a perspective places crime *control* at the margins of concern. In so far as scholars from such traditions have thought of it at all, crime prevention has been regarded as achievable only by changing large-scale economic and social arrangements. Self-evidently, such a position precludes empirical work on crime prevention, and discussion of it will not feature further in this chapter.

In his overview of the field of study of crime prevention, Pease then goes on to focus almost exclusively on what may be termed the strategy of 'primary prevention' or 'situational crime prevention' which addresses the reduction of crime opportunities without reference to criminals or potential criminals and which, in Pease's view, has 'generated a dis-proportionately large amount of good research and evaluation' (Pease 1994: 660). Indeed, there seems little doubt looking back since the late 1970s that situational crime prevention with its techniques of target hardening and implicit appeal to 'actuarial' risk management (based on risk calculation of opportunities, events and deterrents) has had a massive impact on mainstream policymaking in crime reduction and prevention in the UK and beyond (see Gilling 1997; Crawford 1998). In Kevin Stenson's words (1995), the situational discourse and its practical successes transformed 'technical, administrative criminological theory into a governmental tool of key significance'. It matters less for my purposes that Pease's above conclusion about the character of socio-logically informed work on crime control may itself be a parody of (at best) crude Marxist analyses. What is significant in that passage is the logic of the argument for 'excising' macro-sociological structural in-sights from the analysis of both the causes of and strategies for controlling crime from a text that has been marketed as the major work of reference on the main specialist fields of study within criminology. Entering the field of crime prevention in the early 1990s as a researcher 'trained in sociological traditions' was therefore an interesting and challenging encounter!

The overall picture sketched in brief above of a hegemonic situational, actuarial-based criminology of targeted risk and opportunity reduction does of course oversimplify the recent history of fads and fashions in crime prevention practices and theories. Throughout the 1980s and into the 1990s, there were significant social democratic voices in the crimi-nological academy calling for a role for community-based initiatives and, more radically, policies geared to community empowerment and socio-economic regeneration in the fight against crime and victimisation (see Hope and Shaw 1988; Lea and Young 1984). Such social democratic voices would play a key role in some local authority-based policies and initiatives developing around community safety in this period. However, the dominant discourse remained that of a seemingly depoliticised, technicist, risk management set of practices which accorded with the more general neoliberal, marketised philosophy of governments across the anglophone world and would crucially affect how community crime prevention was to be realised (O'Malley 1992). Within this dominant paradigm, the creation of self-help, enterprising communities of 'active citizens' was probably best symbolised by the proliferation of simultaneously fearful and indignant Neighbourhood Watch schemes across the suburban communities of the UK. In such communities in partnership with the police against 'outsider' crime, the logic of community safety as an exclusive 'club good' (rather than a public good) tended to hold sway (Jordan 1996).

Community crime prevention and community safety: the emerging local and international political agenda

On entering into empirical research on local crime prevention and community policing initiatives at the start of the 1990s, it was soon evident that there was much talk both in the police and emergent multi-agency circles about the need for 'community'-based strategies. The impetus for the growing appeals to 'community' in crime control and policing policies and practices in part came from the long-term 'fall-out' of the Scarman Report of 1981 on the policing of 'problem' inner-city communities and its partial legislative embodiment in the 1984 Police and Criminal Evidence Act (henceforth PACE). As a result of PACE, police authorities were required to consult with the local community as 'partners' to find out their views about local crime problems and develop crime prevention measures. Throughout this period, the talk and practice of 'community consultation' and 'community policing' was highly racialised in character (McLaughlin 2002). According to the logic of the Scarman Report the major problems of policing and by implication crime control more generally lay in the strained relations between inner-city 'problem communities' (which translated as 'black') and the insensitive Metropolitan Police. It is therefore vital to note then that much of the impetus for community-based 'solutions' were crucially linked to and inscribed in a broader racialised discourse about managing the 'race and crime' debate in which black communities throughout the 1980s were often pathologised and 'othered'.

By the beginning of the 1990s another report on crime prevention was to prove very influential in the proselytisation of local multi-agency 'partnerships' in crime prevention and community safety. This Home

Office report was to become known as the Morgan Report and was officially entitled *Safer Communities: The Local Delivery of Crime Prevention through the Partnership Approach* (1991). This report in retrospect was arguably the first major triumph of 'New Labour' through the agency of post-Militant, 'neo-sensibilist', Labour-controlled local authorities. It promoted at a local level a multi-agency and increasingly mana-gerialised approach to what it termed 'community safety' (rather than 'crime prevention') and was to prove influential, if in an uneven manner, across local sites of crime control throughout the 1990s until the watershed legislation of the Crime and Disorder Act of 1998. By the mid-1990s multi-agency community safety strategies and community consultative arrangements had become part of the local landscape of crime prevention policy and practice in many parts of the country (Hughes 1996b). During this decade there was ongoing central Conservative government and Home Office (rhetorical) support for community-based, 'self-help' initiatives, not least through appeals to the neoliberal, heroic figures of the 'active citizen' and the self-calculating and prudent 'consumer'. With the benefit of hindsight, the first years of the 1990s also witnessed what may be termed the 'whitening' of the racialised crime and disorder problem in Britain, not least by means of the closely interconnected notions of the 'underclass' and 'social exclusion'. The spectre of the dangerous white underclass was fed by news coverage of the riots and disorders in predominantly white, working-class fringe housing estates across different localities. The talk of dangerous, anti-social or even asocial people was fed by social scientific commentators and journalists of both the right and left of the political spectrum (such as Charles Murray, Norman Dennis and Melanie Phillips on the right and Beatrix Campbell and Nick Davies on the left). Taken together, this discourse contributed to a renaissance of a 'criminology of the other' (Garland 2001). It is now evident that the threat of social disorder from this new, predominantly white (non-)working class and the wish to manage such potentially 'no-go' areas of the socially excluded was a major factor behind the rise of the community safety policy agenda throughout the 1990s and now into the new decade of the 2000s.[3]

Taken together, such developments appear to represent an important political and policy turning point which helps explain the entrance of community crime prevention and community safety in from the cold, both for policymakers and more begrudgingly for criminologists in their work as 'governmental savants'. As Kevin Stenson (1998) argues:

Social scientists have played a crucial role – together with urban managers, police, criminal justice and welfare professionals – in reflecting upon, monitoring, evaluating and driving policies forward. Their discourses play a dual function. On the one hand they constitute attempts to create disinterested, academically driven conceptualisations and analyses within the academy, elite journalistic circuits and policy think-tanks. On the other hand, where they are adopted wholly or in part by policymakers and politicians, they can function as *governmental savoirs* contributing to the knowledge forms which are part of the apparatus of government … The social scientist is, hence, often helping to constitute the realities which he or she describes and explains.

(Stenson 1998: 123)

That noted, the reception given by such leading crime prevention experts in the UK as Ken Pease towards the new discourse of community safety remained decidedly frosty in the mid-1990s. In the same edition of the handbook referred to earlier, Pease notes:

It is of interest that the Morgan Committee preferred the phrase 'community safety' over 'crime prevention' because the latter 'is often narrowly interpreted and this reinforces the view that it is solely the responsibility of the police' (Morgan Report 1991, 3). *The extreme vagueness of the Morgan Committee's definition of community safety gives no confidence that the revised definition will provide a satisfactory focus for the work.*

(1994: 687, my emphasis)

Until the last years of the 1990s community safety would remain quite marginal to the concerns of criminology generally and crime prevention studies specifically. In the eyes of mainstream criminology, it was seemingly fatally flawed in being neither susceptible to technicist-cum-administrative measurement of success or failure, nor focused on clearly targeted crime and victimisation events. Indeed, the resurgence of community crime prevention in both policy and academic circles in the late 1980s and early 1990s was understood largely in terms of what it wasn't (i.e. primary, situational crime prevention) rather than in terms of any clear or positive view of what it was. When it could be pinned down it was, at best, a top-down initiative imposed from above on 'weak' or 'fragile' communities leading to community development-style projects and initiatives and, at worst, pious words of encouragement to poor communities to help themselves through their own endeavours in the spirit of a voluntaristic and moralising communitarian sermon. It is

27

hardly surprising then that most attempts in mainstream criminology at evaluating the 'international' success of community-based crime prevention across different localities have reached the conclusion that its tangible, for which read 'measurable', achievements in reducing crime and victimisation have been negligible (Hope 1995; Ekblom and Pease 1995; Sherman *et al* 1997).[4]

However, looking back at the decade of the 1990s, it is apparent that the wider politics of, and emotive appeals to, community involvement in the 'fight' against crime would not go away. Not least, there were broader international transformations in the governance of crime control which involved both the growing heterogeneity and pluralisation of social control (Newburn 2002) and the privatisation of crime prevention onto the shoulders of 'responsibilised' citizens and their communities (Johnston 1996). Perhaps then the measurable 'success' of community-based crime prevention was not the key issue with regard to this 'species' of crime prevention but instead other political and ideological facets of the phenomenon needed to be explored. Indeed, this point is conceded by Ken Pease in the second edition of *The Oxford Handbook of Criminology* (1997) when he both recognises the growing political salience and rhetorical power of 'community'-based, multi-agency approaches to crime control and regrets the apparent passing of the 'primary prevention'/situational paradigm in crime prevention policy and practice.[5]

The growing importance of 'community'-based forms of crime control has also been widely noted by radical criminologists. According to such commentators, the rise of 'community'-based initiatives in criminal justice and social control more generally since the 1970s has had a massive, if sinister, significance. Driven on by the totalitarian vision of certain readings of Foucault's *Discipline and Punish* (1977) and popularised by Stanley Cohen (1985), most radical commentators have explained such developments as community policing and community-based crime prevention as an invidious extension and blurring of the institutional boundaries of social control into the institutional domain of civil society in general and the lives of the poor, vulnerable and criminalised most specifically (Gordon 1987; Nelken 1985; Pratt 1986). Despite the importance of this radical thesis in connecting trends in crime prevention to wider transformations in social control in contemporary capitalist democracies, this dystopian, totalising picture both overplays the significance of such community-based initiatives and underplays the complexity and contradictory tendencies of such developments in specific contexts and locales. In contrast, I have argued for the need for detailed research based on local studies by means of which a more nuanced and complex picture of the local politics of crime control could be developed (see Hughes 1996a, 1997).

'Coming in from the cold'? Community safety and criminology

At the turn of the millennium, there appears to have been a reluctant recognition in mainstream criminology in the UK of the significance, politically and practically as well as rhetorically, of appeals to community in crime control strategies. This recognition within the academy is explicable in small part as a result of the findings of the local studies of 'community'-based crime control strategies informed by wider intellectual currents from the disciplines of sociology and politics (Crawford 1997, 1998; Gilling 1997; Hughes 1997; Stenson 1998a; Tilley 1994). It is worth noting that the 1999 British Society of Criminology Conference in Liverpool gave its influential seal of recognition for 'all matters community safety' by offering, for the first time, a separate stream of presentations dedicated to this growing area of expertise and research. Furthermore, 1999 saw the launch of a new international journal dedicated to community safety, entitled *Crime Prevention and Community Safety*. Among academic researchers in the UK there are the beginnings of a more comparative research agenda, influenced by contemporary European developments around 'urban security' and 'safer cities', which may foster a warmer reception for research around the policies and practices of community safety and social exclusion (for example, see the European Forum for Urban Security 1994). Important developments have thus taken place in the criminological academy as a result of which community safety has come in from the intellectual cold, although perhaps as a temporary and suspicious lodger rather than a long-lost friend and relative.[6] However, the key factor in the current 'mainstreaming' of community safety across Britain as both policy and research problem is the legislative flagship of 'New' Labour, the Crime and Disorder Act of 1998 and its implications for the local governance of crime and disorder in the first decades of the twenty-first century (see Hughes *et al* 2002a). However, since 1998 we are possibly witnessing yet another discursive shift whereby 'crime and disorder reduction' may be emerging as the new policy field of crime control across different localities in the UK. Both crime prevention and community safety may be in the process of being excised from the new discourse of crime control based on crime and disorder reduction.

Apart from the recent growth industry associated with the policies and practices of what is increasingly referred to as crime and disorder reduction, it is also clear that there is now a hive of research activity

29

associated with the increasingly porous and dynamic contexts of local crime control strategies in the UK and beyond. Within a decade, then, the field is barely recognisable from that which I first encountered in the early years of the 1990s. Not least, there is now a challenging critical culture in the academy, organised around the critical debate with the policies, practices and politics of crime control-cum-safety and security but also engaged with the 'big' questions associated with current thinking in modern social and political theory (Garland 2001; Hughes *et al* 2002a). Although researchers across late modern societies are under pressure to act as 'technicians of the social order' (Haines and Sutton 2000), questions of social justice do now vie with issues of technical efficiency in intellectual debates about crime control and community safety. Nor can normative questions about the 'good society' be easily dismissed. It is to these continuing intellectual developments that this chapter now turns.

Reframing the field of study: towards a replacement discourse of community safety

> To have values or not to have values: the question is always with us. When sociologists undertake to study problems that have relevance to the world we live in, they find themselves caught in a crossfire. Some urge them not to take sides, to be neutral and do research that is technically correct and value free. Others tell them their work is shallow and useless if it does not express a deep commitment to a value position. This dilemma, which seems so painful to so many, actually does not exist, for one of its horns is imaginary. For it to exist, one would have to assume, as some apparently do, that it is indeed possible to do research that is uncontaminated by personal and political sympathies. I propose to argue that it is not possible and, therefore, that the question is not whether we should take sides, since we inevitably will, but rather whose side are we on.
>
> (Becker 1967: 239)

A key theme in my research to date has been the ways in which local multi-agency partnerships in crime prevention, community safety and increasingly crime and disorder reduction are realised in and through relationships of cooperation, collusion, compromise and contestation. In turn such developments are creating new modes of regulation and control and thus the evolution of novel forms of governance with implications for the empowerment, or otherwise, of communities, groups and individuals. According to Becker, the answer to his famous question 'whose side are we on?' was fairly straightforward: the powerless. However, it is less simple to answer whose side are we on in studying community safety when the sides themselves are porous in character, under contested processes of construction and without guarantees.

In the last two decades in the UK and elsewhere in societies engulfed by neoliberalism and market fundamentalism, an increasingly entrepreneurial form of government has taken hold, involving new styles of management and accounting for public finance but also a new approach to governance itself, namely 'partnership' (Powell *et al* 2002). 'Governance' can be defined as the 'control of an activity by some means such that a range of defined outcomes is attained' (Hirst and Thompson 1996: 184). The same authors also point out that we may be witnessing a new political world where we find a 'complexity and multiplicity of levels of governance' (Hirst and Thompson 1996: 183). The reasons behind the promotion of partnerships across the public policy field has of course much to do with the dominant political agenda associated with the economic restructuring of local economies and crucial changes in the organisation and coordination of government at local, regional and national levels. Urban governments are increasingly working through and alongside other interests. As Bailey *et al* (1995: 1) note, by the mid-1990s partnership was seen more and more 'not only as an essential adjunct of policy but as the most important foundation of government's strategy towards urban areas.' And Jewson and MacGregor (1997: 9) are surely correct in their claim that partnership is an attractive concept to government because 'it commits other interests to regeneration (such as the private sector and the local community), it diffuses responsibility for success or failure, and ensures that relatively low levels of public expenditure can be used to lever large amounts of private insurance'. Furthermore it is now widely acknowledged in the research literature on crime prevention/community safety partnerships that the conflict about means and ends associated with these projects and programmes is largely transferred to the agencies within the partnership thereby excluding it from wider public debate. My own work has contributed to this debate by showing that urgent questions also remain about the place and status allowed for democratic procedures and processes within this restructuring of the local governance of crime.

A second and closely related theme to that described above concerns the crucial importance of researchers of trends in crime control re-maining attuned to the importance of local differences and specificities in the working out of what may be supposedly new 'master patterns' from the centre. Detailed empirical research studies of the place of partnerships within specific restructured governmental spaces, both urban and rural, are crucial in helping us remain sensitive to the profoundly uneven, contingent and unfinished processes of national, and increasingly regional and international, programmes of 'reform' and 'modernisation' of criminal justice and social control-cum-welfare agencies. My own case studies into this area of multi-agency partnerships tried to avoid analysing these complex processes and transformations simply as either 'empowering the local "community" ' or as a new 'totalitarianism' of subtle social control. The creative opportunities for individual and community self-government may be overplayed by its strongest advocates such as Charles Leadbetter (1996) and the Blairite think-tank Demos. However, my work and that of others (O'Malley and Palmer 1996; Rose 1996; Stenson 1998a) has pointed to the possibilities of local 'community' representatives, suitably educated and 'empowered' at certain times and in certain contexts, becoming equipped with the essential skills to interact with the new power brokers and gatekeepers for resources. Any optimism must of course be tempered by the recognition that there is also much to fear in the governmental shift towards local and communal modes of government – most obviously the rise of a populist politics of exclusion and sanitisation (Bauman 1999; Reiner 2000).

The third theme to my work may be said to confront both the myth of academic research on crime and disorder and risk and safety being an apolitical and purely technical enterprise (see Becker above), and the tendency of the political left to wallow in 'impossibilism' and the celebration and announcement of dystopia. Instead I have argued for a normatively engaged stance on developments in and beyond crime control, informed by a guardedly optimistic theory of social inclusion and social justice associated with 'radical communitarianism' (Hughes 1996a, and see Jordan 1996; Little 2002). However, most of these accounts tend to fall short of addressing the possibility of a positive and progressive 'replacement discourse' of safety and empowerment (but see van Swaaningen 2002).

A major intellectual and political challenge for radical communitarian work on the possible futures of crime control and community safety is to recognise and think through the complexity and contingency of con-temporary urban forms. Such a recognition thus raises the possibility that cities and other environments might be realised in other ways, if visions of alternative, more inclusive communities were to be recognised and valued. A critical engagement with Basic Income debates across Europe appears to offer one way of moving beyond the 'workfarist' and moral authoritarian project currently hegemonic both in the UK and across neoliberal societies (see Hughes and Little 1999; Jordan 1998; Bauman 1999; Little 2002). Engagement with these increasingly influential debates on guaranteed basic income in turn has implications for rethinking the relationship between crime control, social and economic justice, the recognition of difference and the 'common good'.

The idea of community safety in radical communitarian debates is not simply that of pragmatic institutional policies and practices of local government bodies but is also a vision and progressive political project. As an idea it has close links to the European concept of 'urban security'. Stenson (1998a) notes that the conception of community safety is intrinsically a hybrid, being a right, a commodity and a public good. The appropriation of community safety as a commodity is currently in the ascendancy but the struggle to promote and realise community safety as both a right and a public good is not lost despite the dominant, neoliberal orthodoxy in the USA and UK. The struggle for the 'soul' of community safety is thus 'unfinished' and needs to be fought over (Hughes 2000b). As Stenson (1998a) again cogently observes:

> There is usually a breach between state agencies' conceptions of security and people's needs. This breach is the problem space in which security must be rebuilt, through *local* co-production and dialogue, diagnosis, proposals and assessment, but which simultaneously recognises the European wide commonalities in the causes and nature of social problems and the challenges of managing them. State and EU conceptions of risk and threat have focused on organised crime, illegal immigration, money laundering, drug smuggling or crime which attack the profits of the major corporations. The new discourse, however, spotlights the routine, mass, petty crimes against the person and personal property, often invisible to the criminal justice systems, which corrode confidence in public spaces and also in the neglected domestic spaces: crimes against women, children, the elderly and ethnic minorities.

Such local yet pan-European debates and programmes of public regeneration and safety remain a crucial arena for both research and political engagement from progressive intellectuals involved in the contested politics of community safety and public security. Perhaps the greatest challenge for the new replacement discourse resides in the struggle to counteract the currently dominant, paranoiac and xenophobic response to asylum seekers and immigrants across European countries in debates on safety, security and crime and disorder (Bauman

1999; Düvell and Jordan 1999; Young 1999). Tim Hope (2000) may be correct in warning us that, given the exclusionary impulse in much community safety politics and policy, it is therefore normatively unwise to see community safety as an unalloyed good. That noted, the argument for a 'pan-hazard' paradigm of community safety (Wiles and Pease 2000; Hughes 2000a, 2000b) remains strong. In this new paradigm or replacement discourse, crime and disorder reduction are acknowledged as a major but not the exclusive focus for intervention in community safety. In turn they are viewed as elements within a wider spectrum of harms and hazards to the health, well-being and safety of populations. This replacement discourse of community safety also has potentially important implications for 'joining up' interventions against crime and disorder and other non-criminalised harms with social policies aimed at the regeneration of local communities.

One of the important purposes of any critical normative theory is that of offering an alternative vision of social relations. As Iris Marion Young notes (1990: 256):

Social change arises from politics, not philosophy. Ideals are a crucial step in emancipatory politics, however, because they dislodge our assumptions that what is given is necessary. They offer standpoints from which to criticise the given, and inspiration for imagining alternatives.

Overall radical communitarian thinking seeks to make a contribution to what Nikolas Rose (1999a) terms the 'de-fatalisation' of the present and the opening up of possibilities of 'real inventiveness'. The construction of a progressive, 'pan-hazard' paradigm of community safety can be viewed as a potential invention which both de-fatalises the present and offers new possibilities for the progressive socialisation of criminal justice and crime control.

At the end ... towards an auto-critique

Concepts and theoretical frameworks are in significant ways products of their times and with the benefit of hindsight may be subject to important qualification and revision. In the case of my own work, two key influences are evident, namely the broad sociological thesis of late modernity and risk society and second the moral, political and sociological debate around communitarianism. A brief, critical re-engagement with these two intellectual influences may be especially apposite, not least in the wake of their recent combined association with the politics and thinking of the so-called 'Third Way' (see Giddens 1998; Blair 1997; Rose 1999a).

Revisiting late modernity and the risk society thesis

The twin concepts of late modernity and risk society appear to have entered into the canon of the more theoretically ambitious areas of mainstream criminology (see, *inter alia*, Young 1999; Reiner 2000; Sparks and Garland 2000; Newburn 2002; Garland 2001). Indeed for sceptics it may appear that the ideas associated with the late modernity and risk society thesis – in the shadow of the 'New' Labour's Third Way politics in the UK – merely represent a convenient intellectual bandwagon onto which academic commentators can safely jump. Alternatively it may be argued that these ideas have been employed by scholars in an attempt to infuse the then largely non-sociologically informed field of crime prevention studies with questions of modern social and political theory. However, we might ask are they now concepts which look increasingly tired, washed-out and shallow?

Of late there has been an accumulation of critical responses to these ideas of Giddens and Beck. For some there is no lasting power to the risk society thesis – in Dingwall's terms it is just 'a fin de siècle' fad, with Ulrich Beck cast (or caricatured) as but the latest in a long line of discredited 'gurus' arguing that in the last twenty or thirty years 'traditional' capitalist society changed in some fundamental ways (Dingwall 1999). Whether one accepts Dingwall's dismissal of the risk society theory or not, there is no denying that the late modernity thesis and risk society theory together run the 'risk' of exaggerating both the solidity and certainty of the past and the fragility and uncertainty of the present (see, for example, Young 1999).

Members of the Foucauldian 'governmentality' school of thought have also made some significant contributions to the critique of this work. In an important intervention Pat O'Malley (1999) has argued that Beck's work suffers from a totalising imagery of risk society and from a deterministic approach to processes currently in play. O'Malley notes that for Beck 'risk' seems to lie at the root of almost everything. As a consequence, unforeseen hybridisations are unrecognised. O'Malley instead calls for a less grand and a priori foreclosure of possibilities. 'Whether or not risk consciousness does so structure identities, biographies and solidarities seems to me to be an empirical question' (O'Malley 1999: 144). He rightly points to the possibilities of other bases of identity formation around ethnicity, religion, gender and, I would add, class, age, region and so on. O'Malley also goes on to question the novelty of risk consciousness pointing to its centrality throughout the past century and in particular to the welfare state. Put simply risk management has a long lineage as a technology of government. In a similar vein, Nikolas Rose (1999a: 491) has observed that risk society theorists and proponents of the Third Way such as Giddens (1998) tend to close down what he terms 'inventiveness' in politics and, crucially, fail to 'recognise the forces of injustice are not implacable macro-sociological processes of globalisation, detraditionalisation and risk but are the quite material, micro-sociological and human forces of greed and exploitation, of complacency, prejudice and hypocrisy'.

To return to the specific question of applying the insights of Beck and risk society theorists to current governmental strategies, this work is closely associated with the thesis of the 'new penology' in explanations of current developments in crime control. In particular, it is suggested by such commentators as Ericson and Haggerty (1997) that the governance of all manner of institutional domains is now increasingly organised around risk management rather than the moralised enforcement of social order. Accordingly governmental problems are imagined in terms of potential harms and probabilistic outcomes rather than their trans-gressive nature. Much of this actuarialist thesis remains persuasive although subject to serious qualifications as a totalising explanation which also smacks of excessive determinism.

Despite such broad criticisms, it is difficult to ignore the influence of risk management, particularly in many aspects of the regulation of the 'difficult' members of society (Hughes 2000c). Even a critic such as Rose (1999a: 488), for example, notes that 'the excluded are no longer to be addressed by a collective politics of socialisation, but through discrete and targeted practices of control that seek to monitor and reduce their riskiness and through individualised practices of personal reform'. This argument is in part accurate. It is clear that 'national' notions and programmes of collective risk-sharing are giving way to smaller, more exclusive, 'club'-like risk-sharing collectivities together with a de-creasing confidence in central nation-states' willingness if not ability to deliver effective security and safety for the generality of citizens (Stenson 2000; Jordan 1998). However, proponents of the ascendancy of actuarialist risk management surely underplay the significance of the ambitious, transformative socialising project behind, for example, New Labour's communitarianism and the drive against social exclusion. Indeed the following statement from Rose himself on the Third Way's new 'ethico-politics' seems to confirm the continuing salience of social strategies, albeit targeted rather than holistic in character: 'Through ethical reconstruction, the excluded citizen is to be re-attached to a virtuous community' (Rose 1999a: 489). The case for the hegemony of actuarialism in contemporary strategies of social control – crime viewed as mundane risk to be managed – is overstated by proponents of the thesis (see, for example, Ericson and Haggerty 1997). My own work never concurred with this supposed sweeping truth of a new penology based on actuarialism and instead has highlighted at times the 'rebirth' of rehabilitationism and hydrid forms of restorative justice (Hughes 2001). This trend has since moved on apace, not least as result of a new 'ethico-politics' of communitarian responsibilisation and efforts at coercive social inclusion for the 'underclass' and its 'difficult' members and exclusion via incarceration for its 'dangerous' members as the following discussion makes clear.

Communitarianism and the 'new' politics of community

The popularity and significance of appeals to governing 'through' appeals to community are even more pronounced now than in the mid-1990s. In some ways my work (Hughes 1996a) may be said to have been ahead of the 'criminological pack' in recognising the likely significance of communitarian ideas, and particularly the conservative variant, in informing a new popular, moralising politics.[7] In other words, appeals to community are not just figures of speech but rather may represent key elements of the founding principles which underpin a 'new' politics. In both Anthony Giddens' and 'New' Labour's promotion of a Third Way in politics, we find alongside the social democratic values of equal worth and opportunity for all the rise to prominence of responsibility and community – terms freighted with values – which constitute new ways for governing the behaviour of individuals through acting upon this ethical force field (Rose 1999a: 474). In other words, the possibility is opened up for the attempted governing of citizens through community. According to Rose (1999a: 475–6),

> Community, rather than the 'social' is the new territorialisation of political thought, the new way in which conduct is collectivised … in a double movement of autonomisation and responsibilisation. Once responsibilised and entrepreneurialised, they would govern themselves within a state-secured framework of law and order … Communitarianism thus promises a new moral contract, a partnership between an enabling state and responsible citizens, based upon the strengthening of the natural bonds of community.

37

The dangerously regressive character of this moral voice of community is viewed by Rose (1999a: 486) as being compounded further by its explicitly unitary and Christian character in the UK. It is of course crucial to argue that all is not, to borrow Rose's terms, 'totalised' and 'fatalised'. As Kevin Stenson (1998b) has warned us with regard to the pitfalls of poststructuralist discourse analysis, it is all too easy to find seemingly coherent, totalising 'histories of the present' from texts which may depart dramatically from the contradictory, confusing and uneven material conditions of existence outside the cosy world of the text. This qualification to Rose's compelling account is crucial to hold onto in future work on emergent governmental projects of social reform and re-ordering. For once I would concur with that intellectual 'butterfly', John Gray (1997: 77) in his argument that:

> What we lack are common institutions, which meet enduring human needs for membership and security without smothering the cultural diversity that our society contains. Such institutions cannot be advanced by any project of the Right. Lack of clarity on this fundamental point leaves *the discourse of community up for grabs.*
> (emphasis added)

Rose's own earlier work (1996) and that of other Foucauldian governmentalists (for example, O'Malley 1992) has helped initiate a wider recognition that the changing strategies of governance, including community-based ones, at times open up new opportunities for the empowerment of individuals and groups. Not surprisingly there is little mention of this feature of the thesis in Rose's analysis of the com-munitarian, Third Way politics of 'New' Labour . However, in his text *Powers of Freedom* (1999b), Rose does briefly look at the possibilities of a 'radical ethico' politics associated with non-essentialised, 'becoming communities'. This noted, it remains somewhat unfashionable in the academy to express even an ambivalent interest in the potentialities of community as a site for progressive developments. One is, for example, easily tainted as being 'guilty by association' by sharing the same guiding word and stigmata ('communitarianism') as that of Amitai Etzioni. Jock Young (1999: 153) has rightly observed that 'Writers on the left prioritise justice over community, whereas those on the right grant priority to community over justice'. In response it may be argued that the prioritising of justice over community should not be at the cost of condemning community to the 'bag of tricks' belonging to and deployed by one's ideological enemies on the moral right as has tended to be the case for most intellectuals on the left (but see Little 2002).

Much radical communitarian work implicitly involves a critical encounter with what may be termed aspects of the 'postmodernist turn' in social and political theory. Much postmodernist work, even by those writers who wish to promote political and moral engagement with the (collective?) struggles for justice and tolerance of difference (Young 1990), appears to essentialise difference and at its worst results in self-indulgent solipsism and the (rather ironic) preaching of moral and political disengagement. Furthermore, as Sandra Walklate (1998: 413) perceptively notes, 'although post-modernism encourages us to live without the enemy, it stops short of offering constructive bases for mutual understanding and trust'.

Iris Marion Young (1990: 30) has argued that all forms of communitarianism are committed to the dangerous 'ideal of community'. According to Young (1990: 227) 'This ideal (of community) expresses a desire for the fusion of subjects with one another which in practice exclude those with whom the group does not identify' . She claims such views are predicated on the essentialist Rousseauian dream of the unity of subjects with each other. Young (1990: 231) then goes on to claim that the 'ideal of community denies the ontological difference within and between subjects', a statement which itself appears to be bizarrely essentialist for a postmodernist theorist! As Jock Young (1999: 177) notes, such views suffer from a 'fantasy of unassimilated otherness'. More generally, there are also dangers in the postmodernist promotion of a politics of recognition which is divorced from a wider politics of justice. There is little doubt that diversity is a key element to the 'new contract' of citizenship but such diversity should be understood not as a catalogue of fixed features but rather a 'plethora of cultures, ever changing, ever developing, transforming themselves and each other' (Young 1999: 198). Such a vision is surely preferable to both the stifling conformity to the single 'moral community' of conservative communitarianism and the 'unconnectedness and fixed differences' of postmodernism. It is also crucial to the promotion of and struggle for a progressive replacement discourse on community safety.

Notes

1 There is as yet no adequate history of the development of crime prevention as policies and practices throughout postwar UK society. However, Daniel Gilling (1997: chapter 4) does provide a nuanced account of the changing fortunes of situational and community-based approaches to crime prevention from the late 1970s onwards. He usefully plots the complex interplay

around the Home Office of political, policymaking and research-based interests which lie behind the chequered career of this profoundly contested term (see also Tilley 2002).

2 And that reputation for practising researchers in the field of crime prevention is no doubt made all the more galling given mainstream criminology's more general historical tendency to serve as an at times collusive 'handmaiden' of the state, geared to a largely non-critical, at best reformist and an often administrative project of crime control (Cohen 1981). Mainstream criminology writ large was thus largely untouched until late in its institutional history by the radical intellectual debates in the social sciences more generally (but see Taylor *et al* 1973). However, the 'dismal science' label attached to the field of crime prevention studies may not be necessarily accurate when the history of the subject is explored afresh and future trends in crime control are imagined (see Hughes 1998a, for a somewhat revisionist history of the subject).

3 Many thanks to the participants (in particular Adam Edwards and Kevin Stenson) at the research seminar series *Rethinking Crime Prevention and Community Safety* in 2000 at the Open University for raising this crucial point. My own local research on a relatively affluent 'shire' county in the early-to-mid 1990s did not adequately address the close links between the rise of community safety policy and the managing of the socially excluded 'underclass'. Such battles over 'sovereignty' for the control of troubled/troublesome places and spaces continues apace in the new millennium.

4 Such globalising pronouncements on the 'failure' or lack of tangible successes of 'community'-based crime prevention are themselves not without some limitations even accepting the 'what works is what can be counted' logic. Not least, they tend to ignore and collapse local differences and the crucial importance of the varying contexts to initiatives and policies which much of the work in this volume has highlighted.

5 The fears about the fate of SCP from Ken Pease appear to have been premature and exaggerated. Indeed recent developments in the UK and elsewhere suggest that there has been a renaissance of situational, opportunity-based approaches to crime reduction at the heart of the governmental project of crime control in many late modern societies (see Hughes *et al* 2002b).

6 That noted, when compared to criminological debates, the silence of social policy analysts in the UK with regard to community safety and crime control strategies more generally remains to this day deafening (for some notable exceptions, see Cooke 1997; Jordan 1996 and 1998; Stenson 2000; Gilling and Barton 1997). Kevin Stenson (2000) has convincingly argued that there are historical and institutional factors associated with social policy's close relationship to the Beveridgean social democratic welfare state which have led to the insulation of social policy analysis (as occupying the realm of the 'social') from that of the study of crime control.

7 For example, Young (1999: 22–3) has recently and belatedly noted that Etzioni's 'much vaunted "communitarianism" is not one of integration but of overarching values and sentiments'.

References

Bailey, N., Barker, A. and MacDonald, K. (1995) *Partnership Agencies in British Urban Policy*. London: UCL Press.

Bauman, Z. (1999) *In Search of Politics*. Cambridge: Polity.

Becker, H. (1967) 'Whose Side Are We On?' *Social Problems*, 14, 239–48.

Blair, T. (1997) *The Third Way*. London: Fabian Society.

Cohen, S. (1974) 'Criminology and the Sociology of Deviance in Britain', in P. Rock and M. MacIntosh (eds), *Deviance and Social Control*. London: Tavistock.

Cohen, S. (1981) 'Footprints in the Sand', in M. Fitzgerald, J. Muncie and J. Pawson (eds), *Crime and Society*. London: Macmillan.

Cohen, S. (1985) *Visions of Social Control*. Cambridge: Polity.

Cooke, D. (1997) *Criminal Justice and Social Policy: a New Settlement or the Emperor's New Clothes?* Social Policy Association Conference, University of Lincolnshire and Humberside, July.

Crawford, A. (1997) *The Local Governance of Crime*. Oxford: Clarendon Press.

Crawford, A. (1998) *Crime Prevention and Community Safety*. London: Longman.

Dingwall, R. (1999) 'Risk Society: The Culture of Fear and the Millennium', *Social Policy and Administration*, 33 (4), 474–91.

Düvell, F. and Jordan, B. (1999) 'Immigration, Asylum and Citizenship', *Imprints*: Journal of Analytical Socialism, 4 (1), 13–36.

Ekblom, P. and Pease, K. (1995) 'Evaluating Crime Prevention', in M. Tonry and D. Farrington (eds), *Building a Safer Society*. Chicago, IL: University of Chicago Press.

Ericson, R. and Haggerty, K. (1997) *Policing the Risk Society*. Oxford: Clarendon Press.

European Forum for Urban Security (1994) *Security and Democracy*. Paris: European Forum for Urban Security.

Garland, D. (2001) *The Culture of Crime*. Oxford: Oxford University Press.

Giddens, A. (1998) *The Third Way*. Cambridge: Polity.

Gilling, D. (1997) *Crime Prevention*. London: UCL Press.

Gilling, D. and Barton, A. (1997) 'Crime Prevention and Community Safety: a New Home for Social Policy', *Critical Social Policy* 17 (1), 63–83.

Gilling, D. and Hughes, G. (2000) *Initial Findings of a National Survey of Community Safety Officers*. British Society of Criminology Conference, University of Leicester, July.

Gordon, P. (1987) 'Community Policing', in P. Scraton (ed.), *Law, Order and the Authoritarian State*. Milton Keynes: Open University Press.

Gray, J. (1997) *Endgames: Questions in late Modern Thought*. Cambridge: Polity Press.

Haines, S. and Sutton, A. (2000) 'Criminology as Religion', *British Journal of Criminology*, 40 (1), 146–62.

Hirst, P. and Thompson, G. (1996) *Globalisation in Question*. Cambridge: Polity.

Home Office (1991) *Safer Communities: The Delivery of Crime Prevention Through the Partnership Approach*. London: HMSO.

Hope, T. (1995) 'Community crime prevention', in M. Tonry and D. Farrington (eds), *Building a Safer Society*. Chicago, IL: University of Chicago Press.

Hope, T. (2000) (ed.) *Perspectives on Crime Reduction*. Aldershot: Ashgate.

Hope, T. and Shaw, M. (eds) (1988) *Communities and Crime Reduction*. London: HMSO.

Hughes, G. (1992) *Improving Police/Community Consultation: Report*. Northampton: Nene Centre for Research.

Hughes, G. (1994) 'Talking Cop Shop: A Case-study of Police Community Consultation in Transition', *Policing and Society*, 4, 253–70.

Hughes, G. (1995) *Northamptonshire Corporate Community Safety Strategy: Report on the First Phase of Implementation*. Northampton: Nene Centre for Research.

Hughes, G. (1996a) 'Communitarianism and Law and Order', *Critical Social Policy*, 16 (4), 17–41.

Hughes, G. (1996b) 'Strategies of Crime Prevention and Community Safety in Contemporary Britain', *Studies on Crime and Crime Prevention*, 5, 221–44.

Hughes, G. (1997) 'Policing Late Modernity: Crime Management in Contemporary Britain', in N. Jewson and S. MacGregor (eds), *Transforming Cities: Contested Governance and New Spatial Divisions*. London: Routledge.

Hughes, G. (1998a) *Understanding Crime Prevention: Social Control, Risk and Late Modernity*. Buckingham: Open University Press.

Hughes, G. (ed.) (1998b) *Imagining Welfare Futures*. London: Routledge.

Hughes, G. (2000a) 'Community Safety in the Age of the "Risk Society" ', in S. Ballintyne, K. Pease and V. McLaren (eds), *Secure Foundations: Key Issues in Crime Prevention, Crime Reduction and Community Safety*. London: IPPR.

Hughes, G. (2000b) 'In the Shadow of Crime and Disorder: the Contested Politics of Community Safety', *Crime Prevention and Community Safety: An International Journal*, 2 (3) 47–60.

Hughes, G. (2000c) 'The "Moral Career" of the Community Safety Officer'. Security and Safety in the New Millennium Colloquium, University of Leeds, April.

Hughes, G. (2000d) 'Understanding the Politics of Criminological Research', in P. Francis and V. Jupp (eds), *Doing Criminological Research*. London: Sage.

Hughes, G. (2001) 'The Competing Logics of Community Sanctions', in E. McLaughlin and J. Muncie (eds), *Controlling Crime*. London: Sage.

Hughes, G. (2002) 'Crime and Disorder Reduction Partnerships: the Future of Community Safety', in G. Hughes, E. McLaughlin and J. Muncie (eds), *Crime Prevention and Community Safety: New Directions*. London: Sage.

Hughes, G. and Lewis, G. (eds) (1998) *Unsettling Welfare*. London: Routledge.

Hughes, G. and Little, A. (1999) 'The Contradictions of New Labour's Communitarianism', *Imprints: Journal of Analytical Socialism*, 4 (1), 37–62.

Hughes, G. and McLaughlin, E. (2002) 'Together We'll Crack It: Partnership and the Governance of Crime' in M. Powell, C. Glendenning and K. Rummer (eds), *Partnerships: a 'Third Way' Approach*. Bristol: Policy Press.

Hughes, G. and Mooney, G. (1998) 'Community', in G. Hughes (ed.), *Imagining Welfare Futures*. London: Routledge.

Hughes, G, McLaughlin, E. and Muncie, J. (eds) (2002a) *Crime Prevention and Community Safety: New Directions*. London: Sage.

Hughes, G., McLaughlin, E. and Muncie, J. (2002b) 'Teetering on the Edge: the Futures of Crime and Crime Control', in G. Hughes, E. McLaughlin and J. Muncie (eds), *Crime Prevention and Community Safety: New Directions*. London: Sage.

Hughes, G., Mears, R. and Winch, C. (1997) 'An Inspector Calls: Regulation and Accountability in Three Public Services', *Policy and Politics*, 25 (3), 299–313.

Hughes, G., Pilkington, A. and Leisten, R. (1996) *An Independent Evaluation of the Northamptonshire Diversion Unit*. Northampton: Nene Centre for Research.

Hughes, G., Pilkington, A. and Leisten, R. (1998) 'Diversion in a Culture of Severity', *Howard Journal of Criminal Justice*, 37 (1), 16–33.

Jewson, N. and MacGregor, S. (eds) (1997) *Transforming Cities: Contested Governance and New Spatial Divisions*. London: Routledge.

Johnston, L. (1996) 'Policing Diversity: the Impact of the Public-Private Complex in Policing', in F. Leishman *et al* (eds), *Core Issues in Policing*. London: Longman.

Jordan, B. (1996) *A Theory of Poverty and Social Exclusion*. Cambridge: Polity.

Jordan, B. (1998) *The New Politics of Welfare*. London: Sage.

Lea, J. and Young, J. (1984) *What Is to Be Done about Law and Order?* Harmondsworth: Penguin.

Leadbetter, C. (1996) *The Self-Policing Society*, Demos Arguments 9. London: Demos.

Little, A. (2002 in press) *The Politics of Community: Theory and Practice*. Edinburgh: Edinburgh University Press.

McLaughlin, E. (2002) 'The Crisis of the Social and the Political Materialisation of Community Safety', in G. Hughes, E. McLaughlin and J. Muncie (eds), *Crime Prevention and Community Safety: New Directions*. London: Sage.

McLaughlin, E., Muncie, J. and Hughes, G. (2001) 'The Permanent Revolution: New Labour, New Public Management and the Modernisation of Criminal Justice', *Criminal Justice*, 1 (3), 301–18.

Nelken, D. (1985) 'Community Involvement in Crime Control', *Contemporary Legal Problems*, 85, 259–67.

Newburn, T. (2002) 'Policing and Community Safety', in G. Hughes, E. McLaughlin and J. Muncie (eds), *Crime Prevention and Community Safety: New Directions*. London: Sage.

O'Malley, P. (1992) 'Risk, Power and Crime Prevention', *Economy and Society*, 21 (3), 251–68.

O'Malley, P. (1999) 'Governmentality and Risk Society', *Economy and Society*, 28 (1), 138–48.

O'Malley, P. and Palmer, D. (1996) 'Post-Keynesian Policing', *Economy and Society*, 25 (5), 137–55.

Pease, K. (1994) 'Crime Prevention', in M. Maguire *et al* (eds), *Oxford Handbook of Criminology*. Oxford: Clarendon Press.

Pease, K. (1997) 'Crime Prevention', in M. Maguire *et al* (eds), *Oxford Handbook of Criminology*, 2nd edn. Oxford: Clarendon Press.

Powell, M., Glendinning, C. and Rummer, K. (eds) (2002) *Partnerships: a 'Third Way' Approach*. Bristol: Policy Press.

Pratt, J. (1986) 'Diversion from the Juvenile Court', *British Journal of Criminology*, 26 (3), 212–33.

Reiner, R. (2000) 'Crime and Control in Britain', *Sociology*, 34 (1), 71–94.

Rose, N. (1996) 'The Death of the Social? Refiguring the Territory of Government', *Economy and Society*, 25 (3), 321–56.

Rose, N. (1999a) 'Inventiveness in Politics', *Economy and Society*, 28 (3), 467–93.

Rose, N. (1999b) *Powers of Freedom*. Cambridge: Cambridge University Press.

Sherman, L., Gottfredson, D., Mackenzie, D., Ecke, J., Reuter, P. and Bushway, S. (1997) *Preventing Crime: What Works, What Doesn't, What's Promising*, Research in Brief, National Institute of Justice, Washington DC: US Department of Justice.

Sparks, R. and Garland, D. (eds) (2000) 'Criminology and Social Theory', *British Journal of Criminology*, Special Edition.

Stenson, K. (1995) 'Community Security as Government: the British Experience', in W. Hammerschicht, I. Karazman-Marawetz and W. Staagl (eds), *Jahrbuch für Rechtsand Kriminalsoziologie*. Baden-Baden: Nomos.

Stenson, K. (1998a) 'Displacing Social Policy through Crime Control' in S. Hänninen (ed.), *Displacement of Social Policies*. University of Jyväskylä: SoPhi.

Stenson, K. (1998b) 'Beyond Histories of the Present', *Economy and Society*, 29 (4), 333–52.

Stenson, K. (2000) 'Crime Control, Social Policy and Liberalism', in G. Lewis *et al* (eds), *Rethinking Social Policy*. London: Sage.

Taylor, I., Walton, P. and Young, J. (1973) *The New Criminology*. London: Routledge.

Tilley, N. (1994) 'Crime Prevention and the Safer Cities Story', *Howard Journal*, 32 (1), 40–57.

Tilley, N. (2002) 'Crime Prevention 1975–2010', in G. Hughes, E. McLaughlin and J. Muncie (eds), *Crime Prevention and Community Safety: New Directions*. London: Sage.

van Swaaningen, R. (2002) 'Towards a replacement discourse on community safety: lessons from the Netherlands' in G. Hughes, E. McLaughlin and J. Muncie (eds), *Crime Prevention and Community Safety: New Directions*. London: Sage.

Walklate, S. (1998) 'Excavating the Fear of Crime: Fear, Anxiety or Trust', *Theoretical Criminology*, 2 (4).

Wiles, P. and Pease, K. (2000) 'Crime Prevention and Community Safety: Tweedledum and Tweedledee?', in S. Ballintyne, K. Pease and V. McClaren (eds), *Secure Foundations: Key Issues in Crime Prevention, Crime Reduction and Community Safety*. London: IPPR.

Young, I. (1990) 'The Idea of Community and the Politics of Difference', in L. Nicholson (ed.), *Feminism/Postmodernism*. New York: Routledge.

Young, J. (1999) *The Exclusive Society*. London: Sage.

Chapter 3

'Same bed, different dreams': postmodern reflections on crime prevention and community safety

Eugene McLaughlin

Introduction

I want to use this chapter to argue that it is becoming increasingly more difficult for scholars to acquire a meaningful understanding of New Labour's crime reduction policies by concentrating on the national political level. Some readers may wonder why I am taking such a position. After all, under New Labour, the Home Office – the official site of policymaking – has become more open and transparent and much more willing to consult in the setting of its research agenda. Moreover, never has there been more commitment to supporting a rational 'what works' approach to policymaking. I begin by briefly detailing and critiquing what we might describe as the Home Office's 'high modernist' version of what is happening in the field of crime reduction under New Labour. I then go on to argue the case for using the analytical powers associated with postmodern theorising to highlight the 'irrationalities' linked to the hyper-politicisation of law and order politics and the insights of the governmentality perspective to foreground the deeper rationalities associated with New Labour's commitment to utilising 'community' as a category and potential mode of governance.

The over- and under-representation of 'the rational': 'what works is what matters'

I want to take as my starting point a publication by four Home Office economists published in 2001 entitled 'Evaluation of the United Kingdom's "Crime Reduction Programme": Costs and Benefits' (Dhiri *et al* 2001). This 'in-house' account seeks to explain the defining features of New Labour's crime reduction programme to a primarily North American audience. It describes how the incoming New Labour administration established a cross-departmental review of the criminal justice system as part of a broader assessment of public expenditure. A Home Office working group commissioned an evaluation of the effectiveness of policies for tackling offending which in turn produced a report assessing the research evidence on the possibilities and limitations of different methods of reducing crime. 'Reducing Offending' (Goldblatt and Lewis 1998) concluded that crime could be reduced significantly through the utilization of a coherent evidence-led programme of initiatives. Dhiri *et al* then detail how in July 1998 the government announced a three-year Crime Reduction Programme based on the findings of the review.

> The CRP is intended to contribute to reversing the long-term growth rate in crime by ensuring that the greatest impact for the money spent is achieved and that this impact increases pro-gressively. It will do so by promoting innovation, generating a significant improvement in knowledge about effectiveness and cost-effectiveness, and fostering progressive mainstreaming of emerging knowledge about good practice. Projects will be carefully selected to ensure that they contribute to achieving these objectives. All CRP funded initiatives will be *independently* evaluated.
>
> (pp. 181–2)

Readers are informed that the Crime Reduction Programme was extended in April 1999 with the announcement of a further £153 million investment for CCTV and other initiatives aimed at tackling vehicle crime. This evidence-led approach would also be applied to related programmes that received funding under the Comprehensive Spending Review, e.g. drug use and related crime (£211 million) and constructive prison regimes (£226 million).

In admirable detail, Dhiri *et al* then lay out the multitude of sophisticated, overlapping evaluation principles that will be used by the Home Office to analyse cost effectiveness and cost benefits, measure inputs and costs and outcomes and benefits, and compare costs with outcomes and benefits. In their conclusion they inform readers that:

A sound understanding of the costs and benefits of alternative approaches to reducing crime is fundamental to shaping future policy development. It will help ensure continued improvements in the impact on crime and value for money of policy initiatives both directly, through CRP programmes, and by the incorporation of what has been learned into mainstream government programs in the CJS and other areas of social policy.

The CRP will contribute to a better understanding of what works, where and in what circumstances. Through this understanding, it should help to ensure that crime reduction is viewed less as a series of one-off, discrete projects, and more as a continued and adaptive use of innovative and tailored strategies that can achieve a lasting impact on crime.

(pp. 199–200)

This evidence-led narrative is confirmed if we check the Home Office website. Self-referential text after self-referential text across this website and associated sites stress the need for mutually reinforcing aims and objectives, new funding mechanisms to direct resources strategically and effectively, the embedding of a 'what works' and 'best practice' professional culture and the development of a performance management culture to enhance productivity. It is also possible to map and trace the new systems that have been put in place to drive New Labour's reforms by the Home Office, the Audit Commission and Her Majesty's Inspectorate of Constabulary.

Hence, more than enough heavily hyped data is being generated by Home Office research programmes to provide proof of the government's commitment to institutionalising a 'what works' regime. And New Labour has won high marks from administrative criminologists in the Home Office for adhering to the promises made during the 1997 election campaign.

However, it is clear that those working within the confines of administrative criminology cannot provide adequate representation of the anti-crime project of their political masters. To put it bluntly, the excessive focus on demonstrating the seemingly relentless forward march of the 'what works' programme flattens New Labour's criminal justice project into a non-descript, uninflected narrative devoid of complexity, tensions and contradictions. This account has no use for letting the different facets of the government's crime reduction agenda 'breathe' and no interest in exploring the social and political overtones and undertones of policy, practice and discourse. It is also underpinned by a peculiarly 'high modernist' belief that the capacities of 'administration', 'science' and 'technology' can turn the clock forward to a time when crime will not play such a major role in the conduct of government. Hence, the 'what works' programme has brought together academics, administrators and practitioners from a variety of backgrounds who imagine a relatively crime-free world which can be moulded by 'crime science' – the successor discipline to criminology. In their imagined future 'age of reason', flows of crime data will pass before a new generation of crime scientists and auditors for inspection and evaluation and their work will occasionally be interrupted by the identification of a 'problem' that momentarily disturbs the otherwise relentless progress of the carefully planned and executed national crime reduction programme.

However, as I noted in the introduction, two thematics in particular complicate the claims of administrative criminologists to the imminent dominion of rational policymaking and implementation. First, we have to recognise the impact of the hyper-politicisation of the national politics of law and order that has taken place in the UK. And second, we ought to be attentive to the highly ideological concept of 'community' that lies at the centre of New Labour's governmental project. These run in tandem with the 'what works' policymaking approach, sometimes overlapping, sometimes diverging wildly and at other times standing in stark contrast to each other. It is the multi-levelled complexity of New Labour's policy representation that makes it virtually impossible to read off at the national level what the 'real' position might be in any given locality. Alternative positions are presented to different audiences and one could go so far as to argue that it is becoming increasingly difficult to distinguish between 'rhetoric' and 'reality', 'fact' and 'fiction', 'signifier' and 'signified'. In order to explore 'meaning' it is more important than ever to sound out the 'whether, how and why' localisation and inter-nalisation of national policies and trends.

The 'irrationalities' ensuing from the hyper-politicisation of national law and order politics

The first decisive factor influencing the need to 'go local' is the relationship between New Labour and the national news media. It is a truism to say that the agenda setting powers of the news media enable it to exercise an increasingly pervasive influence on political discourse and public opinion. The majority of public understanding of government policies transpires through the daily reporting and commentary of journalists. Not surprisingly, politicians and their advisors try to influence news coverage of policies precisely because, as many commentators have noted, under the conditions of postmodernity the public 'image' or 'representation' of the policy is the 'reality'. As Angus (1989: 342) has noted:

> Postmodern society is constituted by a media environment characterised by the continuous circulation of signs and messages. The distinctions which are representational distinctions become insufficient to grasp the 'simulation' of signs by the media. They are not copies of 'real' relationships but the simulation of media events that produce real relationships.

At the beginning of the twenty-first century, the relationship between news reporting and political policymaking is growing ever more complex and multilayered. It was during the Reagan presidency that the term 'permanent campaign' was first coined to refer to the combination of image-making and strategic calculation that was turning 'governing' into a perpetual campaign and remaking government into what Heclo (2000) has defined as 'an instrument designed to sustain an elected official's popularity'. Heclo was one of a number of political commentators in the United States who detailed how sophisticated commercial marketing and public relations techniques were being increasingly used by a new breed of political consultants to effectively eliminate the difference between 'campaigning' and 'governing'. During the Clinton presidency the United States witnessed the acceleration and maturation of the 'permanent campaign'.

Although analysts are not sure whether to define it as a 'post-political' or postmodern political moment, there is general agreement that the rise of the 'permanent campaign' is connected to the significant percentage of voters who have given up on the electoral process, the decline in the strength of voters' affiliation with political parties, the institutionalisation of interest groups within the formal political arena, the growth of new 24 hours a day, seven days a week communication and information technologies, and the creation of new political technologies, especially public relations and polling. Newman (1999) details how through the aid of television, computers, database technologies and advertising campaigns politicians are seeking election and governing through the use of sophisticated marketing techniques that drive public opinion and stress image over substance, personality over issues, emotion over rationality and soundbites over meaningful explanation. Attention is drawn by Heclo (2000) to the 'orchestrated appeals' that are used to build and/or maintain the approval of certain publics and targeted audiences for specific policies:

> People in government, interest groups at the fringes of govern-
> ment, and networks of collaboration and opposition stretching
> across both spheres are all part of the non-stop battle for public
> approval that now occurs throughout the political landscape. In
> that sense, the permanent campaign is everywhere, and it is
> nowhere at the same time.
>
> (Heclo 2000: 16)

The claims and counter-claims of competing political parties make it more and more difficult for journalists and commentators to conduct 'reality checks', not least because they are also active participants in key aspects of the 'permanent campaign'. However, certain journalists and commentators have also become increasingly aware of the need for careful analysis of the strategic 'framing' and 'spinning' of policy announcements and to 'sift' and 'read' for 'strategic silences' and 'hidden agendas'.

In the UK, New Labour operates on a scaled-down version of the 'permanent campaigning' mode and there has been considerable commentary, much of it critical, on the party's attempts to control the news media and manage public opinion (Norris 1998; Hefferman 1999; Osborne 1999; Jones 2000; Riddell 2000). New Labour's 'spin masters' – Alistair Campbell, Phillip Gould, David Hill and Peter Mandelson – will always be associated with the 'manufacture' and 'selling' of the re-branded 'new' party to voters during the 1997 general election. One senior advisor subsequently explained how 'communications is not an after-thought of our policy. It's central to the whole mission of New Labour' (cited in *New Statesman*, 18 June 1998).

New Labour's stated intention is to attempt to control the public agenda through a form of mass marketing. Focus groups and public opinion polling data are used to fashion policy announcements; memorable soundbites are written into public statements and speeches; public appearances are carefully choreographed so that core messages are reinforced by visual images; there is the constant search for 'risk-free' policy positions and platforms; policy successes are the subject of endless repetition; 'failed' or 'unclear' policies are relaunched or re-cycled; public fears on controversial issues are exploited; the instant rebuttal of opposition claims occurs through 'fact correction'; 'surrogate speakers' are used to to 'play' different aspects of a policy announcement to diverse audiences; and proof is constantly provided that the party is 'wired in' to public sentiment. New Labour has also shown itself to be the master of what Heclo (2000) defines as 'pseudo-events', e.g. leaks, counter-leaks, exclusive interviews, trial balloons, reaction stories, staged public appearances and made-to-order news events. The party has developed a particular expertise in controlling the news headlines with pre-release publicity blitzes that enable it to dominate headlines again when policy is actually released. Not surprisingly, New Labour interprets policy failures in terms of its 'failure to communicate' rather than in terms of the nature of its initiatives or its strategy for governing.

All of this goes some way to explaining New Labour's propensity towards 'soft' demagoguery on the 'crime' issue. The soundbite 'tough on crime and tough on the causes of crime' is central to New Labour's mythology about how it won the 1997 general election. Because it is charged with multiple meanings it enabled New Labour to compete electorally for the first time on a traditionally Conservative issue. And as the public opinions associated with 'Middle England' have become an increasingly crucial determinant of criminal justice policies, the pursuit of crime policies that are manifestly 'on side' with popular sentiment has become the foremost aspiration of New Labour in government. As many commentators have noted, New Labour cannot resist the populist urge to 'spin' a crime policy proposal if it thinks it will reflect public opinion. The deliberations of New Labour's special advisors on crime remain carefully shielded from public review but the launching of the so-called 'national crime plan' in February 2001 offers an important insight into New Labour's ability and willingness to spin a good crime story irrespective of its commitment to promoting its 'what works' agenda.

In early 2001, New Labour and the Conservative Party moved up a campaigning gear in preparation for what they thought would be an early election. Political analysts were in no doubt that due to the economic performance presided over by the Chancellor, Gordon Brown, New Labour would be re-elected. Indeed, right-wing newspapers began to carry the findings of opinion polls suggesting a second New Labour landslide. However, they also noted how the perception of broken promises could have repercussions on the size of New Labour's majority. Opinion polls also detected a groundswell of public discontent on key issues and unhappiness with the contrived nature of New Labour. This indicated that campaigning would not be problem free and further proof that New Labour's electoral block was potentially volatile and unstable.

Of particular concern was New Labour's record on crime. As a signature issue for New Labour, the party could not afford to be seen to be compromising on its mega-hit soundbite. Reports began to filter through suggesting that party strategists were concerned that although recorded crime had fallen under New Labour, violent crime had continued to rise and the number of crimes solved had fallen, as had the numbers of police officers on the beat. In addition, rumours were circulating that the only one of the five pre-election pledges not to be met before May would be the promise to halve the average time from arrest to sentence from 142 to 71 days for juvenile offenders. New Labour also felt under renewed pressure on crime as the right-wing press acclaimed Conservative Party efforts to reclaim its 'traditional' issue. The Conservatives were making maximum political capital out of controversial issues such as asylum seekers, increased street crime, public campaigns against sex offenders and declining police morale post-Macpherson. Amid unmistakable signs of unease about crime resurfacing as a 'feelbad' issue, newspapers began to carry exclusives on how the Prime Minister had informed the Cabinet that the 'war on crime' would be a central part of New Labour's election manifesto. In the unofficial countdown to the 2001 election New Labour would make a concerted effort to shore up its position on law and order with eye-catching initiatives to reassert its 'tough on crime and criminals' credentials. The government's public statements 'toughened' and the harsh words and promises of more 'cops, courts and corrections' effectively drowned out any 'what works' nuances embedded in their proposed criminal justice reforms.

Hard as it may be for administrative criminologists to accept, in the foreseeable future criminal justice policies will not just be decided by recourse to what is 'rational'. Our society is increasingly organised around the production, circulation and manipulation of symbols and this means that the symbolic, irrational plane of national law and order politics is more important than ever before. The myriad forces and contradictory flows constitutive of the hyper-politicisation of law and order politics have the potential to turn the best laid master plans of administrative criminologists not just upside down but to twist them inside out and outside in.

Hyper-politicisation commits New Labour to constantly having to provide 'evidence' of its 'tough on crime' credentials to the news media. Crime news is news waiting to happen and the 'tough on crime' position is easy to spin. It does not seem to matter that New Labour is promising voters who read right-wing newspapers more 'cops, courts and corrections' and voters who read liberal/left-leaning newspapers that really behind all the 'tough' rhetoric it is committed to rehabilitation programmes. New Labour's political and media advisors seem to be of the opinion that so long as they 'control' the agenda they will not be held to account for spinning contradictory positions. However, we should be concerned about this state of affairs for the following reasons. First, New Labour will always be under pressure to prove its tough on crime credentials and no authoritarian initiative it offers will convince the right-wing media that it is not fundamentally 'soft on crime'. Hence, it runs the real risk of being driven ever rightward by sections of the news media in terms of its permanent campaigning position on crime. Second, the relentless hunt for soundbites runs the serious risk of reproducing crude stereotypical representations of the problem of crime that make rational discussion all but impossible. Third, there is the distinct possibility that political and media advisors will continue to selectively use the findings from Home Office research and official reviews to back up whatever New Labour needs to spin on a given issue. If really pushed, with the proper presentational spin virtually any policy pro-posal, no matter how irrational or authoritarian, can always be made to fit the 'what works' agenda. As we enter the new millennium the process of criminal justice policymaking has been transformed into a full-time marketing campaign and one of the long-term results will be ever deeper public distrust of and impatience with those who claim to offer expert knowledge on the problem of crime.

The governmental rationalities associated with New Labour's rediscovery of 'community'

It must be stressed that the hyper-politicisation of national law and order politics is not the only pressing reason for examining what exactly is taking hold in 'the local'. There is another political dynamic that is caught up in New Labour's cobweb of spins and twists – the classic Foucauldian question of how and what to govern (Foucault 1991; Rose 1999; Dean 1999).

No one should underestimate the extent to which communitarian thought has insinuated itself into New Labour's understanding of the causes of and solution to social disorder and malaise (see Hughes 1996; Levitas 1998). Communitarianism was the conceptual framework within which Tony Blair and Jack Straw forged and popularised the 'tough on crime and tough on the causes of crime' soundbite both to reconnect Labour with its traditional heartland constituencies and to convince the broader electorate of 'Middle England' that the party could be trusted on law and order. I will not digress into a full discussion of New Labour's communitarianism but will simply sketch out the relevant points that are appropriate to its conceptualisation of the problem of crime.

The core messages of Amitai Etzioni's (1993, 1995) 'communitarianism', particularly the emphasis on 'community as a moral voice' and the need for a return to 'core moral values', chimed almost perfectly with the resurgent ethical and Christian socialist wing of the Labour Party. According to Etzioni's analysis, US society is facing an unprecedented crisis of values and loss of virtue because of the breakdown of community. The moral infrastructure has been neglected and undermined as a result of relativistation and pluralisation, the social policies of the liberal left which stress entitlement and the New Right's privileging of and self-interest over the needs of the social order. High levels of criminality and anti-social behaviour are very obvious outcomes of a culture of unrestrained individualism and the quest for instant gratification. In the UK, New Labour has offered a similar diagnosis, arguing that the dangerous social tensions and levels of violent alienation on many council estates pose a strategic threat to the very possibility of governance (see Blair 1993; Mulgan and Wilkinson 1995; Mandelson and Liddle 1996).

'Community' is utilised by New Labour not just in a traditional sociological sense to bemoan fragmentation and breakdown, but also in a governmental manner to signal its determination to use the disciplinary powers of the state to tackle not just 'crime' but to restore order and pro-social behaviour. This civilising mission is a defining difference between New Labour and previous New Right administrations.

The architects of New Labour foregrounded the concept of 'community' as part of their ongoing attempt to forge a distinctive 'Third Way' between what they define as the 'failed' political philosophies of state-centred social democracy and free market liberal individualism. In their overview of the ideological construction of New Labour, Mandelson and Liddle (1996) argued that the concept of 'community' would enable New Labour to reclaim political ground 'that should never have been conceded to our political opponents' (p. 20). They stressed that New Labour did not have 'a soft, romantic' concept of community:

> Community is a robust and powerful idea, and is at the heart of the stakeholder economy New Labour wishes to create. It means teamwork – working and acting together in companies, in local neighbourhoods, in the country as a whole to get things done. It means mutuality – rights and responsibilities going hand in hand. It means justice – that all interests are served, not just those of the

rich and powerful. This tough and active concept of community is more than an individual obligation to be kind, loving and charitable.

(Mandelson and Liddle 1996: 19)

New Labour's attraction to 'community' is intimately connected to its 'Third Way' understanding of the future of the nation-state under globalisation. Globalisation is viewed by New Labour as providing new opportunities and new choices but also bringing the threat of new inequalities and alienation, 'straining or severing bonds of family, community and nation and traditional mechanisms of mutual support and values' (Straw 2000: 4). New Labour believes that diverse societies like the UK have to pay particular attention to the potential for division. Mechanisms have to be found to strengthen the bonds between individuals to create communities – and nation-states – that are not just active but robust and responsibilised enough to withstand the challenges thrown up by the new global economy. For the former to succeed, it has had to engage in the double movement of centralisation and localisation.

The Crime and Disorder Act 1998 is a classic example of this central-local double movement which is intended to strengthen the ties that bind through rebuilding strong families and fashioning safe and active local communities.

Strengthening the family

New Labour believes that 'the family' is the most important mechanism for transmitting moral values and social discipline and the place where a sense of individual responsibility and 'community' is nurtured. The breakdown in law and order is, according to this discourse, intimately linked to the break-up of strong, cohesive communities and the 'loss of community' is a result of the stresses in contemporary family life (Blair 1994; Utting *et al* 1993; Labour Party 1996). It is this that underpins 'welfarist' proposals to provide for the 'deserving': child-rearing education and advice for all parents to enable them to provide effective socialisation and supervision; additional state support to families experiencing difficulties in coping with their children. Guaranteed places for pre-school education for disadvantaged children were also pledged and welfare to work programmes for the young unemployed.

However, for New Labour a key source of disorder is a hard core of 'deadbeat' parents who do not know how to – or are unwilling to –

discharge their parental responsibilities and a generation of delinquent children who are inadequately socialised and supervised, hence the raft of authoritarian 'tough on youth crime' and 'tough love' policies to tackle 'persistent young offenders' and break the cycle of anti-social and petty criminal behaviour. To reinforce moral responsibility New Labour has confirmed that children under 10 are no longer exempt from prosecution. Local authorities have been provided with the power to introduce US-style night-time curfews on children and teenagers. Compulsory programmes force offenders to confront the nature and consequences of their criminal behaviour. New Labour has also defended the need for secure accommodation for the 'hard core' of young offenders. Courts have been given the power to impose Parental Responsibility Orders on parents who refused to accept responsibility for their children's delinquent actions. Under the order, parents are required to attend counselling and guidance sessions to help them to control their children effectively.

Rebuilding safe and active communities

Many of the initiatives unveiled by New Labour pre and post the 1997 election foreground the need for a 'zero-tolerance' approach to tackling the rising tide of public disorder and anti-social behaviour. These highly controversial 'defining deviance up' initiatives provide evidence of the nature of New Labour's unfolding anti-crime agenda and attestation of its readiness to use the legislative powers of the state to sanction intervention in 'disorderly' localities and 'dysfunctional' families in order to shift the balance of power from the 'criminal' and 'anti-social' to the 'law abiding' and 'respectable' (see Labour Party 1994, 1995). Anti-social behaviour orders enable police forces and local authorities to crack down on 'noisy neighbours' and 'families from hell' who indulge in chronic criminal, anti-social, threatening or disruptive behaviour. New Labour has also mandated the police and local authorities to reclaim the increasingly brutalised streets, by cracking down on aggressive beggars, drug addicts, drunks, louts, vandals, graffiti artists and 'squeegee merchants'. This is inspired by the high-profile 'zero-tolerance' or 'quality of life' policing strategy implemented in New York by William J. Bratton, the NYPD Commissioner, and Mayor Rudolf Guiliani. Underpinning this approach was the 'broken windows' thesis of Wilson and Kelling that claimed that low-level disorder and serious crime were inextricably linked (Wilson and Kelling, 1982; see also Kelling and Coles 1996, and Bratton 1997). Overlaying all of this are the coercive plans to resocialise work-deprived, welfare dependent, 'hard of hearing' multi-problem estates and localities which were deemed to be 'outside' conventional society. Thus there is little doubt that since the election of New Labour in 1997, 'problem' families and localities have been subjected to the attention of governmental agencies operating with new powers and techniques and new forms of coordination.

New Labour is also working with an agenda to 'activate' community spirit: 'in which the commitment of the individual is backed by the duty of all organisations – in the public sector, the private sector and the voluntary sector – towards a community of mutual care and a balance of rights and responsibilities' (Straw 1998: 16). For New Labour mechanisms have to be found to strengthen the bonds between individuals to create communities that are not just active but robust and responsibilised enough to withstand the challenges thrown up by the new global economy. Hence, the attempts to revitalise 'the family'. New Labour is also trying to resurrect 'volunteering', which 'brings people together and helps create a sense of citizenship that is often missing from communities today' (p. 7), and revalorise the voluntary sector because it 'builds and strengthens community life like nothing else' (*ibid*). At the time of writing, New Labour is showing increasing interest in inviting 'faith communities' into a formal partnership with the state for the delivery of social welfare services. In March 2001 Downing Street also invited across the American politicial philosopher Robert Putnam to provide an overview of his 'Bowling Alone' thesis. Putnam, like the communitarians, expresses concern that in the United States people are increasingly 'disconnected' from family, friends, neighbours and the social structure. Civic disengagement and disconnection poses a serious threat to school achievement, levels of crime and the health of political democracy. In Putnam's (2000) analysis, there is an urgent need to rebuild strong habits of civic and political participation.

The evidence to date indicates that a communitarian-inspired criminal justice agenda, irrespective of the objective findings of 'what works', will always seek to use the fight against crime and disorder to provide opportunities for active communal bonding. Various policy initiative's and statements suggest a New Labour 'imaginary' where local communities are to be encouraged, via the interventions of various governmental networks, to strengthen their moral and physical boundaries, to be intolerant of and censure anti-social behaviour, to set police priorities, to participate in broader policing initiatives, to determine the nature of punishment and compensation and to stigmatise or expel unrepentant criminals. These self-governing communities will also be rewarded financially for successfully tackling their crime problems. However, 'hard to reach' or 'hard of hearing' pathological localities are to be subject to multiple cross-cutting compulsory interventions. Governance is likely to become more local and intensive in these neighbourhoods as the number of application points grow. In the process, New Labour's programme of 'government through community' is generating new discourses of 'order' and 'control', constructing new criminal subjects and 'new model citizens' and rewriting the script of local governance.

Conclusion: bringing it all back 'home'

There are three general challenges that I want to emphasise initially in this conclusion. The first challenge is to loosen the grip of the 'what works' master narrative which is largely responsible for determining the framework within which much discussion about crime prevention and community safety takes place. Students of criminology should be taught that 'what works' does not reflect some unproblematic, unmediated 'reality out there' but rather is an outcome of particular discursive practices. Consequently, there is no persuasive reason for organising our 'knowledge' of New Labour's agenda primarily according to the terms set down by this narrative. Challenge number two is to explore how the hyper-politicisation of law and order in the UK complicates all attempts to provide a convincing rendition of the national policymaking and policy implementation process. We are increasingly working within a complex series of 'reflections' which mirror 'reflections' of the 'real' and the 'representational'. There is a forceful argument for all of us including a note of caution in anything we write along the lines of: 'What you are about to read may or may not be a work of "fiction". Names, characters, places and events are either the product of the authors' imagination or are used "fictitiously", and any resemblance to "real" persons, living or dead, events, or locales is entirely coincidental.'

The final challenge is to advance the argument for not just researching but theorising the 'little' nooks and crannies where 'crime prevention' and 'community safety' are and are not being 'performed' in a multitude of ways. I believe that we need a criminology that is both of and in 'the local' rather than 'community'. Theorising 'the local' in all its messy complexity is an essential part of attempting to understand and conceptualise the changing post-industrial, postmodern moment we inhabit. 'The local' is the vital production site for those established and emergent everyday practices, social relations, forms of identity and solidarity, and plurality of social interests that might just provide us with situated understandings of the complicated connections and dis-connections between national (and global) agendas and the textures of human experience and existence.

The rest of the conclusion writes itself in the form of a list of research topics that might enable us to generate fragments of critical knowledge about what is happening at particular moments in particular localities. It is vitally important to monitor the strenuous efforts of administrative criminologists to make 'what works' work and consider the degree to which their work is co-terminous with hyper-politicisation. Work also needs to be done to make legible and interrogate:

- the governmental strategies of 'community' that are actually being thought into being and to what effect by the local authorities under the Crime and Disorder Act 1998 and allied legislation;

- the new managerialist modes of governance, networks of partnership-based decisionmaking, interest representation and mechanisms of accountability that are constitutive of the crime reduction project;

- any contestation and resistance, including the perspectives of the marginalised, problematised and criminalised.

We also need to utilise more detailed, portraiture-style methodologies to make these processes legible. Finally, we need to acknowledge that New Labour's governmental project involves the incorporation of a significant number of social scientists as advisors and/or to develop new methods of problem analysis and evaluation and implementation. Critical reflection on the willingness of criminologists to be not just active but enthusiastic participants in the crime reduction programme would suggest that there are convincing ethical reasons for trying to develop a discussion about the governmental activities of ourselves.

References

Anderson, P., and Mann, N., (1997) *Safety First: The Making of New Labour.* London: Granta.

Angus, I. (1989) 'Circumscribing Postmodern Culture', in I. Angus and S. Jhally (eds), *Cultural Politics in Contemporary America.* California, University of California Press.

Blair, T. (1993) 'Why Crime is a Socialist Issue', *New Statesmen and Society*, 29 January, pp. 27–8.

Blair, T. (1994) 'Sharing Responsibility for Crime', in A. Coote (ed.), *Families, Children and Crime*. London: Institute of Public Policy Research.

Blair, T. (1996) *New Britain: My Vision of a Young Country*. London: Fourth Estate Books.

Bratton, W. (1997) 'Crime is Down in New York: Blame the Police', in N. Dennis (ed.), *Zero Tolerance: Policing a Free Society*. London: Institute of Economic Affairs.

Dean, M. (1999) *Governmentality: Power and Rule in Modern Society*. London: Sage.

Dhiri, S., Goldblatt, P., Brand, S. and Price, R. (2000) 'Evaluation of the United Kingdom's "Crime Reduction Programme" ', in B.C. Welsh, D.P. Farrington and L.W. Sherman (eds), *Costs and Benefits of Preventing Crime*. Boulder, CO: Westview Press.

Etzioni, A. (1993) *The Spirit of Community*. London: Fontana.

Etzioni, A. (1995) 'Nation in Need of Community Values', *Times/Demos Lecture*, 20 February.

Foucault, M. (1991) 'On Governmentality', in G. Burchell, C. Gordon and P. Miller (eds), *The Foucault Effect*. London: Harvester Wheatsheaf.

Goldblatt, P. and Lewis, C. (eds) (1998) *Reducing Offending: An Assessment of Research Evidence on Ways of Dealing with Offending Behaviour*. London: Home Office.

Gould, P. (1998) *The Unfinished Revolution: How the Modernizers Saved the Labour Party*. London: Little, Brown.

Heclo, H. (2000) 'Campaigning and Governing', in N.J. Ornstein and T.E. Mann (eds), *The Permanent Campaign and its Future*. Washington, DC: American Enterprise Institute/Brookings Institute.

Hefferman, R. (1999) 'Media Management: Labour's Political Communications Strategy', in G.R. Taylor (ed.), *The Impact of New Labour*. London: Macmillan.

Hughes, G. (1996) 'Communitarianism and Law and Order', *Critical Social Policy*, 16 (4), 17–41.

Jones, B. (2000) 'The Media and the Government' in R. Pyper and L. Robins (eds), *UK Governance*. London: Macmillan.

Kelling, G. and Coles, C. (1996) *Fixing Broken Windows*. New York: Touchstone Books.

Labour Party (1994) *Partners against Crime: Labour's New Approach to Tackling Crime and Creating Safer Communities*. London: Labour Party.

Labour Party (1995) *A Quiet Life: Tough Action on Criminal Neighbours*. London: Labour Party.

Labour Party (1996) *Parenting*. London: Labour Party.

Levitas, R. (1998) *The Inclusive Society?* London: Macmillan.

Mandelson, P. and Liddle, R. (1996) *The Blair Revolution: Can New Labour Deliver?* London: Faber.

Mulgan, G. and Wilkinson, H. (1995) *Freedom's Children*. London: Demos.

Newman, B.I. (1999) *The Mass Marketing of Politics*. Thousand Oaks, CA: Sage.

Norris, P. (1998) 'The Battle for the Campaign Agenda', in A. King (ed.), *New Labour Triumph at the Polls*. London: Chatham House.

Osborne, P. (1999) *Alaistair Campbell, New Labour and the Rise of the Media Class*. London: Aurum Press.

Putnam, R. (2000) *Bowling Alone: The Collapse and Revival of Community*. New York: Simon & Schuster.

Rose, N. (1999) *Powers of Freedom: Reframing Political Thought*. Cambridge: Cambridge University Press.

Riddell, P. (2000) *Parliament Under Blair*. London: Politicos Publishing.

Straw, J. (1998) *Building Social Cohesion, Order and Inclusion in a Market Economy*. Nexus Conference on Mapping Out the Third World, 3 July, http://www.nexus.

Straw, J. (2000) *Human Rights and Personal Responsibility – New Citizenship for a New Millenium*. London: Home Office http://www.homeoffice.gov.uk.hract.

Straw, J. and Michael, A. (1996) *Tackling the Causes of Crime: Labour's Proposal to Prevent Crime and Criminality*. London: Labour Party.

Utting, D., Bright, J. and Henricson, C. (1993) *Crime and the Family: Improving Child-rearing and Preventing Delinquency*. London: Family Policy Studies Centre.

Wilson, J.Q. and Kelling, G. (1982) 'Broken Windows', *Atlantic Monthly*, March, pp. 29–38.

Chapter 4

The rediscovery of learning: crime prevention and scientific realism

Nick Tilley

What made sociology popular among students in the late 1960s was a widespread dissatisfaction with existing social arrangements and an impulse to effect change. While most of us, I guess, began with reformist aspirations, exposure to Marxian ideas eventually led many to conclude that more was needed than the development of a few new policies and practices to ameliorate specific problems. Rather, these individual problems were connected to one another and had a common basis in capitalism. What was needed therefore was less the gradual erosion of specific ills than a fundamental transformation of the whole social order. This was a precondition for creating the good society, where injustice, alienation, exploitation and individual social harms could and would be expunged.

Karl Popper was a controversial critic of Marxian ideas (Popper 1945, 1957). He argued in favour of what he called 'piecemeal social engineering' and against 'utopian social engineering'. Utopian social engineering – the supersession of the existing flawed social order by a new one without the contradictions in the old – unleashed, according to Popper, new social forces that would produce unintended consequences with as many as or even more harms than the old structure. Revolutionaries, disappointed that their creations compromised the ideals they sought, would then be tempted to eliminate, if necessary by force, departures from their vision of the good society. Vestiges of the pre-revolutionary society and aberrant departures from the promise of the new would need to be removed in the interests of the longer-term, greater good. Herein, according to Popper, lie the seeds of totalitarianism. The risks of revolution were worth taking only in 'closed', undemocratic societies where the conditions for piecemeal social engineering are absent.

Piecemeal social engineering had more modest aims. It was concerned with reducing defined problems causing specific harms. Interventions would be tried out to test whether the measures to deal with these harms were having their intended effects and were not inadvertently creating other (worse) harms. If they were found to work they could be adopted generally. Interventions embodied theories. Piecemeal social engineering required the involvement of social scientists to articulate and test the policy theories. It simultaneously offered a practicable way of responding to social harms and a way of testing theory. It was intended in this sense to be realistic, and to pave the way to learning – to progress in understanding.

Popper's prescriptions were attacked by the Marxians. His apparent acquiescence to the existing social order made him implicitly conservative. He was unable to take a properly critical view (e.g. Cornforth 1968). His analytic and policy vision was thereby restricted, and superficial (see, for example, Adorno *et al* 1986).

Popper wrote also about social science methodology in ways that challenged the prevailing Marxian orthodoxies of the time. He advocated methodological individualism: the notion that explanations in social science need ultimately to refer to human agency, even though consequences were often unintended. He proposed the use of situational logic: the idea that human actions need to be understood in terms of their intelligibility in the situations in which they took place. He also defended the 'unity of the sciences': the view that all the sciences are underpinned by the same fundamental logic.

At the same time that his social theory was being criticised, Popper's philosophy of science was also under attack. Popper had argued that scientific understanding progresses through the development of ever more powerful explanatory theories. Theories are not and cannot be proven. They remain forever fallible. Moreover, they cannot be derived from observations – Popper's account of science is the antithesis of the classical positivism of August Comte and his followers. What Popper argues is that scientific theories are invented, and that they must both be testable in principle (i.e. be falsifiable), and also be rigorously tested. Progress is achieved with the supersession of falsified theories with more powerful replacements that must again be subject to rigorous tests and replaced when found wanting. Science proceeds, as the title of one of Popper's books puts it, by a cycle of 'conjectures and refutations' (Popper 1963). Popper was not so naive as to think that theories can be simply refuted by events. Theories being tested and testing methods are embedded in a host of auxiliary theories. Decisions have to be made about what statements to accept on the basis of results of tests. The 'logic of scientific discovery', as the title of another of Popper's books puts it (Popper 1959), is achieved through the imaginative proposal of testable theory, followed by critical tests on the basis of which judgements are made about the adequacy of the theory. Scientific creativity of a high order is needed in the generation of new and more adequate theory.

Popper's 'falsificationist' account of scientific development, however, seemed to be contradicted by the ways in which science actually worked. Kuhn's influential *The Structure of Scientific Revolutions* (Kuhn 1961) appeared to present science as a social psychological process, within which there was no necessary progress and no clear criterion for what would constitute progress. According to Kuhn, one scientific world-view or paradigm succeeds another when a crisis of confidence in the old occurs as it turns up too many unexpected or 'anomalous' findings. Adherents to the old theory are seldom persuaded to abandon the ideas in which they have significant investment, in favour of the new; rather, uncommitted and new scientists are drawn in.[1] The replacement paradigm is different from (incommensurable with) the old; it does not necessarily deal with its problems. Kuhn's version of scientific development was followed by the work of other scholars casting more and more doubt on Popper's ideas. At a philosophical level Paul Feyerabend (1975) produced an avowedly relativist account of scientific knowledge. Sociologists' empirical studies of what scientists actually do also did not find them conforming to Popper's methodological prescriptions (e.g. Latour and Woolgar 1979). Scientists were found to show all the normal human frailties. They were not in the business of trying to falsify theories (Mahoney 1981). They looked at data selectively, manoeuvred to get their ideas accepted, disregarded inconvenient evidence, picked the best bits that fitted their case and so on.[2] Popper's heroic account of the rational scientist did not seem to be matched by the workaday world of real science. Even the heroes of science were not immune from finagling and rhetoric-mongering. The assumptions about science and the status of the knowledge that its methods could generate were thrown in doubt in these post-Popperian studies. If even the natural sciences could not produce anything more than conventionally agreed, socially constructed accounts of the natural world, how much less secure must be other branches of knowledge. Herein lies one of the cornerstones of (philosophical) postmodernism, and the relativist doctrine at its core.

It seemed to me that Popper had been read in a peculiarly conservative way. There was space for left-Popperian social theory and politics where quite radical but realistic harm-reducing policies could be conceived, tried out and implemented. It also seemed to me that Popper's account of science had been read in a peculiarly unsociological way, as if the only way to produce outcomes was as a direct reflection of intentions (Tilley 1982a, 1993a). The identification of patterned unintended consequences from intentional behaviour has been the stock in trade of sociology from the discipline's beginnings. Indeed, mixed in Popper's own work about scientific development were at least two accounts of how the succession of ever more powerful theories was produced. One saw it, indeed, as a result of heroic scientists acting as honourable, rational falsificationists. The other saw it as a community product – the unintended outcome of scientists wrestling not only with ideas but also with one another in the pursuit of reputation (Tilley 1993a). Conjecture and refutation were needed to gain recognition: proposal of one's own conjecture and the refutation of those of others. The so-called strong programme sociologists of scientific knowledge (see Bloor 1976; Collins 1981) had rather missed the point in their rich descriptions of scientists' social constructions during research and their production of reports of it. The scientific establishment, in its objections to the sociologists' subversive account of scientists' activities, similarly missed the point. Or so it seemed to me.

In 1986 I fetched up writing a paper for *Metaphilosophy* that tried to develop these latter arguments in some detail (Tilley 1993a).[3] This paper argued that the succession of new theories and falsification of old ones was an emergent outcome of the self-interested activities of scientists operating according to a set of normative rules within a relatively closed scientific community. In the context of that community structure, the self-interested pursuit of reputation triggered the generation of new ideas and efforts to check out old ones. The risk faced by self-interested scientists of being thrown off course from findings that had been fiddled underpinned strongly enforced mores about truth-telling. Moreover, the interconnectedness of sets of ideas in science and the reproduction of the scientific community through higher education institutions meant that there was an audience that would sort and sift through the literature and adopt what seemed plausible and useful. Scientists might in the grander scheme of things intend to produce new and more powerful explanatory theories but their day-to-day intentions as they conducted their everyday scientific lives were not necessarily (and apparently not generally) the mechanisms through which they achieved this outcome. Ironically, in coming to this view it seemed to me that I had boxed myself into a corner. I had produced a scientific realist (context, mechanism, regularity) account of how falsificationist scientific history was produced! If the explanation for how scientific knowledge is generated is right this casts doubt on falsificationist accounts of science. If falsificationism provides the right master narrative for scientific progress, this leaves little space for scientific realism. The development of a falsificationist scientific realism that would be adequate to describe scientific development and the mechanisms of its generation through the scientific community seemed an awesome prospect. There also seemed to be little interest in it.

One of the reasons my piece in *Metaphilosophy* missed any mark at the time it was published has, I think, to do with what was happening to social theory. While Popper had assumed the primacy of natural science methods and tried to show how these could best be understood and adapted to explain social phenomena, more radical and relativising interpretative and structuralist turns in sociology were gaining ground and subverting any such aspiration. In different ways these represented a turning away from efforts to produce scientifically privileged accounts of social life. Instead all accounts were deemed to be socially situated and socially constructed. There is no point outside these socially located accounting processes. Tests of theories occur within social processes of data construction and interpretation.[4]

Social theory of another kind was also relatively indifferent to systematic data collection, and to aspirations to create a science of social life. This involved the development and deployment of sets of concepts to interpret events in a more or less *ad hoc* way. Though often interesting and apparently insightful, this kind of *post hoc* social commentary, using suites of sensitising ideas to interpret events and apparent trends, was far removed from deductive, testable explanatory theory. The role of such data as are used is to illustrate rather than to provide critical, potentially falsifying evidence.

Applied, Popperian sociology was disparaged (Tilley and Selby 1976). It was taken to embrace reactionary positivism, and to have been overtaken by revolutionary radicalism and relativism. The agenda for sociology was to deconstruct, to relativise and to engage in fundamental criticism of fatally flawed social structures. Much maligned, misread and misunderstood (Tilley 1980, 1981, 1982b), Popperian sociology was out of kilter with the prevailing paradigms.

Meanwhile, the opportunity (funding) for crime reduction research and evaluation became available in the late 1980s, courtesy of the Safer Cities programme. It promised the opportunity to take part in the piecemeal social engineering advocated by Popper, to use social science in an effort to reduce harms of a sort, and to test and hone theory through the evaluation of specific initiatives.

Safer Cities formed the Home Office contribution to Action for Cities, which was a major plank in the then government's efforts in 1988 to address problems of urban decay and deprivation. Safer Cities had three aims: to reduce crime, to lessen the fear of crime and to create communities in which economic and social life could flourish (Tilley 1993b). The first two of these are eminently Popperian aims. In 1989 I became involved as a researcher in an initiative aiming to reduce domestic burglary in one of the poorest areas of Nottingham, St Anns (Tilley *et al* 1991; Gregson *et al* 1992). This entailed an engagement with practitioners and policymakers and their imperatives. It also required that I read some of the crime prevention literature. Situational crime prevention had been developed in the Home Office (Clarke and Mayhew 1980; Clarke 1980) and those appointed to run Safer Cities initiatives were encouraged to use it (though they were not much constrained in the approaches they adopted and turned to other forms of crime prevention also – see Sutton 1996).

The early literature on situational crime prevention came as a revelation. Here was piecemeal social engineering, informed and in-forming developments in social science theory. Here was harm reduction. Here was attention to unintended consequences in the form of displacement and diffusion of benefits. Here was situational logic.[5] Here was radicalism of a sort, challenging assumptions about offenders and ways of reducing offences by treatment or punishment.[6] In short here was Popperian social science in action. More precisely than this, it seemed to me to comprise Popperian sociology. The emphasis on op-portunity rather than individual pathology, the treatment of offenders as intelligible individuals acting out the logic of their situations and the refusal to reify crime and criminal behaviour seemed to me to offer a genuinely sociological rather than moral, legal or psycho(patho)logical account. The more recent accounts of opportunities as causes of crime have further seemed to constitute situational crime prevention as an authentic sociological account (Felson and Clarke 1998). It was ironic that situational crime prevention was largely developed by psy-chologists, given that it has so little interest in individual differences and intra-personal processes. In a snappy play on Marx's famous aphorism Marcus Felson, the sociologist most associated with situational crime prevention, has said of criminal behaviour that, 'people choose but don't choose the choices open to them' (Felson 1986). He captures well the fundamentally sociological orientation.

Situational crime prevention, not surprisingly, elicited also the same kinds of objections that had been made to Popperian social science more generally. It failed to address root problems and left a seriously flawed social structure untouched. The disparaging references to 'administrative criminology' captured just that sneering dismissal of practical, often radical efforts to address real problems in real time that had done for the wider Popperian project. This is notwithstanding (normally unacknowledged) continuities between the critics own work and that which they attacked (Tilley 1997; Ekblom and Tilley 2000; Sullivan 2000).

Work on Safer Cities in Nottingham led to a successful bid to the Home Office to review the progress made by programme cities in embedding longer-term strategic provision (Tilley 1992). This in turn led to an invitation in 1991 to a secondment to the Home Office to try to distil transferable lessons from the scheme-level evaluations that were required as a condition for Safer Cities funding of individual initiatives.[7] This evaluation task was to complement the large-scale evaluation led from the Home Office Research and Planning Unit by Paul Ekblom (Ekblom *et al* 1996). It meant visiting a large number of crime prevention schemes, talking to their architects and those who were implementing them and trying to figure out ways of assembling and analysing data to find out what had been learned.

The Safer Cities work, both in Nottingham and at the Home Office, raised questions of evaluation methodology and purpose. By coincidence Ray Pawson, a long-time colleague and collaborator (Pawson and Tilley 1982), was also having to confront evaluation issues. He was working with Stephen Duguid examining the effects of prison education in Canada (Duguid and Pawson 1998). We went to a Social Research Association seminar on evaluation in 1989 or 1990 and frankly could not believe our ears. It was as if the debates over methodology and the developments in social theory over the previous twenty years had not happened. The assumption was that programmes could be treated as variables, that the task of evaluation was to isolate the programme as an independent variable and that the programme aims were the dependent variables. A programme could be deemed to 'work' if it was found to be associated with attainment of programme aims. The trick was to perform an 'experiment', by which was meant random allocation to treatment or non-treatment in the best of circumstances or something as close as possible where random allocation was impracticable. The discussion was all about technical problems and technical solutions in doing this. The assumption seemed also to be that the results of these so-called experiments could provide grounds for policy adoption. There was even unselfconscious talk about programmes being 'proven' and 'unproven', with the implication that experimental methods, if implemented properly, could do the proving.

This seemed to us to be palpable methodological nonsense. It took time to grasp the policy nonsense consequences. It was even longer before the dangerousness of the nonsense became apparent. To us as sociologists the previous twenty years of our discipline had underlined the need, for explanatory purposes, to treat individuals as situated (partially) knowing agents, not as passive deliverers of or objects of programme stimuli. That failure to understand this was systematically feeding into policy adjudication, through the prevailing methodological orthodoxy, came as a shock.

At the Home Office, I was confronted with many, many evaluations of the separate Safer Cities schemes, very few of which had used technically satisfactory social science research methods. Those habits of thought that any reasonably competent jobbing social scientist picks up were characteristically missing. Writers of the evaluations unsurprisingly fell into all those traps that lie in wait for lay folk (see Tilley 2000a). While Ray Pawson and I have been critical of crass experimentalism, we would still share with proponents of that method many assumptions about data collection and use, as well as their ethics about publication and critical discussion.

So, what made Ray Pawson and I so dissatisfied with the experimental methods conventionally deemed the gold standard of evaluation? Basically we thought the so-called experimental approach did violence to science, causation, programmes and policy (see Pawson and Tilley 1997).

1. *Science*. Rather little natural science experimentation resembles the methods used in experimental evaluation. Use of the term 'experimental' is, thus, largely rhetorical (see Tilley 2000b).

2. *Causation*. 'Experimental' evaluations use a successionist account of causality. They focus on temporal association. 'Realist' philosophers of science prefer a generative account of causality. This tries to explain associations by reference to real causal powers or mechanisms. So, for example, the association of physical attributes of parents and children are explained by underlying genetic causal mechanisms. Understanding the association involves identifying these. In the case of social programmes, our first example was CCTV in car parks (Tilley 1993c, Pawson and Tilley 1997). Cameras cannot directly impede car crime. If they have an effect, they do so by virtue of the underlying causal mechanisms activated. These may include increased perceived risk of apprehension to the offender, increased caution by the driver who is reminded to lock the car and remove

stealable goods from sight, or changed usage of the car park as risk-averse drivers squeeze out those indifferent or blind to crime risks, etc. Behaviour germane to crime patterns is altered through changes in the reasoning and resources of those involved.

3. *Programmes.* Social programmes are not like peas in a pod. In crime reduction, security upgrading, prison education, therapy, property marking, alarms and so on are each quite heterogenous. Take seemingly simple CCTV in car parks again: the numbers of cameras to cover a given area, their siting, their range, their accessibility, their maintenance, whether they are monitored continuously, the use of signs, the capacity and speed of pan, tilt and zoom, the skills and training of operators and so on will all vary enormously. They cannot be lumped together, and the findings for one set-up cannot automatically be read to another. Moreover, the context for the introduction of measures varies widely, in ways that are liable to play a part in affecting which causal mechanisms, if any, are triggered. In the case of CCTV, lighting levels, local offending and offence patterns, lines of sight, patterns of usage, nature and levels of publicity, relationships to supplementary policing and security services and so on will again vary widely. Even within the apparently simple and mechanical there is huge variation. These variations may be significant for mechanisms triggered and hence outcomes brought about. So-called experiments that allocate to treatment and non-treatment and simply compare before and after measurement differences across each cannot cope with this diversity. They typically railroad over it (Pawson and Tilley 1997, 1998).

4. *Policy.* The rationale for evaluation studies is better to inform policy and practice so that they can improve. The problem in this for 'experimental' evaluations is that findings are typically mixed. If positive findings are acted on, if they are taken to suggest replication, what then happens is that differences in impact are found. The policy and practice is initially misled and then confusion reigns, with suggestions for further studies that typically further increase confusion! There is no route to resolution in experimental method. This is true for property marking, lighting, mandatory arrest for domestic violence, the Kirkholt burglary reduction project etc. (see Tilley 2000c) as well as CCTV. Methodological muddle is followed by muddled findings and these in turn generate policy and practice muddle. It's not hard to see why. Measures can work in various ways. Their mode and circumstances of implementation vary and this will

affect what causal mechanisms are liable to be activated. And this will shape outcomes. Homogeneous outcomes cannot and should not be expected. 'Experimental' methods assume they should. Policy and practice will be misdirected if they make the same assumption.

I mentioned earlier the danger that lurks in experimental methods. This is worth stressing, since one of the classic and commendable rationales for rigorous evaluations is to avoid harm. Drugs and other medical treatment regimes are systematically tested to ensure that they do have their expected effects and do not have unwanted and unacceptable side-effects. Unfortunately misleading experimental results in criminal justice have fed dangerous practice in the case of mandatory arrest for domestic violence. A randomly controlled trial in Minneapolis suggested that the rates of repeat domestic violence in cases where discretion could be used were lowest where arrest was actually made. This led to a rapid increase in the number of cities in the United States implementing mandatory arrest policies. Replications of the Minneapolis experiment found mixed results. As often as arrest reduced rates of repeat domestic violence, it increased it. It was speculated that arrest angers some while it shames others. It stimulates repeat domestic violence in the one group and inhibits it in the other. It depends on the circumstances. For those who are employed in stable communities, it inhibits through shame. For those who are unemployed in marginal communities, it provokes through anger. The conclusion drawn is that police use their discretion in an informed and intelligent way (Sherman 1992). The policy adopted as a result of the findings of the first Minneapolis study led some to experience violence they would otherwise have avoided. It caused harm.

In place of what we believed to be a discredited and discreditable experimental orthodoxy, Pawson and I advocated what we termed 'realistic evaluation' rooted in scientific realism. This enjoined evaluators not to ask crudely whether or not a programme 'works', but instead to ask, 'What works for whom in what circumstances, and how?' Just as regularities in nature are only brought about when contextual contingencies are conducive to the release of causal powers or mechanisms, so too in social life regularities are generated by the context-dependent activation of causal mechanisms. Policies and programmes are about trying to effect change. Their efficacy depends on the changes wrought in causal mechanisms activated. The measures introduced will work differently in different places, at different times, and among different groups. The trick of evaluation studies is to understand the ways in which programmes trigger sets of causal mechanisms in the various saliently differing programme contexts to yield patterns of intended and unintended consequences. Mechanisms in social science, we suggest, comprise the reasoning and resources of active agents (thus distinguishing the matter of social science from that of natural science). Programmes generally operate thus ultimately through changing the reasoning and resources of the individuals implicated in them.[8] Our idea was that decisions on programme futures – modification, continuation, extension and cancellation, etc. – would be informed by an understanding of how the programme worked. An evaluation that merely reported net effects without regard to context, notably in the contrived conditions in which pilot and early stage programmes are normally operated, would mislead.

Unsurprisingly what we deemed the best of evaluations had already tacitly used realist thinking. Gloria Laycock (1992) and Janet Foster and Tim Hope (1993), for example, had produced realist work before Pawson and I had begun to formalise the method. Dennis Rosenbaum, though a highly skilled exponent of experimental evaluations himself, had noted the problems of black box experimentation and in this way had opened the door to realism (Rosenbaum 1988).

We are still working through the implications for realist evaluations. We have written individually, for example, about replication (highlighting the impossibility of doing exactly the same and hence the need to distil crucial elements of context and programme to effect changes in causal mechanisms operating – Tilley 1996) and about meta-evaluation (or evaluation review, stressing the scope for looking across programmes at families of interventions, context types and forms of intended and unintended consequence – Pawson 2000a). There is certainly more to be done, but the basic elements of realistic evaluation are laid out in Pawson and Tilley (1997).

The products we envisage at varying levels of specificity are 'Context, Mechanism, Outcome Pattern Configurations' (CMOCs). These comprise models that link contexts to mechanisms to outcome patterns. They formalise the ways in which programmes bring about effects in specified types of situation. A range of conjectured CMOCs can be tested in the course of a study. CMOC conjectures can be elicited from programme stakeholders, from past studies, from theoretical literature or from common sense. The point is to find ways of testing them within programmes by identifying varying subgroups among which changes would or would not be expected in relation to CMOCs. More general CMOCs describe types of context, forms of intervention and broad outcome pattern variations amongst subgroups. Specific CMOCs will refer to more detailed particulars of programme subgroups and the variations that might be expected among them. In no case can CMOCs be proven. What the judicious collection of data and comparison of subgroups can achieve are findings that can corroborate or refute CMOC theories.

Let us turn now to the implications of the realist position, as Pawson and I have developed it, for learning. We have cast doubt on experimentation as a source of valid lessons for policy and practice. We've suggested that it will mislead. We've suggested that conclusions that a particular programme, treated as a variable, was or was not associated with a suite of changes comprises an inadequate basis on which to draw inferences about what effects might be brought about were the programme to be put in place at another time or place.

The realist position in evaluation, as against the so-called experimental one, however, raises some uncomfortable issues for policy and practice.

Policy

The experimental position promises a measurement of net impact. In so far as policies are general they attach to classes of person or place or condition. They comprise rules whose consistent application to relevant categories provides for fairness. The experimental approach may railroad over difference in a way that mirrors or is mirrored in the tendency of policies to railroad over difference. Indeed, at its 'best' the experiment will attempt to achieve just that level of railroading constituted in policy and implement it in the experiment. Variation within is in this case not deemed of interest, since it is assumed that the policy will be applied invariantly to the relevant class. It does not matter that policies work through in different ways for different subgroups. The realist might be right that there is patterned variation. It is just not relevant.

The realist position does imply attention to difference in how measures work within different subgroups to produce a range of intended and unintended outcomes. This is, in the first instance, in the interests of better understanding how programmes are working for whom. At the same time it will suggest refinement in the scope of policies and their ways of implementation in order most effectively to achieve a given end. Here, variation is crucial, while net effects mask the ways policies and programmes work through to generate their effects. The realist position yields tested theories which need to be applied with understanding. It does not legitimate blunt instruments. As concluded by Sherman following mixed findings about the consequences of arrest in cases of domestic violence, it would seem to suggest increasing use of educated discretion.

What's to be done about blunt policy instruments? Do we need railroading evaluations of them to find net effects? Or do we conduct evaluations to refine the classes used for policies and programmes, and to use discretion in an educated way, informed by empirically tested theory. The problem with the former, even if the aspiration is accepted, is that of open systems. The contingent conditions for patterns at one time may not exist at another. Moreover, as Paul Ekblom (1997) has argued, in the case of crime and crime prevention changes that at one point may inhibit crime may cease to inhibit it in the future as motivated offenders probe the measures to find new weak spots. Indeed preventers and offenders are involved in a continuous process of mutual adaptation, as each tries to outdo the other, rather as in nature some species adjust to one another, only far more slowly. The association of crime reduction with the introduction of a particular measure at Point 1 in Place A does not entail that the same sequence will be found at Point 2 in Place A, or, for that matter, at any time in Place B. A sequence of events at one spatio-temporal point is not a good guide to series of events at other spatio-temporal points. For example, the introduction of steering wheel locks in West Germany was associated with a sustained fall in total numbers of thefts of cars. This was not the case in Britain. In Germany they were introduced to all cars, in Britain only to new ones. In Britain there was ample scope for displacement to older cars, but this was not the case in Germany (Webb 1994). In Britain scope for displacement provided continuing rewards for car theft, a continuation of recruitment into car theft and time for offenders to adapt to the new protection furnished by steering wheel locks (Clarke 1995). In Germany the steering wheel locks inhibited car theft sufficiently to interrupt recruitment of new offenders and a sustained fall in offending was achieved. In crime reduction, rather than simple, universal policies that promise permanent solutions, processes of continuous research, development, adjustment and imagination are needed. Policy in a world of contingency and emergence may need to look rather different from policy in a stable state. Much policy and the evaluation research examining it and feeding into it seems to assume a steady state and a closed system.

For the realist the problem of change and open systems can partially be ameliorated through the development and testing of middle-range abstract CMOCs, which may have wide relevance, but at some remove from the particulars of specific interventions. Some fairly basic mechanisms, for example shaming, perceived risk increasing, reinforcement, incapacitation, capacity-increase, angering, dissonance-reduction/production and so on, may be activated in a range of conditions and times in crime reduction or many other programme settings. It may also be possible to develop models of the kinds of conditions in which these sorts of mechanisms will be triggered. Perhaps effective shaming needs conditions where subjects share moral standards with agencies delivering the shaming and have significant others who also share those moral standards, and where there are no significant countervailing sources of moral identity. The presence of specific initial conditions for shaming may be ephemeral across time and across particular settings, for example education, rail company performance, equal opportunities practices, criminogenic retail methods, corrupt police officers, young offenders, old offenders, sex offenders and so on. Yet an abstract tested model can provide (realistic) grounds for deciding whether, for whom and how a shame-triggering set of measures might help attain a given end.

Practice

There is often discretion in practice. Decisions have to be taken at the point of intervention. Ill-informed use of discretion opens the door to arbitrary decisions. As we saw in the case of domestic violence elimination of discretion brings danger. Recognising what is salient in a practice context, understanding change-induction as a matter of activating an alteration in the balance of causal mechanisms triggered and grasping what those mechanisms might be is tricky. It calls for an understanding of theory and of tested principles. It means coming to grips with CMOCs and being able to work through what applies in particular practice settings. Developing these skills is unlikely to be easy. Rather than simple procedural routines applied from the manual, what is needed is informed reflection and creative application. There is liable to be a tacit dimension, as Michael Polanyi (1958, 1967) terms it, where elements of judgement are subtle and often difficult if not impossible to formulate. As abstract principles are translated in local settings into application, a kind of informed intuition comes in to play. Apprenticeship, experience and contact with those with expertise are liable to be needed. This is not to make of practice something that is merely airy-fairy personal magic. It is to acknowledge the devil in the detail of deploying abstract knowledge. Harry Collins (1985) found that the first lasers could not be built without personal contact with those who had already produced them. Even in the physical world, in science and engineering, where impersonal laws are being applied, there is a tacit dimension.

Practitioners need, thus, a grasp of research-based CMOC principles, and to develop the capacity to deploy them appropriately, using imagination and intelligence. They do not need mechanical 'what works' rulebooks.

There is an affinity between realistic thinking and problem-solving approaches to dealing with social problems in general and with crime and disorder in particular. In advocating problem-oriented policing, Goldstein (1979, 1990) commended careful and clear delineation of problems and the construction of responses rooted in their systematic analysis. There are continuities between this and the approach adopted in situational crime prevention, where likewise problem analysis is advocated following which decisions about plausible situational measures can be taken (Tilley 1999). Both also acknowledge limitations to what can be achieved through the criminal justice system though neither wants completely to eschew its use. Though situational crime prevention clearly privileges situational approaches to prevention, neither approach is pre-committed to ascribing particular roles to specific agencies or citizens. Rather, the question is a pragmatic one: given this problem and this understanding of the problem, what points of leverage are there to deal with it, or to pre-empt it? In realist terms, the question is that of what measure(s) in this context can be introduced to trigger which causal mechanisms to generate what expected intended and unintended outcomes.

Ethical and practical questions arise, of course. Within the range of potential means of dealing with a problem, what can be done ethically in practice? What comprise legitimate problems for attention? How are problems prioritised? What forms of aggregation and analysis are politically acceptable? How are the expected intended and unintended consequences, including forms of displacement and diffusion, to be weighed and balanced? What level of risk is acceptable to whom? Who can reasonably be assigned responsibility to bear the costs of change? Though some precede it, these questions largely follow and are raised by problem-identification and analysis. Decisions about what to do do not precede analysis. Normative issues arise in relation to means, which are otherwise open provided they are ethically proper. In this sense there is no a priori commitment, for example, to a grass roots community, agency police or other enforcement response, or to a neighbourhood, household, individual, 'virtual' (non-geographic) community, or manufacturer problem-definition.

If we look specifically to community-based control, tricky issues of efficacy and equity arise, that can only be touched on here. The track record of characteristic community-based measures such as standard versions of neighbourhood watch is not good (Bennett 1990, Laycock and Tilley 1995). Community policing, now widely promulgated in the

United States, has been found to be disappointing in implementation and effectiveness (Rosenbaum 1994; Skogan and Hartnett 1998; Skogan *et al* 1999). Moreover, community-related measures appear more easily to be seeded in less needy places and to be operated more successfully there too (Skogan *et al* 2000).

One of the mechanisms generating the inequitable distribution of crime and disorder may comprise the varying capacity to control and resist them among those from differing socio-economic groups (see Barr and Pease 1990). If we take crime and disorder as (at least in part) distributive ills, over-egging community responses may not be the most effective way of remedying social injustice – at worst it may reinforce it by channelling well-considered prevention towards those who are better off, less at risk and more able to orchestrate self-protection. This is not to say that community efficacy in effecting control is irrelevant. Indeed, there is evidence to suggest that it is important. The point is not to see this as the only means of effecting prevention, and to acknowledge that injecting it, where it is absent, may be easier said than done. The best research literature finding community efficacy to be significant sadly fails to suggest how it might be facilitated (Sampson *et al* 1997; Sampson and Raudenbush 1999).

Finally, many problems of crime and disorder are faced by travelling victims – those in but not of the physical communities within which they are victimised, for example students, holidaymakers, shoppers or travellers. Community-generated controls and priorities are likely to overlook these vulnerable groups.

There are good grounds for subordinating community-based control to problem-oriented approaches and to treat it as a means that may sometimes, but not always, make sense in terms of social justice and effectiveness.

Conclusion

I began with Popper and piecemeal social engineering. It captures well the modest, reformist aspirations of situational crime reduction. Yet is has never been able much to capture imagination. While it calls for bold theorising, it calls for it on a small canvas. If offers no panaceas. It makes no assumptions about the perfectibility of individuals or societies. It is a theory of adjustments to deal with harms. It contains no grand moral vision of the constituents of the good society. It calls for real, particular achievements to deal with particular problems. It presents no vision. It also invites us to bow to the authority of science in understanding human relations and methods of changing them. In bowing to the authority of science it assumes that scientific knowledge is possible, and that scientific knowledge enjoys special status. Yet the authority of science at any given point lacks finality. All knowledge-claims are fallible. They will, for the most part, be found at some time to be flawed. The knowledge-claims are just good enough for now, even in the face of as severe a set of tests as we can muster. They are certainly the best we have, for now, to explain and to inform policy and practice. So it is also with situational crime prevention – an approach with minimal assumptions about offenders, with no claims to solve the crime problem, with no great moral vision, using the methods of science to test out theory and practice. It wants effectively to reduce crime-induced harms. This modesty and lack of drama again is unlikely to capture the imagination. In crime, above all, it appears that finding a point of blame – the individual or society – and offering a method of reform or punishment are *de rigeur*.

The kinds of practice and programming suggested by a middle-range realist approach[9] are likewise rather modest, perhaps more so. 'What works for whom and in what circumstances' is hardly a rallying cry. It calls for patient analysis and hard thought. It eschews the undifferentiated, blanket response. Even here, the specific dividends may be short-lived. In a relatively fast-changing world, what goes for today in terms of specific effects is unlikely to go in the same way for tomorrow and the next day. The mix of contingency and emergence make for unstable effects.

The best that realistic evaluation, piecemeal social engineering and situational crime prevention, the three linked sets of ideas that have animated my working life, can offer are a method and set of principles to guide decisionmaking to deal effectively with emerging harms and threats. Though the thinking can often be profound and highly radical, perhaps more so than much wide-sweep theorising, they leave the bigger picture unaltered. It is backroom theorising, backroom theory testing and backroom improvement.

For ambitious social scientists the bigger picture is paramount, as it is for most politicians. Newspapers and the chattering classes they cater for are also interested in diagnosing contemporary ills, assigning blame for 'where we went wrong', and pontificating on 'what do we do next'. Those involved in day-to-day policy and practice are left coping with rather more prosaic problems. The humdrum business of working out how to decide what to do is important. Improving learning here will improve all our lots. It will not, though, hit the headlines.

Finally, what are the prospects for realistic, middle-range applied criminology? The criminological community is probably no more or less susceptible to the self-interested manoeuvrings that sociologists of scientific knowledge have described in the doings of natural scientists. Strategic neglect, refusals to debate issues, *ad hominem* argument, denied platforms, the politics of citation, appointment and promotion, refereeing prejudice, ideological commitment, selective use of evidence, misrepresentation, investment in sets of ideas to which personal credibility is attached, refusal to take seriously the radically challenging and personal abuse can all be found in criminology among much kindness, openness and encouragement. The diversity of the criminological community and the flows of work into what seems to promise interest and fruitfulness, again as with the natural scientific community, look more plausible as mechanisms for sorting and sifting the worthwhile from the worthless than cool, disinterested reason on the part of individual criminologists. One part of me holds to the hope that this good work will drive out bad. Another recognises that in the more ideologically infused realm of the social sciences, matters are normally rather different. Research is always situated in a political and normative setting. Researchers themselves frequently have political and normative preoccupations. The context for research is one in which factors other than practical and scientific fecundity tend to prevail in shaping the dominant agenda.

It may be that the patient modesty of situational crime prevention, piecemeal social engineering and realistic evaluation will confine them permanently to a precarious position, and even then only at the margins. As ever these positions do, of course, carry some normative freight. Some particular applications, especially of situational crime prevention, raise specific significant normative issues. Recent literature, especially Garland (2001) and von Hirsch *et al* (2000), has begun to tease out a range of normative issues raised by situational crime prevention. Their detailed discussion lies beyond the scope of this essay. The best claims of piecemeal social engineering, situational crime prevention and realistic evaluation to attention, however, lie in their explanatory power and practical application for harm reduction, and even these are (properly) contested. Promising possibly and fallibly to reduce specific harms in a piecemeal way is not much of a come-on, evidently even to the research community in criminology!

There's no escaping politics in crime reduction. I hope they don't squeeze out other, scientific discourses in shaping the criminological agenda. Indeed, I hope that the science may inform (but not overwhelm) the politics, as in some modest way I've tried to show in the parts of this essay referring to community crime prevention. I'm not optimistic. The establishment in 2001 of the Jill Dando Institute of Crime Science at University College London, however, offers some hope.

Notes

1 Max Planck had commented some years earlier that, 'A scientific truth does not triumph by convincing its opponents and making them see the light, but rather because its opponents gradually die' (Planck 1950).
2 A large literature appeared in the 1980s. The distinguished historian of science, Gerald Holton, provided telling detailed accounts of some major events in the history of science (e.g. Holton 1986). Sociological readers, drawing together some of the main research and thinking, include Knorr-Cetina and Mulkay (1983), and Knorr, Krohn and Whitley (1981).
3 The long gap between submission and appearance was neither a function of repeat revisions nor of a peculiarly long list of papers waiting to appear. As the editor's footnote said, 'Publication of this article was delayed by an editorial oversight, for which I apologise to the author and readers' (Tilley 1993a). I'd been too diffident to chase it up. I'd assumed the editor had had second thoughts.
4 For a Popperian way of construing and responding to this, see Tilley (1980).
5 As part of situational logic, Popper advocated use of the 'rationality principle'. According to this, agents in their situations are assumed to act in a (weakly) rational way (see Popper 1967). All this accords remarkably well with the assumptions made in situational crime prevention and the rational choice approach that has developed to underpin it (see Newman *et al* 1997).
6 A recent book highlighting the radicalism of situational crime prevention, a radicalism deemed to be a step too far for full implementation, is Sullivan (2000).
7 In the end there were about 3,500 schemes in Phase I of Safer Cities. (Phase II was run rather differently, with management contracted to third parties – Crime Concern, the National Association for the Care and Resettlement of Offenders (NACRO) and the Society of Voluntary Associates (SOVA). Phase I was directly managed by the Home Office.)
8 This is not entirely true. Incapacitation comprises one of the mechanisms through which some criminal justice sanctions, such as incarceration and execution, may bring about effects other than through alteration in agents' reasoning and resources.
9 See Pawson (2000b) for a general statement on this.

References

Adorno, T. *et al* (1986) *The Positivist Dispute in German Sociology* [1969]. London: Heinemann.

Barr, R. and Pease, K. (1990) 'Crime Placement, Displacement and Deflection', in M. Tonry and N. Morris (eds), *Crime and Justice: A Review of Research*, Vol. 12, Chicago: University of Chicago Press.

Bennett, T. (1990) *Evaluating Neighbourhood Watch*. Aldershot: Gower.

Bloor, D. (1976) *Knowledge and Social Imagery*. London: Routledge.

Clarke, R. (1980) '"Situational" Crime Prevention: Theory and Practice', *British Journal of Criminology*, 20 (2), 136–47.

Clarke, R. (1995) 'Situational Crime Prevention', in M. Tonry and D. Farrington (eds), *Building a Safer Society: Strategic Approaches to Crime Prevention*, Crime and Justice, Vol. 19. Chicago: University of Chicago Press.

Clarke, R. and Mayhew, P. (eds) (1980) *Designing out Crime*. London: HMSO.

Collins, H. (1981) 'Stages in the Empirical Programme of Relativism', *Social Studies of Science*, 11.

Collins, H. (1985) *Changing Order: Replication and Induction in Scientific Practice*. London: Sage.

Cornforth, M. (1968) *The Open Philosophy and the Open Society*. New York: International Publishers.

Duguid, S. and Pawson, R. (1998) 'Education, Change and Transformation', *Evaluation Review*, 22, 470–95.

Ekblom, P. (1997) 'Gearing up Against Crime: a Dynamic Framework to Help Designers Keep Up with the Adaptive Criminal in a Changing World', *International Journal of Risk, Security and Crime Prevention*, 2 (4), 249–65.

Ekblom, P. and Tilley, N. (2000) 'Going Equipped: Criminology, Situational Prevention and the Resourceful Offender', *British Journal of Criminology*, 40 (3), 376–98.

Ekblom, P., Law, H. and Sutton, M., with assistance from Crisp, P. and Wiggins, R. (1996) *Safer Cities and Domestic Burglary*. Home Office Research Study 164. London: Home Office.

Felson, M. (1986) 'Linking Criminal Choices, Routine Activities, Informal Control and Criminal Outcomes', in R. Clarke and D. Cornish (eds), *The Reasoning Criminal: Rational Choice Perspectives on Offending*. Berlin: Springer-Verlag.

Felson, M. and Clarke, R. (1998) *Opportunity Makes the Thief*, Police Research Series Paper 98. London: Home Office.

Feyerabend, P. (1975) *Against Method*. London: New Left Books.

Foster, J. and Hope, T. (1993) *Housing, Community and Crime: the Impact of the Priority Estates Project*, Home Office Research Study 131. London: HMSO.

Garland, D. (2001) *The Culture of Control*. Oxford: Oxford University Press.

Goldstein, H. (1979) 'Improving Policing: A Problem-Oriented Approach', *Crime and Delinquency*, 25, 236–58.

Goldstein, H. (1990) *Problem-Oriented Policing*. New York: McGraw-Hill.

Gregson, M. and project team (1992) *St Ann's Burglary Project Report March 1990–March 1992*.

Holton, G. (1986) *The Advancement of Science and its Burdens*. Cambridge: Cambridge University Press.

Knorr, K., Krohn, R. and Whitley, R. (eds) (1981) *The Social Process of Scientific Investigation*. Dordrecht: Reidel.

Knorr-Cetina, K. and Mulkay, M. (eds) (1983) *Science Observed: Perspectives on the Social Study of Science*. London: Sage.

Kuhn, T. (1961) *The Structure of Scientific Revolutions*. Chicago: University of Chicago Press.

Latour, B. and Woolgar, S. (1979) *Laboratory Life*. London: Sage.

Laycock, G. (1992) 'Operation Identification, or the Power of Publicity', in R. Clarke (ed.), *Situational Crime Prevention: Successful Case Studies*. New York: Harrow & Heston.

Laycock, G. and Tilley, N. (1995) *Policing and Neighbourhood Watch: Strategic Issues*, Crime Detection and Prevention Series Paper 60. London: Home Office.

Mahoney, M. (1981) *Scientist as Subject: The Psychological Imperative*. Cambridge, MA: Ballinger.

Newman, G., Clarke, R. and Shoham, S. (eds) (1997) *Rational Choice and Situational Crime Prevention*. Aldershot: Ashgate.

Pawson, R. (2000a) *A Realist Approach to Meta-Analysis and Research Review*. Paper presented at the Annual Conference of the UK Evaluation Society, Church House, Westminster, 6–8 December.

Pawson, R. (2000b) 'Middle Range Realism', *Arch. Europ. Sociol.*, 41 (2), 283–325.

Pawson, R. and Tilley, N. (1982) *Monstrous Thoughts: Weaknesses in the Strong Programme of the Sociology of Science*, Occasional Paper No. 14. University of Leeds Department of Sociology.

Pawson, R. and Tilley, N. (1997) *Realistic Evaluation*. London: Sage.

Pawson, R. and Tilley, N. (1998) 'Caring Communities, Paradigm Polemics, Design Debates', *Evaluation*, 4 (1), 73–90.

Planck, M. (1950) *A Scientific Autobiography and Other Papers*. London: Williams & Norgate.

Polanyi, M. (1958) *Personal Knowledge*. London: Routledge & Kegan Paul.

Polanyi, M. (1967) *The Tacit Dimension*. New York: Anchor.

Popper, K. (1945) *The Open Society and its Enemies*. London: Routledge & Kegan Paul.

Popper, K. (1957) *The Poverty of Historicism*. London: Routledge & Kegan Paul.

Popper, K. (1959) *The Logic of Scientific Discovery*. London: Hutchinson.

Popper, K. (1963) *Conjectures and Refutations*. London: Routledge & Kegan Paul.

Popper, K. (1967) La rationalité et le statut de principe de rationalité', in E. Classen (ed.), *Les Fondements Philosophiques des Systèmes Economiques*. Paris: Payot.

Popper, K. (1972) *Objective Knowledge*. Oxford: Clarendon Press.

Rosenbaum, D. (1988) 'Community Crime Prevention: a Review and Synthesis of the Literature', *Justice Quarterly*, 5, 325–95.

Rosenbaum, D. (ed.) (1994) *The Challenge of Community Policing*. Thousand Oaks, CA: Sage.

Sampson, R. and Raudenbush, S. (1999) 'Systematic Observation of Public Places: a New Look at Disorder in Urban Neighborhoods', *American Journal of Sociology*, 105 (3), 603–51.

Sampson, R., Raudenbush, S. and Earls, F. (1997) 'Neighborhoods and Violent Crime: a Multilevel Study of Collective Efficacy', *Science*, 277, 918–24.

Sherman, L. (1992) *Policing Domestic Violence*. New York: Free Press.

Skogan, W. and Hartnett, S. (1998) *Community Policing, Chicago Style*. New York: Oxford University Press.

Skogan, W., Hartnett, S., DuBois, J., Comey, J., Kaiser, M. and Lovig, J. (1999) *On the Beat: Police and Community Problem Solving*. Boulder, CO: Westview.

Skogan, W., Steiner, L., DuBois, J., Gudell, J., Fagan, A., Kim, J. and Block, R. (2000) *Community Policing in Chicago, Year Seven: An Interim Report*. Chicago, IL: Illinois Criminal Justice Information Authority.

Sullivan, R. (2000) *Liberalism and Crime: The British Experience*. Lanham, MD: Lexington.

Sutton, M. (1996) *Implementing Crime Prevention Schemes in a Multi-Agency Setting: Aspects of Process from the Safer Cities Programme*, Home Office Research Study No. 160. London: Home Office.

Tilley, N. (1980) 'Popper, Positivism and Ethnomethodology', *British Journal of Sociology*, 31 (1), 28–45.

Tilley, N. (1981) 'The Logic of Laboratory Life', *Sociology*, 15 (1), 117–26.

Tilley, N. (1982a) 'Rational Scientific Development: a Sociological Comment', *Knowledge: Creation, Diffusion, Utilisation*, 3 (4), 453–64.

Tilley, N. (1982b) 'Popper, Historicism and Emergence', *Philosophy of the Social Sciences*, 12 (1), 59–67.

Tilley, N. (1992) *Safer Cities and Community Safety Strategies*, Crime Prevention Unit Paper 38. London: Home Office.

Tilley, N. (1993a) 'Popper and Prescriptive Methodology', *Metaphilosophy*, 24 (1/2), 155–66.

Tilley, N. (1993b) 'Crime Prevention and the Safer Cities Story', *Howard Journal*, 32 (1), 255–72.

Tilley, N. (1993c) *Understanding Car Parks, Crime and CCTV: Evaluation Lessons from Safer Cities*, Crime Prevention Unit Paper 42. London: Home Office.

Tilley, N. (1996) 'Demonstration, Exemplification, Duplication and Replication in Evaluation Research', *Evaluation*, 2 (1), 35–50.

Tilley, N. (1997) 'Realism, Situational Rationality and Crime Prevention', in G. Newman, R. Clarke and S. Shoham (eds), *Rational Choice and Situational Crime Prevention*. Aldershot: Ashgate.

Tilley, N. (1999) 'The Relationship between Crime Prevention and Problem-Oriented Policing', in C. Brito and T. Allan (eds), *Problem-Oriented Policing: Crime Specific Problems, Critical Issues and Making POP Work*. Washington, DC: Police Executive Research Forum.

Tilley, N. (2000a) 'The Evaluation Jungle', in S. Ballintyne, K. Pease and V. McLaren (eds), *Secure Foundations: Key Issues in Crime Prevention, Crime Reduction and Community Safety*. London: IPPR.

Tilley, N. (2000b) 'Experimentation and Criminal Justice Policies in the United Kingdom', *Crime and Delinquency*, 46 (2), 194–213.

Tilley, N. (2000c) 'Doing Realistic Evaluation in Criminal Justice', in V. Jupp, P. Davies and P. Francis (eds), *Doing Criminological Research*. London: Sage.

Tilley, N. and Selby, J. (1976) 'An Apt Sociology for Polytechnics', *Higher Education Review*, 8 (2), 38–56.

Tilley, N., Webb, J. and Gregson, M. (1991) 'Vulnerability to Burglary in an Inner City Area: Some Preliminary Findings', *Issues in Criminological and Legal Psychology*, 17, 112–19.

von Hirsch, A., Garland, D. and Wakefield, A. (eds) (2000) *Ethical and Social Perspectives on Situational Crime Prevention*. Oxford: Hart.

Webb, B. (1994) 'Steering Column Locks and Motor Vehicle Theft: Evaluations from Three Countries', in R. Clarke (ed.), *Crime Prevention Studies*, Vol. 2. Mosey, NY: Criminal Justice Press.

Chapter 5

Power, politics and partnerships: the state of crime prevention on Merseyside[1]

Roy Coleman, Joe Sim and Dave Whyte

> I tell my people on briefing parades, when they start complaining about a lack of resources, that with 6,000 people in the organisation and all the equipment and assets we have at our disposal, we could invade a small South American country. Although we're not going to ... not tonight!
>
> (Norman Bettison, Chief Constable of Merseyside Police, quoted in *Liverpool Echo*, 18 November 1999)

We seem to have reached a point at which, as Hughes has pointed out, 'multi-agency crime prevention now has the status of a taken for granted "fact of life" in the crime control business in the UK' (1998: 77). New Labour's (NL) preoccupation with 'joined-up thinking' in government has prompted a renewed emphasis upon 'multi-agency' working. This is clearly indicated by the introduction of the Crime and Disorder Act which imposed a statutory duty upon local authorities and police forces to develop joint local crime prevention and community safety strategies. The Act gives wide discretion to the police and local authorities to invite other 'partners' to join Crime and Disorder Partnerships as they see fit.

Utilising the discourses of partnerships and joined-up government, as Norman Fairclough has noted, is a central part of the 'language of government' employed by NL. These discourses have been particularly useful in constructing a 'corporate populism' which has resulted in both a strengthening of, and a 'transformation in, the nature of central control' (2000: 120–1).

In this chapter we build on Fairclough's insights by tracing the development of community crime prevention strategies on Merseyside using closed circuit television (CCTV) cameras as a focus of analysis. In developing this analysis we will be situating our argument firmly within a neo-Marxist theoretical perspective in order to get beyond both the narrow and endless empirical debates that have dominated this area (do cameras reduce/displace crime?) and the arguments generated by a number of governmentality and postmodernist writers who have air-brushed the power of the local, national and international state from theoretical and political scrutiny. The chapter is divided into five parts. First, it explores the development of multi-agency crime prevention on Merseyside. Second, it contextualises emergent crime prevention partnerships within the process of urban regeneration, with particular reference to the use of CCTV. Third, it discusses how CCTV has been used to reproduce a politically insulated and exclusionary crime control agenda. Fourth, the chapter establishes a set of themes for under-standing and analysing the strategic role played by local crime control partnerships. Finally, it considers the implications of our analysis with respect to the question of the state both as an interventionist force and as a constructor of a consensus around the nature of crime and appropriate responses to it. Inevitably, this will bring us back to questions of democratic accountability and social justice.

The origins of multi-agency strategies on Merseyside

The Safer Merseyside Partnership (SMP) has, since 1994, provided a powerful stimulus to the emergence of criminal justice partnerships on Merseyside. The roots of the current SMP structure can be found in the mid-1980s in a series of responses to a sustained legitimacy crisis in the Merseyside Police. Central to this crisis were allegations of widespread brutality, racism and corruption (Gifford *et al* 1989; Scraton 1985).

Despite the abolition of Merseyside County Council – as part of the Thatcher government's attack on local authority power – Merseyside local authorities retained close links in the administration of criminal justice policy. The financial and political stimulus for SMP emerged from these early attempts to create a Merseyside-wide partnership approach to crime prevention. In 1991, heavily influenced by the Morgan Report, the Police Authority set aside £250,000 for developing 'community safety'. The five local authorities on Merseyside were given £50,000 to employ a community safety officer in each authority. The five officers collaborated with the police to develop a range of projects aimed at augmenting police crime reduction strategies at a local level. Importantly these mechanisms were formatively influenced by the prospect of considerable government resources for similar projects that were to be made available via 'Safer Cities' and the Single Regeneration Budget (SRB). Developing bids for these emerging large-scale pools of funding was to be a central task for the new local criminal justice professionals.

In 1994, the five Merseyside Community Safety Officers succeeded in gaining £5m in funding from the SRB. In 1997, the SMP was awarded a further £5m to run the community safety strategy into 2004. The fact that these funds came from the SRB, a Department of Environment fund that was established to stimulate economic development in the inner cities – and in many ways was the antecedent to NL's current Neighbourhood Renewal initiative, to 'reinvigorate' (attract private investment) to the urban centres – was important for two reasons. First, it consolidated the position of the emergent layer of new criminal justice professionals organically linked to Merseyside Police and administered by local authorities, and secondly, it formally coupled together the bureaucratic management and control of local crime prevention with Merseyside's economic regeneration programme, a point that we will return to at the end of this paper.

The construction of local agendas

To some extent, the political development of SMP's crime control agenda and its relation to wider state priorities can be observed empirically by analysing the areas of work that SMP is involved in, alongside the imperatives of the government's agenda. The Home Office's current priorities as defined by the Crime Reduction Programme (2000) have much in common with the major initiatives developed by SMP (Safer Merseyside Partnership 1996 and 1998). Indeed, SMP is presently funding initiatives that directly address 9 of the 11 priority areas identified by the Home Office (Whyte 2001).

At the same time, there does exist some scope for developing local initiatives alongside Home Office priorities. While SMP initiatives are able to marshall considerable funds to respond to local priorities, they rarely breach the boundaries of what constitutes the local 'public good' as constructed by the police and the Police Authority. SMP initiatives – without exception – augment strategies of 'intelligence-led' and 'problem-solving' policing rather than encourage community developed and administered alternatives to these fashionable shibboleths of police work. The partnership has also been known to channel funding to policing activities more directly. For example, SMP has provided resources to fund the EuroNav III navigation system for the force helicopter which, it is claimed, will assist the police in 'Fighting crime from the skies' (Safer Merseyside Partnership 1998: 2).

Among the most important projects resourced by SMP is the development of Geographical Information Systems (GIS) by academics working at the University of Liverpool which have attempted to establish patterns of offending and repeat offending for each ward within the five local authority areas (Hirshfield and Bowers 1998; Bottoms and Wiles 1997: 316–30). Processing data using this technique has resulted in a complex map which identifies crime 'hot-spots' to areas as small as 100 square metres. The data used in crime prevention GIS systems are derived from police recorded data. The GIS on Merseyside thus includes: 600,000 records of police command and control incidents; 140,000 police recorded offences; 60,000 police recorded offenders (including address/age/sex/occupation of the offender); victim details (including age/sex/occupation of the victim); offence details (including time/date/location/nature of offence). These data are cross-referenced with a myriad of other types of geo-coded information on properties (schools, pubs, doctors' surgeries, youth clubs and social meeting places), infrastructure (roads, bus routes and bus stops), geographical boundaries (police beats/divisions, local authority areas, Objective One Single Regeneration Budget Areas), census indicators, and 'lifestyle' area profiles ('affluent professionals', 'settled suburbans', 'blue-collar workers' and so on) (Hirshfield and Bowers 1998: 198–9).

Within government circles, the proponents of GIS systems have a receptive audience. The Merseyside GIS system has been highly praised by the Home Office. The Guidance for Crime and Disorder partnerships has highlighted the system specifically, holding it up as an example of best practice and has enthusiastically outlined its practical merits (Home Office 1998a: box 1.6). As Hughes (2000) has noted, under NL community safety means what works is what can be counted (see also Allen 1999). Elsewhere, it has been noted that one litmus test being applied to Crime and Disorder Audits on Merseyside is whether they will prove useful in bids for Home Office funding under the Crime Reduction Programme – a process within which Chief Constables are formally made the gatekeepers of official bids (Whyte 2001). With these observations in mind, it is therefore hardly surprising that each of the Merseyside Crime and Disorder audits and strategies is based almost entirely upon police command and control data (Metropolitan Borough of Wirral 1998; CitySafe 1998; Knowsley Metropolitan Borough Council 1999; Sefton Metropolitan Borough Council 1999).

Thus, as with the funding of the Safer Cities programme in the early 1990s (King 1991: 88), behind the work of contemporary partnerships there is a powerful structural imperative demanding that the law and order problem should be constructed almost entirely around police recorded crime statistics. Perversely, it is the fluctuations in these data that are also used to evaluate the effectiveness of crime prevention initiatives. This local geography of crime has a number of important implications for the construction of the city centre and its immediate surroundings as key sites for the development of crime prevention strategies and, as we will detail in a later section, wider 'social ordering practices' (Lacey 1994: 28).

City centre commerce and crime prevention strategies

As noted above, the emphasis upon 'situational' crime prevention is evident in the strategic role of GIS data in the assessment and refinement of local crime control priorities and has been reinforced by the recruitment of private sector support for many of SMP's initiatives. Outside the confines of Crime and Disorder partnerships, SMP aims to attract £1,775,000 for its own initiatives in funding from the private sector between 1997 and 2004 (Safer Merseyside Partnership 1996). Latterly, encouraged by Home Office guidance, local Crime and Disorder partnerships have sought the active participation of local businesses:

> It will be absolutely essential to ensure that there is proper input into the strategies from the local business sector. Businesses are central to the life of their communities and of course, suffer from the consequences of crime.
>
> (Home Office 1998a: para. 2.33)

It is in the context of Safer Cities that Crawford points out: 'private sector input inclines towards situational rather than social prevention', favouring CCTV and other short-term measures that may be easily tailored to protect commercial premises and spaces (1997: 227).

The opening paragraph to SMP's 1996 Challenge Fund Submission highlights the centrality of commercial interests to the debate:

> The government and the community of Merseyside recognise that crime adversely affects quality of life. Rising crime and the fear of crime can deter inward investment and ultimately hinder the progress of urban regeneration on Merseyside.
>
> (Safer Merseyside Partnership 1996: 2)

Defending commercial space: the city centre partnership and CCTV

The key example of how those interests have become closely intertwined around the evolution of crime control policy on Merseyside is evident in the new urban management consortia that fund and manage CCTV. In 1994, the Liverpool City Centre Partnership (LCCP) (now known as Liverpool Vision) was established in Liverpool's commercial centre. Those involved included local business interests (the Liverpool Stores' Committee), the local authority, the police, the city's two universities, the chamber of commerce, local media representatives and transport companies. For the partnership, a prerequisite for sustaining consumption and attracting investment to the city was challenging the images of 'dangerousness' which were thought to be damaging to the emergent urban aesthetic. CCTV was to be the centrepiece of this strategy. SMP supported this development politically and also funded schemes to enhance training and codes of practice for CCTV operatives in the city centre (*ibid*: 9).

The new CCTV network enabled Merseyside Police to simultaneously bolster their support from local commercial elites and, as one urban development manager noted, enter 'the investment machinery' in Liverpool (research interview). Merseyside Police now provide business networks with data on local crime hotspots, secondments to key partnerships and delegates to major business conferences in the city (Coleman and Sim 2000). Alongside CCTV two other bodies were developed by Liverpool Stores' Committee: Crime Alert (a body of private security concerned with targeting CCTV) and Townwatch (a body concerned with litter control, monitoring homeless people and tourist information). According to a city centre manager, in working closely with the CCTV network, these bodies have been utilised in targeting 'wrongdoers, known shoplifters and people who are banned' so that they 'cannot walk around the city centre with impunity' (research interview). Exclusion Notice Schemes primarily aimed at shoplifters sit alongside by-laws aimed at prohibiting drinking in city centre streets. Beggars have also become an important focus for city centre policing and surveillance, this group having been deemed a significant enough problem to warrant attention from the small squad of 12 police officers funded by the local authority to police the city centre 'Gold Zone' established by the LCCP (Liverpool City Council 2000; *Big Issue in the North*, 4–10 December 2000). This development represents a major break in the police funding regime.

The cost of establishing Liverpool City Centre's CCTV system in 1994 was £396,000, £100,000 of which came from central government, £158,000 from the European Regional Development Fund and £138,000 from the private sector (Coleman and Sim 2000). This paid for 20 cameras in Liverpool's main shopping area. LCCP, which developed and currently manages the system, was created at the behest of Liverpool's business community and has an annual budget of £1 million. Ostensibly established as an independent body free from local political red tape, the LCCP, in the words of one urban development manager, acts to 'promote the product of Liverpool city centre' (research interview). It aims to attract tourists and consumers while regulating areas of street security, cleanliness and entertainment. For urban managers CCTV represents a new-found confidence in their power to intervene – acting as a vehicle for the promotion of a desired urban order. Though initially trumpeted on the back of promoting the safety of women and children (Coleman and Sim 1998), the system was underpinned by a deeper rationale concerned with the promotion of commercial and managerial competence to inside and outside potential investors. Therefore the idea that Merseyside can be seen as a 'safe place to do business' has been promoted in numerous documents through Merseyside Police's Community Strategy Department as well as within the local media. In this sense, the city centre became the arena within which common objectives were forged through the operationalisation of discourses around economic growth and social development.

In October 2000, a proposal to extend and integrate the camera system was approved through the Home Office Crime Reduction Programme. The programme allocated £1.7 million to develop a further 70 cameras in the city centre. They will link with independent surveillance systems, providing a total of 140 cameras (CitySafe 2000).

Alongside these moves Merseyside Police have requested Liverpool City Council to make CCTV cameras compulsory in pubs and clubs as a condition of licence to provide 'almost total coverage of the city centre with police access to all footage' (*Daily Post*, 18 August 2000). In addition every school in Liverpool is now covered by the cameras (*Liverpool Echo*, 29 July 1999).

The long-term aim of these initiatives is the integration of the system whereby a central control room will oversee up to 240 cameras in the city centre and the outlying residential areas of Kensington, Old Swan and Dingle. It is important to note that Kensington has been officially designated a crime 'hotspot' under Labour's Crime Reduction Programme and has received £30 million to fund 'a new high-profile approach' or zero-tolerance approach to policing the area (*Liverpool Echo*, 13 November 1998). Under the New Deal, £67 million has been allocated to fund the work of five police officers in the area (*Liverpool Echo*, 30 January 2001).

These developments are supported by the police crime reduction campaign 'bestreetsafe'. The campaign has all the hallmarks of a corporate public relations strategy and is carefully aimed at building collective solidarity around 'tactics to identify, confront and arrest offenders'.[2] Photographs and descriptions of ten of 'Merseyside's Most Wanted' (mostly unconvicted) appear on the campaign website.

The campaign draws attention to the dangers of street robbery and street violence and issues the usual diet of crime prevention advice: avoid high-risk areas, do not wear expensive jewellery prominently, and so on. It also seeks to responsibilise potential victims into action. 'Know your rights: You may use as much force as you need to stop yourself or somebody else being attacked, or to detain the offender, but you must not use more force than you need. You must use anything or anyone to help you; however, you must not carry a knife or anything else you intend to use as a weapon.' This tone of cautious intervention is carefully repeated: 'Don't fight back unless you are certain that you can over-power the offender without injuring yourself', while warning that prospective have-a-go heroes should 'avoid getting so drunk that it adversely affects your decision making reactions.' Using public focus groups to test out publicity ideas and high-profile advertising cam-paigns, bestreetsafe is aimed explicitly at 'education of the public' and 'improving public reassurance' using its corporate 'brand' name to promote high-visibility patrols in fluorescent jackets supported by dogs and officers on mounted horseback. It is also the vehicle for the launch of new high-visibility (fluorescent yellow) mobile patrol CCTV vehicles that can record footage on location as and when required. This strategy thus has two clear aims: to build a consensus around the ever expanding deployment of coercive and invasive technology in order to mitigate a supposed growing threat to law and order; and to use a strategy of responsibilisation to push forward this consensus.

Beyond the city centre: community, crime prevention and social harm

The regeneration of Liverpool city centre has, as elsewhere, become the hub of region-wide regeneration efforts and is based on a market ethos of 'trickle down': 'if we get it right in the city centre, other areas will see benefits too' (research interview, urban development manager). Thus, the process of regeneration ostensibly is one from which everyone stands to benefit: the wealth generated in the centre will somehow fan out into the residential areas of the city, spreading jobs and improved services in its wake. Yet, this view ignores the fact that resources are channelled towards and concentrated in the hands of 'urban elites'. A local campaign group in Liverpool has noted: '… a recent report shows architects, surveyors, lawyers, letting agents, and specialist consultants are all collecting fees on an "unprecedented scale". Meaning the latest flow of money from Europe will not go on local people to improve our lives, it will go on people who are already some of the highest earners in Liverpool' (*People Not Profit Newsletter*, issue 2, February 2000). In March 2001, an investigation by a local newspaper revealed that the bureaucracy created by regeneration funds had in turn created a new layer of professionals whose salaries alone cost the taxpayer £2 million a year (*Daily Post*, 14 March 2001).

In addition, funding can be directed *away* from traditional and well proven measures of crime prevention and redirected *towards* those that fit with the partnership ethos. For example, as the plans for erecting CCTV cameras in the Dingle area of Liverpool were being finalised, the local authority announced that it had decided to withdraw funding from the only local youth centre, the Dehon Centre, along with six other youth centres on Merseyside. The argument developed by the campaign to save the centre made explicit reference to local partnership rhetoric around crime prevention and community safety. The closure of the centre, according to this group of local residents, was likely to greatly exacerbate the problem of youth crime in the area. An explicit link was made between local service provision and the ability of the community to deal with the alienation experienced by young people in the area. For example, the unemployment rate for Riverside (which includes the Dingle area) was running at 11.6 per cent, more than three times the national average (Merseyside Trade Union Community and Unemployed Resource Centre 2001). In addition, the community's prospects for reducing crime were being diminished as local services were also withdrawn. Local people made reference to CCTV not as something that could deal with or ameliorate the problem, but rather as a strategy that provided a justification for the local authority to divert resources away from youth services. According to one of the campaign's leaflets:

The facts are very clear. To close the youth centre will result in:
- soaring crime rates by bored children
- increased drug and solvent abuse by 11–16 year olds
- lack of extra curricular activities
- increase in mental health service use

…The actual amount needed from the local council to keep the Dehon open is £30,000. This amount is a drop in the Mersey compared to other spending areas … not much to ask for the safety of the children of Liverpool.

(Save the Dehon campaign leaflet, Autumn 1999)

These concerns should be seen in the context of broader concerns around the direction and trajectory of the network's gaze and the narrow definition of community safety which is reinforced by this gaze. For example, from various vantage points in the Dingle, it is possible to look upriver along the Mersey to the multiple flares and stacks of the refineries and chemical plants of Runcorn and Ellesmere Port. The Mersey basin, stretching out to Widnes and Warrington, is one of the most highly concentrated sites of chemical production in Western Europe. Chemical spills and leaks of toxic substances are a regular occurrence in the area. This is a place where corporate illegalities are committed with alarming regularity and with largely unknown, but potentially deadly, effects. The Environment Agency's list of the worst environmental offenders was topped by ICI Runcorn in 1999. ICI were convicted 12 times in 1997 and 1998 for offences at the Runcorn plant (Personal Contact with Regional Solicitor, Environment Agency, 10 March 2000). The Shell plant at Stanlow was fourth on this list (*Daily Post*, 22 March 1999).

In addition to the long list of illegalities committed in the chemical cities of the Mersey basin, highly toxic air pollution also occurs as a result of *legitimate* omissions. Associated Octel in Ellesmere Port and ICI in Runcorn are licensed to pollute the area with 5,000 and 2,000 tonnes of carcinogenic chemicals every year respectively (www.environment-agency.gov.uk). Local press reports have raised the possibility that this may account for the abnormally high levels of lung cancer in the area (*Daily Post*, 11 February 1999). Furthermore, estimates by the Department of Health propose that the total number of premature deaths attributable to industrial and transport pollution is likely to be anything exceeding 10,000 in the UK (*The Guardian*, 1 September 2000). The geographical location of the Mersey basin industrial complex suggests that the death toll on Merseyside may be a disproportionately high one. In addition to this hazardous burden, Liverpool currently has the highest levels of traffic pollution for any city outside of London. Thirty-seven streets are expected to exceed government nitrogen limits before 2005 (Department of Environment figures cited in *The Observer*, 21 March 1999). These major threats to the safety and health of the community are (despite the fact that many of them are unequivocally the result of *illegalities*) completely absent from current crime prevention partnership priorities and continue unchecked by the gaze of an elaborate and grossly expensive CCTV camera system that is currently being erected in the residential areas of Merseyside.

Taken together the processes described above not only construct very precise definitions of what is (and is not) a responsible strategy for crime prevention, but they are also based on a very precise definition of what is harmful to the communities subjected to these strategies. Overall, therefore, these inclusionary and exclusionary practices can be understood as part of a wider social ordering strategy which is legitimated by the moral and intellectual project of social and economic regeneration. Thus the 'empowerment' of communities in turn is legitimated with reference to a generalised notion of the public interest which both mystifies and marginalises debates around 'safety', 'crime' and 'order'.

Partnerships as social ordering strategies

Cementing the local and the national

Contrary to the claims of current governmentality and risk theorists (Barry *et al* 1996; Ericson and Haggerty 1997; Hirst 1994; Rose 1999) the evidence presented here suggests that new local modes of government – formal statutory and non-statutory partnerships – are increasingly forming the central pivot for *cementing* relations between central and local state structures in both policy formation and ideological terms. Rather than representing a fragmentation of the traditional centres of political power, the development of crime prevention partnership networks in Liverpool, as in other places in the UK during the 1990s, has proved to be an effective arena for the consolidation of existing local power structures. Crime control partnerships have mobilised and engineered local social ordering strategies between local and national authorities. While new participants from the private spheres of commerce, production and civil society are recruited to ever expanding partnerships, these mechanisms merely augment and extend (rather than challenge) the sovereignty of local and nation-state decision-making structures.

As noted above, politically and ideologically, Crime and Disorder partnerships remain largely organised around police data, refined by GIS systems. The definitional status of these data is nurtured carefully by – as is the very power to shape agendas derived from – the centrally ordained partners in the Crime and Disorder partnerships: the police and the local authority. These data are subject to new forms of centralised control. Audits are then written using these data and Home Office approval is granted (either in terms of political or financial rewards) on the basis of what they reveal about local recorded crime patterns.

This definitional process is, of course, moderated by the political imperatives of regeneration. As Ian Taylor has argued, conflicts surrounding the definitions of, and policies towards, crime prevention and urban regeneration 'are one of the main sites, or locales, for a very contemporary political struggle over notions of the public as well as the private interest' (Taylor 1997: 70). As Taylor pointed out, local crime rates and other indices of security became central to local coalitions in their bids for increased investment, and were linked in with discourses concerning 'quality of life' – a key signifier within contemporary regeneration vernacular. The changed nature of political space and power at the local level, through the development of partnerships, reinforces and is reinforced by legislation and guidance from central government that have together set an agenda for the formalisation of local crime prevention strategies.

Many of the informal processes that we have referred to have become formalised. In attempting to bring coherence across an expanded scope of state institutions the Home Office plays an important role:

> We are here to short-circuit the learning curve. Central government supports the partnership concept and we want to raise the standard in building on the good work already underway at the local level. It's not about throwing it all on to you. We are here to help formalise and coordinate and give you the tools to do the job more effectively.
>
> (Home Office representative, speaking at the
> Liverpool Chamber of Commerce, 6 October 2000)

The responsibilisation of the actors involved in local crime control projects can therefore be understood as intrinsic to wider social ordering strategies. This project is underpinned by a logic of social and economic regeneration that attempts to forge and disseminate a market orientated and entrepreneurial inspired notion of the 'public interest'.

Partnerships, coercion and legitimacy

Police involvement in these processes has bolstered their 'symbolic authority' to make 'legitimate pronouncements' on crime and disorder

(Loader 1997: 2) through the wider regeneration agenda. This authority has manifested itself in, and has proceeded through, powerful coalitions concerned with regeneration and has placed the police alongside other powerful private interests in the business of creating, assessing and allocating resources from the Single Regeneration Budget and Objective One European Community funding. Thus, the use of situational data systems and CCTV may prove significant in recruiting the support of local business as part of a broader bid for legitimacy by the local state. Local crime prevention partnerships play a similar role in organising a range of powerful actors in the public and private sectors behind community crime prevention strategies. In this sense, we have to understand partnership structures as providing new concrete mechanisms for local hegemony building, in particular with respect to policing. Two aspects of local policing render the maintenance of police legitimacy vulnerable: firstly, the extraordinary high resources demanded by the force; and secondly, the force's frequent and public exposure for its use of coercive tactics utilised in the maintenance of public order.

In 1999, there was one officer for every 331 people living on Merseyside. This compared with a national average of 427. Merseyside has, with the exception of the Metropolitan force, remained, by this indicator, the most heavily policed area in England and Wales since its inception. Since the 1970s, Merseyside has had the highest number of police per head of population outside London. While the dramatic increase in police resources has been marginally slower on Merseyside than the national average, the force has since the advent of the new police authorities in 1974 consistently held its place as the second highest spending force in England and Wales. Only the Metropolitan Police has a higher per capita spending pattern. In 1997/8 the force cost the public £158 per person, 38 per cent higher than the average cost per person for all forces in England and Wales. Between 1996 and 1999, council tax contributions for the police rose by 34 per cent.[3] Furthermore, as we noted above, in a significant break with previous funding arrangements, 12 extra police officers were funded by the local authority in October 2000 at a cost of £350,000 'with officers' time being rented for shifts during the most disorderly parts of the day and evening' (*The Guardian*, 6 October 2000). According to Lady Doreen Jones, Liverpool City Council Executive Member for Community Safety: 'These 12 police officers, along with a radical CCTV system which is being installed in the city centre, will make the city safer for our citizens, visitors and for business. That will help Liverpool's continuing regeneration' (Liverpool City Council 2000: 26).

Since the disturbances of 1981, Merseyside Police have remained under public scrutiny in 'public order' situations. In recent years there have been several high-profile moments of exposure for the force. In particular, the mobile response unit, Operational Support Division (OSD), has been exposed for its heavy-handed tactics. During the dock workers industrial dispute in 1995/6, the police in general and the OSD in particular were frequently accused of using excessive force and inciting peaceful picketlines into conflict. These accusations led to no fewer than four local Members of Parliament demanding a public inquiry into the policing of the dispute (*Liverpool Echo*, 5 February 1998).

One incident where OSD officers have used violence in the city centre included an alleged unprovoked attack upon an 'essentially good-natured crowd' (*The Times*, 6 September 2000) of football supporters enjoying a drink in Slater Street after a game. Among those injured were the clientele of several pubs, a 15-year-old boy and a man in a wheelchair. Public criticism in the local press led to the removal of seven officers and the replacement of the commanding officer (*Liverpool Echo*, 14 September, 16 September and 5 October 2000), although there was widespread criticism that an internal investigation and an investigation by the Police Complaints Authority failed to identify and deal with most of the officers: 'investigations have been hampered because officers wore masks and riot gear which covered up individual markings' (*Liverpool Echo*, 1 May 2000).

The Merseyside force is also distinguished by the regularity of successful cases brought against officers for the misuse of CS Gas (see *Liverpool Echo*, 12 April and 14 April 1999; and Police Complaints Authority Press Statement, 9 June 2000). The force boasts the highest number of complaints about the use of the gas in the country with 60 complaints made in 1998/9 and 62 in 1999/2000, 50 per cent higher than any other force (*Liverpool Echo*, 5 March 1999 and 27 March 2000; *The Guardian*, 24 January 2001).

The eagerness of the local state to resort to coercion reaches beyond policing activity alone, and is reflected in the strategy of local government. The first civil action for anti-social behaviour in the UK was taken against three teenagers in June 1999 by Liverpool City Council. After conducting a covert surveillance operation, the council claimed the teenagers were guilty of loitering with large groups of other youths, jumping onto burnt out cars and urinating in the street (*Liverpool Echo*, 1 September 1999). Gaining distinction as the first local authority to use these new coercive powers was of symbolic importance to the local authority which had made considerable resources available for this purpose: 'Liverpool City Council is leading the field with a 12-

strong anti-social behaviour unit, which included lawyers, a police officer and housing enforcement officials' (*The Guardian*, 11 June, 1999).

Furthermore, the punitive powers of the police continue to be used indiscriminately and disproportionately against black people. According to the force's own figures for 1999/2000, the stop and search ratio of blacks to whites is 7.5 : 1, and the arrest ratio 6.5 : 1. In the same year, the police stopped more than a fifth of the black population on Merseyside, the highest stop and search rate for black people in the country (Home Office 2000).

These processes are continuously reinforced by the ongoing militarisation of the force (Coleman and Sim 1998), particularly with recourse to the use of armed police patrols, initially justified on the basis of wanting 'people to feel safe to come and shop and socialise in Liverpool city centre' (Assistant Chief Constable, cited in *Liverpool Echo*, 23 December 1996). Such militarisation underlies the desired ambience of consumer- and business-orientated regeneration and represents a rarely acknowledged 'but ubiquitous role of state repression' within strategies for ordering 'the theme park city' (Parenti 1999: 95).

The politics of responsibilisation

The process of building legitimacy for the coercive tactics of the local state should be understood within the context of the regeneration project. This has involved a struggle for coherence and unity of purpose which has witnessed the promotion of official discourses around the notion of local 'regeneration' and what is assumed to be in the interests of 'the city as a whole'. These discourses have been concerned with a strategic designation of the objects of partnership power. Furthermore, they 'are not neutral'. Rather, 'they construct problems, solutions and actions in particular ways that are congruent with existing relations of power, domination and distribution of resources' (Atkinson 1999: 70).

In Liverpool a series of formal and informal networking processes have, through partnerships, been orientated towards the construction of a politics of responsibilisation. The coordination of these partnerships has involved channelling funds to 'reliable', 'credible' and 'responsible' partners. This process has attempted to define a local 'collective will' and promoted strategies deemed to serve it. After the police were subjected to a barrage of complaints in the wake of the Slater Street incident, the leader of Liverpool City Council Mike Storey left no doubt that his greatest concern was not the conduct of the OSD, but the threat to the local discourse of regeneration: 'Any disturbance causes me concern because of the wrong impression it can create of the city centre' (*Liverpool Echo*, 14 September 1999).

Partnership has set in train procedural mechanisms, which are at the same time ideological in promoting 'the focusing of minds and the negotiation of sensible terms of reference' along with the 'commitment of resources to agreed packages' (research interview, Government Office for the Regions spokesperson). The (unwritten and unofficial) conditions for inclusion in partnerships may therefore prevent the inclusion of organisations and community interests that are critical – or that are likely to raise uncomfortable questions that expose the locally powerful. Strategies to neutralise resistance via the assimilation of dissenting voices into the mechanism of the local state characterised the state's attempt to negotiate with racially excluded communities in the UK in the 1970s and 1980s. Thus, a generation of black activists were to be dealt with by drawing them into the relatively benign and controllable structures of local state-sponsored community and race relations organisations (Sivanandan 1982; Gilroy 1987). The selective inclusion (and exclusion) of black community groups has been more recently identified as a common problem with community-based partnerships by the MacPherson inquiry into the racist killing of Stephen Lawrence (1999: paras 45.19 and 45.20).

However, strategies of responsibilisation that strictly define in official terms the appropriate recipients of funding or the legitimate participants in local crime control partnerships do not necessarily proceed unchallenged. Despite the seemingly overwhelming ideological force of political assertions around the problem of crime, it is important to recognise that the legitimate area of local law and order maintenance is always a contested one (Girling *et al* 2000). The contest for an alternative strategy for crime prevention in the Dingle was one of the common – but rarely reported in the local media – instances of the local struggle to define the appropriate work of crime control partnerships. On other occasions, it has been possible for communities to secure media coverage of local protests around the failure of the local authority or the police to protect them from speeding motorists. Two prominent campaigns to close roads to traffic and introduce speed restrictions emerged in the Northwood and Norris Green areas of Merseyside within weeks of the implementation of the Crime and Disorder Act in 1999. In both cases, the protests involved local residents blocking roads (*Liverpool Echo*, 27 May and 3 June 1999). It is perhaps unsurprising that protests have also started to emerge in residential areas, since after Greater London and Cheshire, Merseyside has the third highest accident rate in the country with 13.4 accidents per thousand registered vehicles

(Department of the Environment, Transport and the Regions 1999: Table 45).

This is only one of a number of issues that highlight how the priorities of crime prevention partnerships continue to sweep aside the priorities identified by local communities. As this *exclusionary* process is reproduced in other locales around other concerns (such as the provision of services for young people) the locally powerful may find that the inclusive rhetoric of partnerships will be turned around and used against them. In this sense, while the cementing of local and national interests around the right to define the crime problem may involve the 'closing down' of the law and order debate to some extent, partnership structures do at the same time create new (if still disconnected) arenas for community-based resistance.

Conclusion: the dialectics of crime prevention

Regeneration and the reconfiguring of the local state

This chapter has challenged some of the orthodoxies that prevail in current criminological and community safety literature. One of the most remarkable recent developments in social and criminological theory has been the marginalisation of the local, national and international state from theoretical scrutiny. As noted above, under the auspices of partnership, strategic alliances between key local elites – business, police, media, local government and other key institutions such as universities and travel companies – have been evolving during the last decade. The central concern of these alliances has been to materially and ideologically reconstruct a geographical sense of place utilising European, central government and local business funding cocktails to drive forward the notion of 'regeneration'. The emergence of these partnership networks has been important in reconfiguring local state structures of rule and as a consequence has opened up spaces for powerful private authorities to both articulate and have a practical impact upon problems of crime and disorder within a wider discourse of healthy 'social development'. Importantly these forms of partnership rule in urban centres 'do not need to exert total power *over* the city's population to act effectively (i.e. whether through the ballot box or other means), but rather they merely need the power to act' (Hall and Hubbard 1996: 156, emphasis in original).

What this chapter has argued therefore is that the newer developments concerning crime prevention and CCTV have *not* run parallel with developments in the 'older' mechanisms and strategies of social control but have been *dialectically* interrelated with them so that one supports and reinforces the other in the construction and reproduction of state institutions and policies. There are three observations to be made about the political conditions that underpin this dialectical process. First, the rhetoric of partnerships, devoid of any political context, claims empowerment of the local will lead to the empowerment of all through the development of autonomous authorities committed to the supposedly apolitical goals of regeneration and crime reduction. In practice, however, the partnership approach has not only consolidated the formal and informal power of local elites but has been successful in generating a new local crime control industry. This industry both mirrors and reinforces the ideological perspective of this local elite and the perspective of central government who lay down the rules and sanctions within which this industry operates. Second, and allied to this, has been the *formalisation* of the old *ad hoc*, informal model of multi-agency co-operation and its reorientation towards a business and entrepreneurial rationale for urban rule. This powerful ideological message, promoted by the idea and practice of orderly regeneration, is increasingly proscribed by government. New Labour's commitment to Local Strategic Partnership planning provides evidence of this. Third, these increasingly formalised partnership structures are playing a key role in anintensification in the neoliberal hegemony that has happened in the last three decades. One effect of this process which has deleterious consequences for notions of social justice is the ongoing change in the balance of state forces from an institutional matrix shaped around postwar welfarist strategies to one shaped by business-oriented managerial strategies.

Partnerships, as powerful institutional ensembles, thus reconfigure the boundaries of state action and effectivity. Organised around the local institutional elites of state, capital and civil society, partnerships extend the reach of government into new spheres of influence, ordained by old and new moral entrepreneurs and cemented into a local historical bloc by the doctrine of corporate and market populism (Fairclough 2000; Frank 2001).

Hegemony and crime prevention

The developments in crime prevention and CCTV discussed in this chapter are overwhelmingly concerned with traditional and conventional definitions of crime and have marginalised a range of social activities that are equally if not more socially harmful to the local population. In making this point we want to make two important qualifications. First, we are not denying the impact of conventional crimes such as burglary on the socially and economically powerless. Second, we recognise that at particular moments the present government has attempted to introduce crimes such as racist violence, domestic violence and rape onto the political and social policy agenda which previous governments have systematically ignored. Having said this, it is equally important to point out that a range of private and public actions which have immensely deleterious effects on society in general, and the relatively powerless in particular, remain on the margins of the crime prevention debate.

This analysis also challenges the official discourses of 'empowerment' that surround camera networks and finds support in other kinds of research that have questioned the power and trajectory of CCTV in relation to women's safety (Brown 1997) and the disempowerment of young people under the cameras' gaze (Norris and Armstrong 1999). The use of cameras to monitor workplaces – invariably pointed at workers rather than managers – could be added to these concerns. This has serious consequences for reinforcing and exacerbating social processes of inequality and alienation. Thus, for example, given the unequal social relations of workplace production, it is likely that cameras will be used to discipline and punish workers rather than support the prosecution of a corporation over a breach of health and safety or environmental law.

It could be argued therefore that the crime control partnerships in general and the use of CCTV cameras in particular will reproduce the 'ideological mystification' (Box 1983) surrounding crime and punishment. Thus, concerns around public criminality will be built upon a narrow definition of what constitutes community and public safety so that the other social harms described above will also remain on the political and ideological margins as politicians (and many academics) continue to be transfixed by the behaviour and activities of the powerless and the detritus generated by the social arrangements of twenty-first-century capitalism. However, as Gramsci argued, the construction of consensus will always be underpinned by the use of, or the threat of, coercion. As we have outlined in the previous section, on Merseyside the coercive capabilities of the state continue to intensify and expand to the point where punitive and militarised strategies are increasingly more visible and normalised. Paradoxically, this intensification in coercion remains invisible in the crime prevention and community safety literature.

Finally, we would argue that the nature and direction of crime prevention strategies should be firmly situated within the coruscating divisions that dominate the local and national landscape of the UK. These divisions are sustained by a local and national state form that operates outside of the structures of democratic accountability and marginalises debates around social justice that theoretically govern liberal democracies. Consequently, crime prevention strategies are filling this political and ideological vacuum and their normalisation is likely to continue for the foreseeable future. This allows politicians to claim they are taking action to deal with the 'crime problem' while simultaneously ensuring that scores of academic researchers are employed writing grant applications for evaluation studies that will feed back into the ossifying world-view of these same politicians. This structure of power is seriously hindering the development of Gramscian 'good sense' around law and order. Breaking it down is no easy task. The alternative, however, is the maintenance of the circumscribed, commonsensical and pessimistic visions of crime, punishment and social order that have dominated the majority of political and academic debates for the last two centuries which modern crime prevention strategists and their technological acolytes have uncritically accepted and continue to reproduce.

Notes

1   This paper is based on statistical and interview data collected in the course of two research projects into CCTV and community safety carried out at the Centre for Criminal Justice, School of Law, Liverpool John Moores University. In the text 'research interview' is used to make reference to qualitative data gathered in the course of those projects.
2   All quotes in this and the following paragraph are taken from Merseyside Police's bestreetsafe website (www.bestreetsafe.co.uk).
3   Merseyside Police Chief Constables Annual Reports, various years; Personal Communication with the Office for National Statistics, 15 February, 1999; Audit Commission (1999: 52); Minutes to the Merseyside Police Authority (1998–99); Report by the Chief Constable to the Merseyside Police Authority meeting, April 1995.

References

Allen, R. (1999) 'Is What Works What Counts? The Role of Evidence-Based Crime Reduction in Policy and Practice', *Safer Society Magazine*, February, 21–3.

Atkinson, R. (1999) 'Discourses of Partnership and Empowerment in Contemporary British Urban Regeneration', *Urban Studies*, 36 (1), 59–72.

Audit Commission (1999) *Safety in Numbers: Promoting Community Safety, National Report*. London: Audit Commission for Local Authorities.

Barry, A., Osborne, T. and Rose, N. (eds) (1996) *Foucault and Political Reason: Liberalism, Neo-liberalism and Rationalities of Government*. London: UCL Press.

Bottoms, A.E. and Wiles, P. (1997) 'Environmental Criminology', in M. Maguire, R. Morgan and R. Reiner (eds), *The Oxford Handbook of Criminology*. Oxford: Oxford University Press.

Box, S. (1983) *Power, Crime and Mystification*. London: Tavistock.

Brown, S. (1997) 'What's the Problem Girls? CCTV and the Gendering of Public Safety', in C. Norris, J. Moran and G. Armstrong (eds), *Surveillance, Closed Circuit Television and Social Control*. Aldershot: Ashgate.

CitySafe (1998) *Crime and Disorder Audit for Liverpool*. Liverpool: Liverpool Community Safety Partnership.

CitySafe (2000) *CCTV in Liverpool Briefing Paper*. Liverpool: Liverpool Community Safety Partnership.

Coleman, R. and Sim, J. (1998) 'From the Dockyards to the Disney Store: Surveillance, Risk and Security in Liverpool City Centre', *International Review of Law, Computers and Technology*, 12 (1), 27–45.

Coleman, R. and Sim, J. (2000) '"You'll Never Walk Alone": CCTV Surveillance, Order and Neo-liberal Rule in Liverpool City Centre', *British Journal of Sociology*, 51 (4), 623–39.

Crawford, A. (1997) *The Local Governance of Crime: Appeals to Community and Partnerships*. Oxford: Clarendon Press.

Department of the Environment, Transport and the Regions (1999) *Road Accidents in Great Britain: 1999 – The Casualty Report*. London: Stationery Office.

Ericson, R. and Haggerty, K. (1997) *Policing the Risk Society*. Oxford: Clarendon Press.

Fairclough, N. (2000) *New Labour, New Language?* London: Routledge.

Frank, T. (2001) *One Market Under God: Extreme Capitalism, Market Populism and the End of Economic Democracy*. London: Secker & Warburg.

Gifford, Lord, Brown, W. and Bundey, R. (1989) *Loosen the Shackles: First Report of the Liverpool 8 Inquiry into Race Relations in Liverpool*. London: Karia Press.

Gilroy, P. (1987) *There Ain't No Black in the Union Jack*. London: Hutchinson Education.

Girling, E., Loader, I. and Sparks, R. (2000) *Crime and Social Change in Middle England: Questions of Order in an English Town*. London: Routledge.

Hall, T. and Hubbard, P. (1996) 'The Entrepreneurial City: New Urban Politics, New Urban Geographies?', *Progress in Human Geography*, 20 (2), 153–74.

Hirshfield, A. and Bowers, K. (1998) 'Monitoring, Measuring and Mapping Community Safety', in A. Marlow and J. Pitts (eds), *Planning for Safer Communities*. Lyme Regis: Russell House Publishing.

Hirst, P. (1994) *Associative Democracy: New Forms of Economic and Social Governance*. Cambridge: Polity.

Home Office (1998a) *Guidance on Statutory Crime and Disorder Partnerships: Crime and Disorder Act 1998*. London: Home Office Communication Directorate.

Home Office (1998b) *Community Crime Reduction Partnerships: The Retail Contribution*. London: Home Office Communication Directorate.

Home Office (2000) *Statistics on Race and the Criminal Justice System: a Home Office publication under section 95 of the Criminal Justice Act 1991*. London: Home Office Research, Development and Statistics Directorate.

Hughes, G. (1998) *Understanding Crime Prevention: Social Control, Risk and Late Modernity*. Buckingham: Open University Press.

Hughes, G. (2000) 'The "Moral Career" of the Community Safety Officer'. Paper presented to Insecurity and Safety in the New Millennium: a colloquium held at the Centre for Criminal Justice Studies, University of Leeds, 23 March.

Jessop, B. (1990) *State Theory*. Cambridge: Polity.

King, M. (1991) 'The Political Construction of Crime Prevention: a Contrast Between the French and British Experience', in K. Stenson and D. Cowell (eds), *The Politics of Crime Control*. London: Sage.

Knowsley Metropolitan Borough Council (1999) Knowsley's Crime and Disorder Reduction Strategy, http://www.knowsley.gov.uk/community/safer/strategy/action, downloaded, 12 June 1999.

Lacey, N. (1994) 'Introduction: Making Sense of Criminal Justice', in N. Lacey (ed.), *A Reader on Criminal Justice*. Oxford: Oxford University Press.

Liverpool City Council (2000) *Liverpool City*, Issue 11. Liverpool: Liverpool City Council.

Loader, I. (1997) 'Policing and the Social: Questions of Symbolic Power', *British Journal of Sociology*, 48 (1), 1–18.

MacPherson, Sir William (1999) *The Stephen Lawrence Inquiry*, Cm 4262. London: Stationery Office.

Mersyside Police Community Strategy Department (1998) *Merseyside: A Safe Place to do Business?* Community Strategy Department, Merseyside Police.

Merseyside Trade Union Community and Unemployed Resource Centre (2001) *Unemployment Statistical Factsheet No. 134*. Liverpool: Merseyside Trade Union Community and Unemployed Resource Centre.

Metropolitan Borough of Wirral (1998) *Your Community, Your Security, Your Voice: Tackling Crime and Disorder Together*. Wirral: Metropolitan Borough of Wirral and Merseyside Police.

Norris, C. and Armstrong, G. (1999) *The Maximum Surveillance Society: The Rise of CCTV*. Oxford: Berg.

Parenti, C. (1999) *Lockdown America*. London: Verso.

Povey, D., Cotton, J. and Sisson, S. (2000) *Recorded Crime Statistics, England and Wales, April 1999 to March 2000*. London: Home Office Research, Development and Statistics Department.

Reiner, R. (1992) *The Politics of the Police*. London: Harvester Wheatsheaf.

Rose, N. (1999) *Powers of Freedom: Reframing Political Thought*. Cambridge: Cambridge University Press.

Safer Merseyside Partnership (1996) *New Solutions, Further Actions: Challenge Fund Submission*. Liverpool, Safer Merseyside Partnership, September.

Safer Merseyside Partnership (1998) *Annual Report 1997/98*. Liverpool: Safer Merseyside Partnership.

Safer Merseyside Partnership (1999) 'Single Regeneration Budget Plan: Merging SRB Resources Approved under Round 1 and 3 of the Challenge Fund'. Unpublished, February.

St Helens Metropolitan Borough Council (2000) 'Crime and Disorder Audit' (Executive summary of an unpublished update).

Scraton, P. (1985) *The State of the Police: Is Law and Order Out of Control?* London: Pluto.

Sefton Metropolitan Borough Council (1999) *Sefton Crime and Community Safety Strategy*. Southport: Sefton Council and Merseyside Police.

Sivanandan, A. (1982) *A Different Hunger: Writings on Black Resistance*. London: Pluto.

Smart, C. (1984) *The Ties That Bind*. London: Routledge.

Taylor, I. (1997) 'Crime, Anxiety and Locality: Responding to the "Condition of England" at the End of the Century', *Theoretical Criminology*, 1 (1), 58–75.

Whyte, D. (2001) 'Criminal Justice Partnerships on Merseyside'. Unpublished paper, Liverpool John Moores University Centre for Criminal Justice.

Chapter 6

Community safety in Middle England – the local politics of crime control

Kevin Stenson

Bronx End

A worried resident has compared her village to the Bronx after seeing youths openly selling drugs in the street ... (she said) ... living in the village feels like something out of a Charles Bronson movie.

(*The Bucks Free Press*, 3 August 2001)

Introduction

Risible comparisons between Bourne End, a pretty, affluent, Thameside Buckinghamshire village, and the Bronx were rightly downplayed by the local community police officer. Yet such reports are not a rarity in this part of Middle England, a region that has done well economically from the great Thatcherite neoliberal revolution since 1980 in loosening up markets and encouraging enterprise. Notwithstanding far-fetched analogies, these sentiments indicate that pretty rural villages and fast-expanding towns have experienced some of the ingredients of dramatic changes to be found in the inner city. These experiences are often manifest in widespread feelings of fear and insecurity that colleagues and I encountered frequently in a series of studies undertaken in the predominantly wealthy Thames Valley (Oxfordshire, Berkshire, and Buckinghamshire) from the early 1990s. They helped to provide a stimulus for a steadily rising body of research from slender beginnings in a part of the UK that has been strangely neglected by academics and also by policymakers. The work in question, undertaken by the Social Policy Research Group at my academic institution, consists of a series of empirical, policy-oriented studies. These issues relate to the social control of youth, social deprivation and regeneration initiatives, community safety, the policing of paedophiles, family support and anti-social behaviour initiatives.

This book provides researchers with an opportunity to draw wider theoretical and methodological lessons about their work. However, I hope that these reflections, emphasising the need to focus on the political nature of crime control, will be useful, not just for scholars, but also for practitioners. In part this is because there is an increasing focus on crime control in the agenda for government at every level. With the growth of inter-agency work, and statutory requirements to consult the community, undertake audits of social problems and develop and monitor a series of local policy strategies, practitioners are now pushed increasingly into the terrain of political struggle. For example, police superintendents are no longer just middle managers, protected within a huge bureaucracy; they increasingly function as key local political players in negotiating with a range of authorities and reacting quickly to trouble. Moreover, economic development specialists in local government are usually acutely aware that conditions and feelings in poorer neighbourhoods are sensitive barometers of the state of and changes in the local economy.

With increasing global interdependency, many trends are familiar internationally. Predictably, analysts have attempted to describe and explain these trends by means of general or grand theoretical story lines. In this chapter I will reflect on the two general theoretical story lines about crime control, or narratives to use the more upmarket term, that have had most influence on my work. Firstly, there is a broadly Marxist account that highlights political economic forces in explaining social change and the workings and effects of the apparatuses involved in crime prevention, policing and criminal justice (Jessop 2000; Hay 1996; Hogg and Brown 1998). Secondly there is the 'governmentality' approach, to which I have a closer allegiance (Dean 1999). This is inspired by Michel Foucault's later work, that attempts to chart and explain the great shifts in mentalities and modes of governance and public government in the advanced liberal democracies. By liberalism I mean not a point on the political spectrum, but rather the institutional and moral underpinnings and rationales of the major modern, law-governed democracies. For me, governmentality studies should not only make liberal democracy – in the broadest sense – its major object of analysis. It should also be wedded to a firm normative commitment to update, defend and enhance the vigour of a liberal democratic way of life (Stenson 1998). I complement this agenda with a focus on political economic factors, but in ways that contrast with Marxist perspectives.

In a liberal culture there should be checks and balances to authorities of all kinds, and tolerance and respect for open debate and the rights of individuals and minorities. Many of the most significant developments in liberal government involve attempts to deal with crime and insecurity and involve a bewildering range of partnerships between statutory, not-for-profit and commercial organisations, and the rise of new forms of knowledge and expertise. These are often well beyond the purview or grasp of elected representatives of the citizenry and present major challenges for social scientists and political theorists in rethinking how to recreate a proper separation of and accountability for the new governmental powers in twenty-first-century liberal polities. Hence, the critic in criminology can play a crucial role within liberalism. Indeed, I see most of the established critical academic postures, however they tag their 'ism' of the moment, as variations on a grand liberal tradition of critique stretching back to the eighteenth-century Enlightenment, even if the critics can also be prone to intolerance of dissent from their views and sorely in need of critique themselves.

If the main explanatory emphasis in the Marxist narratives is on the role of economic forces and class conflict, in the governmentality school the focus is on politics: on governance, government and political conflict. However, I argue that too much attention has been paid to issues of government from above, as represented in official discourse produced by agents of government. This is at the expense of the messier and murkier fields of political conflict and informal processes of governance that help to shape the governing process. General narratives have their place and remind us of the international or global nature of the forces and problems that we grapple with, and I have contributed to these from a governmentality perspective (e.g. Stenson 1993, 1996, 1998, 2000a, 2000b, 2001, 2002). Policymakers and concerned citizens in a democracy should be prepared to learn the lessons of good and bad practice elsewhere, and there is a burgeoning import/export trade between the major countries in policy ideas and technologies of implementation in this, as in other, policy fields. These range, for example, from tough, zero tolerance approaches to policing to the manifold initiatives of local community crime prevention, conflict mediation, problem-oriented and intelligence-led policing and community justice (Stenson 2000b, 2002).

Local problems and issues are seldom unique to a given locality and there is no need to continually reinvent the policy wheel. Yet, there is always the danger that we construct theoretical narratives and one-size-fits-all policy frameworks of supposed universal relevance out of narrow empirical cases, or a highly selective review of work that disproportionately highlights particular social problems, populations and geographical areas and jurisdictions. In addition, our theoretical and methodological tools are not innocent or neutral and even in particular empirical case studies we may see and generalise from only what our chosen spectacles allow us to see. It would be premature to claim to have found definitive ways to disentangle the particular from the general, but I hope that this chapter contributes a little to the wider pool of knowledge and reflection about crime control, particularly as it is manifested in debates about community safety.

This term is notoriously slippery and resists precise definition since it is used and applied at local levels in a variety of ways. It often refers to a range of ways to reduce crime, disorder and the fear of crime, with the recognition that concerns about these issues are deeply intertwined with concerns about traffic and a host of environmental and other issues (Audit Commission 1999). Yet it is not devoid of stable meaning. Its ethos was crystallised in the work of mainly progressive, Labour local authorities from the late-1980s who wished to move beyond the Home Office emphasis on bolts and locks and situational approaches to crime prevention and develop a more holistic, multi-agency approach to the prevention of crime. This formed part of a revival of the old municipal socialist tradition and, with limited help from macro state policies, paralleled municipal attempts to revive local economies. There was a growing view, increasingly shared by Liberal and Tory authorities, that situational strategies and tough approaches to policing and criminal justice neglected the deeper, complex roots of criminality, especially among young people in poorer areas who were usually seen as the main source of trouble (White 1998). Hence, to tackle car crime, drug dealing, burglary, mugging, criminal damage and anti-social behaviour requires a recognition of the need to tackle the interaction between what is seen as poor parenting, housing, health and educational attainment, a deteriorating environment and so on (Home Office 1991).

In addition, these approaches emphasised the need to involve local citizens, and also required grants from the government's Safer City and Single Regeneration Budget initiatives for community regeneration. All these ventures required research to help diagnose problems and policy options, and underpin applications for grant aid – in short a new knowledge base for 'joined-up social policy' (Stenson 1996; Hughes 1998). These developments helped to spawn a new body of professional workers committed to work and develop expertise within the community safety ethos. Yet ironically, as leading players in community safety within the Thames Valley have noted, New Labour in office have sent out ambiguous signals (Thames Valley Partnership 2001). On the one hand, the work of the government's Social Exclusion Unit promotes holistic, multi-agency, 'joined-up' solutions to social problems, in harmony with a community safety perspective. On the other hand, the Home Office's evidence-based crime reduction strategy and performance targets announced in 1998 and the Crime and Disorder Act 1998 focus more narrowly on reducing volume crime, with a particular emphasis on burglary, auto-crime and anti-social behaviour (Goldblatt and Lewis 1998). As usual, white collar and corporate crime seem to be defined out of the concerns that must be addressed locally by statutory agencies. Here was yet another pro-business government not wanting to ruffle the feathers of local business communities.

My sympathies lie strongly with a holistic notion of community safety, albeit one that fully recognises the need for tough, sovereign law enforcement where necessary to secure public order and the physical security of vulnerable citizens. However, I recognise its contentious nature and in this chapter will use the term crime control as a more generic term to refer to the continuum of strategies and technologies that are involved in the struggle to prevent and reduce crime, and impose sanctions on offenders.

Notwithstanding their virtues, I emphasise the similarity in the limitations of the general narratives on which I focus. I also emphasise the importance of building bridges between them in trying to find ways to identify and explain general trends, while also recognising the diverse ways that these trends impact on and interact with local cultural, economic and political conditions. An inherent problem with the general narratives is that they recognise that part of the story is the increasing policy focus on local crime control. This operates through strategies to gather information locally about problems of crime and disorder and to develop ways of dealing with these issues at that level. These developments, in turn, are partially explicable in terms of the declining faith in the effectiveness of macro economic and social policies employed by the state.

However, at the level of a town or region, in this case the Thames Valley, we face richly varied contexts, historically, culturally, economically and politically. Hence to make sense of policy and practice at the local level we need intellectual tools beyond the capacity of the general narratives to help us understand the links between more general national and international trends and those which are more locally specific. It would be invidious to characterise this complex, under-researched, varied region as having a unified social structure. However, in the third section of the chapter, I will selectively indicate some of the features that differentiate it from other, more obviously deprived and problematic regions and cities that have attracted greater attention from government and researchers. I also explore some of the dilemmas associated with a policy climate that prioritises the need to target resources narrowly to those populations and areas defined as having the highest level of need or as constituting the highest level of risk. Given the limited range of empirical evidence so far about crime control in the Thames Valley and the necessarily selective use of evidence in a brief review, I use some poetic licence to push forward the analysis. Though this is not a substitute for a more comprehensive and detailed regional study. I will first explore the first two general narratives in the light of my research experience.

Narratives of crime control – Marxism

Marxist conflict theories, make sense of the linkages between changes in socio-economic relations and governmental and policy changes with respect to crime control by arguing that new forms of production and exchange in a knowledge-based and more fragmented economy need new modes of regulation. These can include the new forms of commercial discipline imported into the public sector, crystallised in the management target-oriented 'performance culture', to regulate the regulators (McLaughlin and Murji 2001). At route these modes of regulation, while not reducible to state activity, are orchestrated and co-ordinated through ever-evolving state agencies, on the premise that the principle function of the state is to serve the dominant coalition of economic interests within the changing capitalist economy (Hay 1996). These Marxist analyses can be sophisticated, but I would argue that, in the final instance, a key feature that makes them Marxist is the tendency to view the key political actors as bearers or manifestations of deeper structural tendencies in the unfolding historical development of capitalism. This contrasts with the approach to governmentality studies that I prefer, which puts much greater emphasis on political agency, conflict and choice.

A second key Marxist feature is the view that the language of liberalism functions largely as an ideological fig leaf that disguises and renders respectable and acceptable systems of control whose function is seen as defending an increasingly ruthless and exploitative capitalism, globally and locally. In this view, the agencies of crime control and justice, with their liberal vocabularies of due process, the rule of law, human rights, problem-oriented and intelligence-led policing, community safety and justice, and so on, disproportionately advance the interests of the big corporations and the classes that benefit most from them, while claiming to represent the public interest. A virtue of this broad characterisation of a Marxist-based political economy model is that it recognises that regulation in the sphere of crime control includes both punitive methods of policing and criminal justice to subdue those seen as threats to the class interests of the affluent majority and public order, as well as the more subtle, social oriented methods of regulation, which aim to build up popular consent for crime control.

In this perspective, the growing strength of the transnational corporations, aided by the dominant western states and their client international agencies, have shifted the focus from (if not entirely displacing) 'social' modes of governance, codified in theory as the 'Keynesian Welfare State' (Hay 1996). This refers to the techniques and modes of professional expertise of fiscal and monetary policy and social management crystallised in the work of the economist Keynes and his acolytes during the high period of the postwar welfare states between the 1940s and late 1970s. Keynesians in 'Fordist', large factory-based economies ameliorated capitalism by state taxation and investment and the manipulation of consumer demand in order to: provide public sector and shore up private sector employment; iron out the cycles of boom, slump and inflation; and create public structures to collectivise, through state agencies and national insurance, the management of risks. The latter are associated, for example, with old age, sickness, unemployment and criminal victimisation. In various ways, the 'social' vision formed a part of an optimistic faith in the capacity of the state to promote social justice, social solidarity and equality in the distribution of the goods of life. This was seen as a third way between unbridled capitalism and the planned, illiberal state socialism of the soviet countries. In varying ways and to varying degrees, welfare state policies provided some space for policies and professional expertise that tried to use criminal justice – especially in relation to young offenders – as a means to deal with social and psychological problems, in addition to enforcing a penal sanction and channelling and taming the thirst for revenge.

Clearly, fast-growing, prosperous capitalist societies are criminogenic, providing burgeoning opportunities for acquisitive crime and the money for alcohol, illegal drugs and the violent crime associated with their abuse in the public and domestic spheres (Felson 1998). Yet in a deeper sense, following Marxist logic, Keynesian economic and social regulation could be said to have contained particular forms of criminality now usually associated with economic decay and the collapse of old community structures. At the core of social, Keynesian government was an acceptance that the state is the employer of last resort, and must support industries that maintain the livelihoods and household and community structures of the male working classes, particularly in what are now described as the declining, old-technology, 'smokestack' industries. Let us remember that for generations these industries and the (predominantly) men who worked within them as 'breadwinners' earning a family wage and struggling for a better life provided the bedrock of support for the labour movements and parties of the left.

However, the neoliberal transformation of the agenda for government ushered in by Reagan, Thatcher and their allies in the 1980s means that capitalist states – especially in the anglophone world – now downplay responsibility for maintaining employment and promoting equality and social justice through macro economic and social policies. In the UK, for example, 100,000 manufacturing jobs were lost between January and July 2001, with another 250,000 jobs under threat from a cyclical downturn reinforcing long-term structural decline (*The Guardian*, 7 August 2001). The new regulatory focus replaces demand management with a 'supply side' economic focus (Jessop 2000). This envisages that the state's primary economic responsibility is to enhance the quality of the supply of labour, entrepreneurship and other means to enable a population to compete in a more open global economy. Hence the focus is on economic restructuring and growth instead of solidarity and social justice, and at the price of dramatically widening gulfs of inequality between rich and poor and the collapse of relatively well paid, 'breadwinning' work for millions of working-class men of all ethnicities.

In the English speaking world this has meant that even the parties of the left have followed the Thatcherite dictum that it is pointless to support smokestack industries, since globally footloose capital will always shift production to where labour is cheap and pliable. This signals the abandonment by the left of its traditional, core constituencies. Hence, for example, in the UK, recent administrations have been characterised by low income taxes, an overvalued currency hastening the decline of manufacturing industry unable to sell its products, underfunded public services and the privatisation of state assets.

Recent UK administrations have favoured the affluent majority, increasingly dependent on the new service and hi-tech sectors of the economy. Not surprisingly poorer citizens, dependent on now less unionised and protected, blue-collar and public sector employment and state welfare, are increasingly reluctant to participate in elections in which few tribunes voice their interests. The election campaign of 2001 highlighted the extent to which the New Labour administration, winning only a quarter of the total possible vote, had abandoned the goals of equality and social justice in favour of 'meritocracy' and opportunity – values thought to be more congenial to the affluent majority (Kellner 2001). This has involved a diminishing commitment to universal, tax-funded services and welfare safety nets.

The costs to declining inner city and social housing neighbourhoods are heavy. The abandonment in these areas by commercial organisations of production, transport and retailing parallels a growing neglect by state agencies, contributing to a feeling of ungovernability. Into this vacuum step illegal economies, particularly related to the global drugs economy, prostitution and a host of spin-off illegal economies in which agencies of official government can be poor competitors with criminal forms of informal governance and conflict resolution. These illegal economies and the fast-growing commercial security industry which is largely parasitic on them are associated with less educated white men and those from ethnic minorities suffering from economic and social exclusion (Davies 1997; Rose, D. 1996; Winlow 2001). In undertaking research in Buckinghamshire social housing estates, we encountered concerns among residents and local professionals about the strength of such illegal economies, the under-reporting of crime, and the difficulties of persuading victims and witnesses to give evidence against powerful local figures who engaged in deviant, informal governance (Stenson and Watt 1999b).

Hence, in this narrative, neoliberal policies reinforce a deeper logic of change by creating and exacerbating destabilising inequalities. This creates major problems of public disorder, crime and community conflict, evident, in the UK, in the riots in poor areas in 1981, 1985 and 1991, and more recently in declining, industrial northern towns with large ethnic minority populations in the spring and summer of 2001. These developments thus require ever strengthening state power to contain dissent and the organised criminality that emerges among the poor, the ambitious and the desperate in their struggle to survive and achieve the goals of the consumer dream that saturate the media. This is seen as at the expense of principles of justice and civil liberties and usually accompanies an indifference towards the crimes of government, the corporations and the rich. Thus new forms of crime control are seen as a function of the growth of increasingly *authoritarian states* (Hogg and Brown 1998; Hudson 2001).

The Marxist-based grand narrative has great persuasive force in trying to make sense of developments in poorer countries too. As in richer countries, neoliberal intellectuals in the western ministries and the World Bank have declining faith in the probity and capacity of state governments to effect change through macro economic and social policies, and a preference for locally based initiatives, using the libertarian rhetoric of empowerment and citizen action. There is encouragement for initiatives organised by commercial firms and by not-for-profit, non-governmental organisations. This was reinforced by the experience of criminologists (including myself) invited as academic observers to the historic UN conference on crime prevention in Vienna in April 2000. Western policymakers advised their counterparts from poorer countries that adopting the western repertoire of local crime control measures, including criminological technologies like local crime surveys, hotspot analysis and so on, is the key to attracting western state aid and inward investment by the big corporations. Presenting Singapore as a role model, the emphasis was less on human rights and democracy than on the enforcement of discipline and the rule of law, especially in public places, and in the control of the drugs economy, bribery and corruption.

Crime control and targeting

This narrative, in the UK and other advanced societies, highlights the targeted, local initiatives to identify and manage the areas and populations represented as posing the highest risks to the state and the economy. These are often legitimated through the use of the new technologies of risk analysis developed by criminologists, geographers and other social scientists to identify the hotspots of crime and social dislocation. These accounts highlight the repressive role of the state, in the form of tough, 'zero-tolerance' tactics and a growing punitiveness in the treatment of the poor and minorities (Hogg and Brown 1998; Cuneen 2001). The huge growth in incarceration in advanced societies, particularly in the USA and the UK, even during periods when official crime rates have dropped, can be viewed as methods to contain and suppress dissident or marginalised classes (Parenti 1999).

Clearly there are other more seemingly liberal aspects to crime control, usually associated with profligate use of the term 'community': community, problem-solving and intelligence-led policing; crime prevention and reduction; community safety, regeneration and justice; mediation; restorative justice; and mentoring. These developments are usually viewed as the velvet glove which hides the iron fist of coercion (Gordon 1987). Moreover, the Marxist narrative dovetails nicely with those produced by anti-state, anarchist intellectuals who explain these developments, along with CCTV and other surveillance technologies, as manifestations of the huge growth in the international crime control industries, authoritarian state bureaucracies, the widening of the net and thinning of the mesh of social controls (Christie 1993; Cohen 1985).

The most persuasive Marxist or anarcho-Marxist accounts focus on situations and places which afford opportunity to highlight social conflict and extreme differences of interest, in volatile, conflictual and deeply unequal cities like Los Angeles and Liverpool (Davis 1992; Coleman and Sim 1998). Thus, multi-agency coalitions of crime prevention are presented as alliances of urban managers, retailers and other corporate interests, concerned to discipline and exclude the homeless, the poor and other groups defined as troublesome from shopping malls, city centres and other urban spaces; these are designated as sites for the spectacle and conduct of consumption. It is tempting within this grand narrative to view these locations and the forms of often repressive social control that operate there as representing the deep truth of capitalism, in the same way that the use of brutal riot police to suppress anti-globalisation protesters at meetings of the G7 and the World Trade Organisation can be represented as the true face of the major corporations and their client western state governments. Hence the grand, macro narrative coincides with and reinforces the narrative of the local setting; the latter is a dramatic instance of the former. Each particular instance represents the visible face of the deeper essential reality of capitalism.

Narratives of crime control: governmentality

The governmentality narrative about the changing forms of crime control explains them as elements of the shift from welfarist policies, so in this respect finds common ground with the Marxist narrative (Rose, N. 1996, 2000). However, governmentality writers challenge the view that these shifts can be understood principally in terms of changes in the economy and state. Their privileged explanatory status is replaced by focusing on political action and government. Hence, the lines of causality are reversed in that domains like the economy – agencies of production and distribution in the market – are themselves produced and reproduced as relatively separate spheres by political action. In this narrative, economic relations and activities, while crucial, can not be understood as existing beyond the political and cultural realm. They are not the products of the workings of the capitalist system conceived as a machine-like structure that determines our lives. Rather economic relations and production and market activities are intrinsically cultural, political and emotionally laden activities. The same is true of relatively autonomous spheres like the law, policing and criminal justice, with their special forms of professional expertise. Hence the regulatory agencies involved in crime control are not simply cogs in a giant machine of control, but extremely complex, locally varied cultural institutions.

Moreover, in this perspective policy strategies are not just responses to external social problems. Rather, the 'problems' they address are given shape and recognition by the emerging policy discourses in which academic theories and research can play a critical role (Stenson 1991). Hence, crime control strategies embody *governmental savoirs*, intellectual instruments of government (Foucault 1977). These embody reflections on the arts of government: governmental philosophies, or rationalities, together with the policy strategies and technologies that they deploy or with which they become aligned. They forge new ways to make populations thinkable and measurable for the purposes of liberal government: what Foucault described as *governmentality* (Foucault 1991; Stenson 1991, 1998, 2000b). This is a gloss for a series of processes through which populations, at every spatial level, are categorised, differentiated and sorted into hierarchies. The everyday processes of public *government*, the exercise of publicly financed and organised power, are underpinned by censuses, official and academic surveys of crime and other social problems. These do not simply describe the world, they also create – in this policy field – their own regimes of what counts as the accredited 'truths' about the nature, causes and remedies for crime (Stenson 1991).

However, these public forms of government are part of a larger sphere of *governance*. For me, the term refers to the more or less rational means to shape human conduct, by trying to structure the field of constraints and possibilities within which action takes place (Gordon 1991). It ranges from self-governance to the governance of family life, commercial firms, voluntary associations, religious and international organisations (Shearing 1996). Hence, the key players in the local politics of crime control may be many and varied, even where they are not formally brought into the official process of democratic government (Stenson 1998; Stenson *et al* 1999a). Liberal polities from the beginning have generated multiple sites of governance, but the great neoliberal revolution has reinforced this and led to a reinvention of the nature of public government.

There has been a redistribution of the tasks of government and an accompanying growth in new forms of expertise, in crime prevention and control, as in other policy fields. These new governmental forms cross the boundaries of the statutory, commercial and voluntary sectors, promoting the involvement of active citizen groups of various kinds. The changes in governance and government are also associated with the break-up of large, hierarchical organisations into leaner, adaptable network-based organisations and practices. In these new social forms, influence and command increasingly operate indirectly, at a distance and through the fostering of self-regulation in accordance with centrally set benchmarks and goals (Stenson 1996).

Advancing the governmentality perspective

I wish to mention and respond to a series of criticisms that can be made of governmentality studies. Firstly, governmentality narratives have neglected political economic processes. I have tried to redress this by focusing on these topics, but emphasise the role of politics, choice, discourse and culture (Stenson and Watt 1999b; Stenson and Edwards 2001). I stress (echoing Max Weber) that Marxists have no monopoly on the description and explanation of political economy. Secondly, the governmentality narratives have been criticised for being overly abstract and exaggerating the role of rational policy discourse at the expense of messier, contingent emotional and political influences on policy (Crawford 1997).

Thirdly, like the Marxist narrative, this general narrative often glosses over local variations in the unfolding forms of liberal government. Wider influences operate through the filter of local political cultures and forms of habitus (Bourdieu 1990) or shared emotional and cognitive dispositions. Within these local political cultures, there is scope for discretion and choice, in which political leadership and decisionmaking are crucial in shaping policymaking and practice (Stenson and Edwards 2001). At national level global economic influences are interpreted differentially in the light of different cultural dispositions and political coalitions (Hirst and Thompson 1995). For example, in Western Europe the British, whether Tories or Labour are in power, occupy the Thatcherite end of the continuum of political culture and choice. A consequence which has had profound implications for issues of crime control is that in other Western European countries there has been a greater political determination by state governments to apply Keynesian policies and support the public services, coal, steel and other smokestack industries, and the working-class constituencies that depend on them (Hutton 1995).

Fourthly, within the governmentality school, I have argued that we need to go beyond an overemphasis on history and a reliance on archives and policy texts as providing key evidence of the existence and effects of liberal mentalities. These operate also within our living cognitive procedures and form part of shared oral cultures. This narrow textual, historical bias is associated with an attempt to distance this approach from realist social science, as if it were possible to detach the study of reflections on the nature of liberal rule from the social contexts in which rule operates. On the contrary, I have argued for the use, in governmentality research, of a range of data sources and methods, including ethnographic exploration of mentalities and practices in oral culture and visible, practical settings. In political and policymaking processes, the key discourses usually unfold in a complex interplay between talk and text. Policy documents can never be understood in isolation from the practical contexts in which they are produced and interpreted.

This was particularly brought home to my colleagues and I in studying attempts by statutory authorities to govern unpopular and stigmatised areas of social housing in Buckinghamshire (Stenson and Watt 1999a, 1999b). We analysed shifts in local economic and community development policy through focusing on key texts. But this was also informed by our knowledge of local social history, our interviews and our close relationships with a range of local government and other key players in the statutory services, and also by our attendance at meetings where disputes and compromises were ironed out before the production of tidy policy texts. We also attended public meetings, interviewed residents and observed patterns of interaction and the built environment in key areas. In our study of young people's perception and use of public spaces and their patterns of informal governance, in addition to semi-structured interviews we employed ethnographic observation. As researchers, we were at times participant observers. Our role in the local governmental process presented risks at times to our academic independence yet gave us access to data and information that would otherwise be denied to us. In brief, I advocate a rapprochement with realist, institutional analysis that can enable us to go beyond abstract grand narratives to look at the interaction between general trends and local settings (Stenson 1998, 1999; Stenson and Watt 1999a; Stenson and Edwards 2001).

Fifthly, I have argued that that governmentality studies have failed to recognise the centrality of sovereign modes of government – through policing and criminal justice as well as military means (Stenson 1999, 2000b; Waddington 1999). This refers to the use or threat of use of coercion to maintain control over geographical territory in the name of sovereign law. Although my notion of sovereignty is broader than that within the Marxist narratives and goes well beyond the explanation of class and state domination, it has been a strength of those narratives that they have linked policing and criminal justice to sovereign domination (Grimshaw and Jefferson 1987). Moreover, a key element of New Labour's Third Way version of the neoliberal agenda is the attempt, for example through anti-social behaviour orders, curfews and other measures introduced in the Crime and Disorder Act 1998, as well as frequent reference to the virtues of 'zero-tolerance' approaches to crime control, to retake sovereign control over perceivably disorderly inner-city and social housing areas (Stenson 2000b; Stenson and Edwards 2001). Thus New Labour aims to reconnect with its core constituency via law and order policies.

Targeting and the social

This emphasis on sovereignty forms part of the shift towards the targeting of policy and resources towards poorer areas and marginalised groups and away from universalist policies that aim to create a more equal society. This stems from the break-up internationally of the political alliance between the poor and the affluent and relatively contented majority of voters, and the consequent diminishing electoral support for parties that promise to tax and spend in order to help the poor and those otherwise excluded from the good life (Galbraith 1992). Hence, a profound meta-dilemma of centre-ground governments, which provides a frame for crime control and other areas of policy, is that *they must struggle to reach out to the disaffected 'excluded' populations while not unduly hurting the pockets of the economically comfortable majority* (Stenson and Edwards 2001).

The vestiges of the universalistic, social democratic programme are reformulated within the 'Third Way' agenda of New Labour as a strategy to target help to the marginalised and those considered to represent high levels of risk to themselves and others. Central to this is the construction of knowledge about high-risk populations through the use of new technologies and policies of risk assessment and management (Feeley and Simon 1994; O'Malley 2001). This strategy includes attempts to discourage welfare dependency and encourage and reward those willing to help themselves through improving their marketability to employers. Analysis of local social policy by Paul Watt and I in High Wycombe in Buckinghamshire reinforces the case that these are attempts to reconstruct a form of holistic, 'social' policy through 'joined up' targeted approaches to regeneration policy. We argue that public sector agencies return to centre stage as coordinators of regeneration. However, we noted the tension between targeting the poor and risky and the commitment to a 'social' form of universalism, in equitable service provision, which remains central to the professional identities and statutory requirements of local government officers (Stenson and Watt 1999a). In addition, Adam Edwards and I have pointed to the competitive and destabilising tensions opened up by targeting resources for community safety. It is always open to citizens from non-targeted areas and groups to question the equity, morality and legality of targeted provision (Stenson and Edwards 2001).

The government's Social Exclusion Unit has orchestrated much of this strategy under the New Labour government. Targeted provision works through a plethora of initiatives, ranging from working family tax credits to Health and Education Action Zones to the New Deal for Communities targeting marginalised neighbourhoods. However, these policies have not stopped the gulf of inequality widening. In part this is because the notions of exclusion embedded in policy have tended to highlight issues of crime, anti-social behaviour and other behavioural characteristics rather more than issues of poor housing, low pay and other issues relating to inequality (Watt and Jacob 2000). Analysts remain sceptical about the government's goal to take a million children out of poverty by 2004 and to reduce widening inequalities in health and education without significant redistributive policies and progressive taxation (*The Guardian*, 13 July 2001).

I have tried to build theoretical bridges between the governmentality perspective with Marxist perspectives by focusing on political economy, albeit in a culturally and politically sensitive and less mechanistic way. I highlight the need to recognise the role of local cultures, processes of governance and political conflict. Now let us explore these issues further with a closer look at some selective features of crime control in the Thames Valley.

Thames Valley: restructuring and relative deprivation

The Thames Valley police service serves three English counties, Oxfordshire, containing one of the world's greatest seats of learning, Berkshire, whose wealthy inhabitants include the Queen at Windsor, and Buckinghamshire, whose boundaries include Chequers, the Prime Minister's official country residence. This part of mainly Tory voting, Middle England includes 2.1 million people (and rising) in 2,200 square miles of predominantly rural landscape, with the most beguiling stretch of the River Thames and extremely pretty English villages that attract media stars and many of the wealthiest people in Europe. This area has been a prime beneficiary of Thatcherite neoliberalism, attracting new corporations at the cutting edge of the global economy. These have benefited from the long international stock market boom, with rising employment levels and prosperity associated with falling rates of officially recorded crime. The region is associated not only with farming and rural tourism (it experienced an estimated 6 million visitors in 2000 according to police figures), but with the rapid expansion of hi-tech based and financial and other new service industries. The corridors around the M25, M4 and M40 motorways are acknowledged to be at the European cutting edge of business expansion, where Thames Valley meets Silicon Valley. The key economic players are global corporations, whose managers carry clout with local statutory authorities and central ministries. Its economy has shifted rapidly towards hi-tech and service industries and away from older, smokestack industries.

Its settlements do not score high enough on the standard measures of deprivation, particularly the government's 'Index of Local Conditions', in order to have attracted significant EU or central government grants for regeneration. Moreover, neither Conservative nor New Labour administrations have provided much assistance to declining industries here and the populations which depended on them. Hence, in this region, markets were allowed to find their own levels to the benefit of the majority in material terms. Let us focus now on restructuring in rural and secondly in urban settings.

Rural socio-economic change

At first sight, this region provides a classic example of white flight. Through rapid internal UK migration large numbers of educated, skilled middle- and affluent working-class people have joined the longer settled affluent rural and suburban populations. In addition to seeking employment, they could be seen as fleeing the cultural diversity and social problems and conflicts of the cities, seeking secure work and the chance to participate in the dream of the culturally homogeneous, English rural idyll (Stenson and Watt 1999b). However, a closer look reveals worms in the darling buds. The government's own Countryside Agency, in a major report, has shown that rural areas include significant threads and pockets of deprivation, hidden from view but familiar to local police and other agencies (Countryside Agency 2001). In partial support of the foregoing political economy narrative, many of these problems can be traced to profound economic and social restructuring that have affected rural life (Dingwall and Moody 1999).

In the last thirty years, a general decline in agriculture in areas like

Berkshire and the introduction of labour-saving technologies have increased rural unemployment (GO-SE 2000: 76). This can be related to tensions between settled and travelling populations. The latter, pejoratively termed 'Pikies' in the Thames Valley, are widely perceived as a source of criminal threat and intimidation. In part this tension stems from diminishing demand for the unskilled agricultural labour traditionally provided by travellers. Moreover, the sale of rural social housing and the invasion of villages by wealthy commuters have increased property values. These factors have combined to polarise many villages along class lines and progressively push the rural poor into the nearby urban areas. Moreover, as we found in a study of a sharply polarised village, which included an isolated, unpopular estate of social housing, marginalised populations can be pushed out into the countryside from the town (Stenson and Watt 1999b). In such neighbourhoods – as in parallel urban areas – the police and other governing agents seldom visit. Troubles are rarely reported to officialdom and informal modes of governance, in the forms of vigilantism, organised crime and patriarchal domestic violence, partially fill the vacuum.

Furthermore, there are tensions over the politics of local economic and demographic development. Here, the central issues include how far to allow growth in business and residential development that conservationist lobbies argue transcend the capacity of the geographical environment and material infrastructure to sustain (Stenson and Watt 1999a).

Urban socio-economic change

Despite the rural image of the region, there are substantial towns and cities, notably Oxford, Reading, Slough, Aylesbury, Milton Keynes and High Wycombe, that play a central role in the region and account for a high proportion of officially recorded crime and related social problems, including the most visible and concentrated areas of deprivation. Slough, Oxford and Reading return Labour MPs to parliament, reflecting concentrations of working-class and ethnic minority voters. These urban areas have experienced considerable economic restructuring and demographic change. In addition to absorbing the rural poor and waves of immigration from the Celtic fringes and Ireland, they have absorbed large numbers of new Commonwealth immigrants, who originally worked in the less attractive manufacturing sectors and, more recently, with the proximity of Heathrow, large numbers of Balkan and other refugees. Hence, the class and ethnic polarisation found in major cities is paralleled in this region too, generating anxiety, fear and resentment in the suburban and rural populations adjoining the urban areas. These tensions are exacerbated by the sales of social housing and the diminution of its stock. This has led to the concentration of people with a variety of perceived problems, including the mentally disturbed released into the community, in the remaining areas of social housing. This increases the potential for social conflict (MacVean 2001; Jones 2001).

Skills gap

Many of the traditional manufacturing sectors have experienced decline, or technological change resulting in reduced opportunities for 'breadwinning', secure, well paid blue-collar jobs for those who lack the skills, qualifications or aptitude to adjust to the new labour markets. This is obscured to a degree by the increasing availability of low-paid, insecure jobs in the service sector opened up in part because of the high levels of disposable income of the newly affluent. The poor pay and prospects of those trapped in these jobs create major barriers to penetrating the expensive housing and other key markets in the region (GO-SE 2000). For example, the traditional town and gown tensions of Oxford have been exacerbated by the rapid expansion of a wealthy professional class. Their lifestyles contrast sharply with those who remain dependent on the shrinking Fordist manufacturing base clustering around the car industry and the low-paid reaches of the service sector. Oxford and the surrounding villages, like the other major towns in the region, have experienced a rapid expansion in illegal drugs economies and the related crime patterns with which they are usually associated (Rose 2001). Furthermore, public order disturbances on the city's Blackbird Leys social housing estate in the early 1990s showed that social dislocation is not confined to deindustrialising northern towns.

Slough had been an unlovely powerhouse of 1930s industrial renaissance earning John Betjeman's poetic injunction to suffer a rain-storm of bombs. But it has experienced rapid expansion of IT-based industries, of affluent neighbourhoods like Caversham and an ongoing urban facelift, while employment in chemicals and the industries clustering around Mars, the confectionery giant, has contracted. Directly or indirectly the tensions from economic restructuring have manifested in the predominantly white Britwell and predominantly Asian Chalvey social housing estates located near the main industrial estates. Both these areas have experienced high levels of criminal victimisation and some ethnic tensions, and its populations are familiar to the range of local regulatory agencies. Similarly, the poorer areas of Reading reflect the contraction of employment in traditional manufacturing in, for example, food production and transport, while hosting some of the most significant corporate players in the new economy: Microsoft, IBM and Cisco Systems. The latter already employs more than 4,000 workers and has bought numerous houses for employees, hence further fuelling a frenetic housing market.

My colleagues and I in our Social Policy Research Group were commissioned by Wycombe District Council and other statutory agencies in the mid-1990s to undertake two major studies of social deprivation in the area and propose anti-deprivation and community regeneration strategies (Stenson *et al* 1996; Watt *et al* 1997; Watt and Stenson 1996). This district includes a ring of wealthy, white commuter villages around the historic town of High Wycombe, a major industrial centre that had been the centre of the UK furniture and allied industries. About 20 per cent of the town's population are from the visible ethnic minorities, the bulk of whom are of Pakistani Muslim origin. These groups and the poorer white people living in the three major areas of social housing were the principal casualties of the sharp decline in large-scale 'Fordist' furniture manufacturing, paper mills and allied industries.

Focusing on the smallest level of analysis, the census enumeration district, and through combining data sets from statutory agencies, our research revealed high levels – by national standards – of deprivation, crime and victimisation in particular areas and groups, especially among ethnic minorities. Echoing other Thames Valley towns, these groups lacked the education and skills that would enable them to adapt to the burgeoning hi-tech and services-based labour markets and they were also vulnerable to discriminatory employment practices in a local economy dominated by small to medium-sized firms. Indicators of deprivation, typically, were hidden in aggregated, district-wide data sets, that, as used in central government's assessment of the local authority, ranked it as the 15th wealthiest in the UK.

From our research it became clear that, in an area where living costs are much higher and transport and other public services more threadbare than in poorer parts of the country, the conditions of deprived people are grim. Furthermore, the presence of great wealth can create a profound sense of relative deprivation. Social division in Buckinghamshire is reinforced by a school system that has retained grammar schools and is polarised at both primary and secondary level along class and, to a degree, ethnic lines. A study we undertook of the perceptions and uses of public space by young people in High Wycombe demonstrated the effects this can have in reinforcing social differentiation and conflict between groups of young people (Watt and

Stenson 1998). Predictably, in addition to hot spots of volume crime, the town centre experienced periodic episodes of public order disturbances, as did one of the estates with high levels of crime and deprivation. In 1998 the problems of this estate were the subject of a BBC TV documentary and the topic of acrimonious local debate (BBC2 1998).

In surveys of citizens' community concerns and opinions of public services conducted by local and county councils in the region – now a normal part of the Best Value reviews required by the government of public serve provision – crime routinely comes in the top few topics of concern. This can be to the exasperation of the police, who sometime complain that this pressures them to divert resources from poorer to wealthier, low-crime areas. However, Richard Sparks has warned that it is misleading to view fear of crime in such locations as irrational in relation to statistical risks of victimisation (Sparks 1992). Rather, fear and anxiety that focus on crime and incivilities crystallise a range of shared concerns within local cultures about a complex of interrelated social changes. Hence, problems related to crime are compounded, for example by traffic congestion and pollution, high accident rates, the steady deterioration of rural transport and other public services. These concerns until recent years were poorly, or only partially, articulated and represented within the formal political process. Furthermore, the logic of targeting resources to the marginal has meant in academia that, by contrast with northern towns and inner cities, this rapidly growing region has attracted scant research funding for social problems research. It is easier to attract both research funding and also funds for community development from the EU and central government when established indicators of deprivation provide prima facie evidence of deprivation and related ills.

Local political culture: managing social dislocation

With an emphasis on political culture and agency, I argue that there is no mechanistic link between the nature of the local economy and the local political cultures that provide filters for the perception of social problems, the local interpretation of central government policy and development of local policy responses. With historic roots, political cultures vary richly at the levels of county and local district and borough, in addition to the particular cultural milieux one finds in voluntary sector, police and other statutory sector agencies, presenting much potential for turf wars and misunderstandings. In addition, and on a more positive note, the development of multi-agency partnerships has created additional discretionary space for relatively autonomous professional perspectives across agency and district boundaries (Edwards and Benyon 2000). The shift in some areas to 'unitary' local authorities, which are responsible for the whole range of services, rather than dividing responsibilities between district and county levels, can facilitate holistic, joined-up approaches to community safety and other policies. For example, Milton Keynes and Slough, which have taken this route, have been able to develop a range of innovative multi-agency programmes to deal with local illegal drug markets and use, and other problems involving children and young people.

Local shifts in political coalitions can also make a significant difference. For example, after decades of Tory rule, a Liberal Democrat/ Labour council was elected with a slender majority in Wycombe in 1995. This led to the commissioning of our deprivation studies. The data underpinned a successful bid that yielded over £1.5 million under the government's Single Regeneration Budget. This led to other research and closer involvement with a range of local policymakers. Government grants helped to finance and legitimate community regeneration and community safety work across a broad political spectrum, and in highlighting relative deprivation in affluent areas our research has had significant influence across the region.

There was no structural inevitability about this process; it involved considerable political negotiation, contingency and chance. In line with governmentality theory, the fruits of this research helped to facilitate a shift in the local governmental, intellectual and policy climate. This made the poor and marginal more visible in the region and helped to create new intellectual instruments and knowledge to make populations thinkable and measurable for the purposes of government. I must emphasise that the production of social data is not a neutral, bureaucratic exercise. What information to gather, beyond data that is statutorily required, and how to organise and present it, are intensely political, complex issues in local as well as national politics. Local authorities and central governments will be keen to gather data on issues that they are willing to devote resources to and less keen to gather and highlight information about issues that they are less willing to spend money on. In turn this is dependent on the local balance of political forces and the effectiveness of political representation for different population groups and neighbourhoods.

Nevertheless, we must recognise limits to the discretionary power of local government to redistribute resources at local level to public institutions and the poor. In Victorian Britain great municipal reformers like Joseph Chamberlain in Birmingham possessed considerable scope to raise local taxes in order to create the extraordinary, but now decaying, public infrastructure that became the underpinning to the welfare state. Local wealth could 'trickle down' to the poor and to the common weal. However, Mrs Thatcher's introduction in the 1980s of 'rate capping' and the unitary business rate protected businesses from local taxation and greatly reduced the possibility of local 'trickle down'. Hence central government restrictions have limited the ability of local authorities, even in the affluent Thames Valley, to raise and spend significant sums on economic and community regeneration. There are hosts of worthy schemes and initiatives (too numerous to analyse here) to reskill the labour force, promote regeneration, reduce illegal drug use and promote community organisation and capacity (Jones, 2001). These demonstrate what can be achieved through creative effort. Nevertheless, without impugning the commitment or motives of those involved in these efforts, I argue that in this region the funding base for these initiatives has so far been inadequate to the huge challenges faced.

Liberal enclaves and the protective shield of the social

It is notable that in a Tory heartland, Thames Valley Police, by national standards, has a considerable reputation for its liberal commitment to problem-solving and intelligence-led policing, and gender sensitivity in dealing with rape and domestic violence. Its Chief Constable has been a leading critic of zero-tolerance and other punitive approaches to policing and criminal justice (Pollard 1997) and the force has pioneered the use of restorative justice in the UK. Nevertheless, poor funding handicaps the police service's policy responses to crime problems. With only 3,971 officers for over two million residents in a large area with clogged roads hampering response times to incidents, it has one of the worst ratios of officers per citizen in the UK. This partially derives from the increasing proportion of Home Office funding allocated by reference to measures of deprivation in a force area. Low scores on the government's 'Index of Local Conditions' for local authorities in the police region fail to trigger additional funding for the police service. This is despite the fact that many mobile offenders travel in from deprived areas and, as I argue, the state's measures of deprivation fail to reveal the hidden threads and pockets in a region like this. One way around this problem has been to obtain funding to pilot and benchmark progressive innovations like restorative justice. Besides, as police managers recognise, to apply the tough reactive policing strategies favoured by many councillors would require dramatic increases in police numbers. This remains an unlikely political prospect.

In addition, the importance of leadership and political culture is reinforced by the enterprising and dynamic activities of an agency as firmly devoted to a holistic, social 'joined-up' conception of community safety as the aforementioned pioneering Labour local authorities: the Thames Valley Partnership. Under the charismatic leadership of its director, with a board of trustees from the major statutory agencies and a team seconded from the police and other criminal justice agencies, it provides regular fora for all the relevant key stakeholders and professional personnel, networking opportunities, means of communicating across agency and disciplinary boundaries, and disseminating good practice. It also engages in and commissions research.

Its philosophy strongly emphasises the need for consultation with all sections of the population and their involvement in initiatives. It has pioneered, for example, the promotion of 'early interventions' targeted at families and communities at risk (Stenson 1997; Ball and Awan 2001), in addition to efforts to reduce school exclusion, domestic violence and auto-crime, to work with school-age children and the mentally disordered, and so on. It also campaigns for local authorities and other agencies to implement section 17 of the Crime and Disorder Act 1998 that requires community safety issues to be 'mainstreamed' as central to corporate agency strategies, rather than being ghettoised as particular department responsibilities. In this regard the modernisation strategy for local authorities embodied in the Local Government Act 2000 and which introduces a cabinet-based and more thematic approach to responsibilities, is viewed as providing new opportunities to pursue a holistic path.

The partnership has helped to generate and maintain a considerable degree of consensus among agency personnel in favour of a broad, holistic philosophy and a number of authorities in the region have moved along this path. However, as I indicated in the introduction, New Labour's emphasis on targeted crime reduction and strengthening local sovereignty in troubled areas through curfews, anti-social behaviour orders and other measures threaten to dent the protective shield of local, holistic community safety policies. As a recent Partnership discussion paper noted, the data gathered for the crime audits in the region required for the Crime and Disorder Act 1998 'had focused almost entirely on recorded crime – and in some cases led to a more narrow interpretation of the areas of local concern ... [moreover] ... there is less emphasis currently being placed on responding to local needs and consultation with local communities, and more on achieving identified reductions in levels of particular crimes' (Thames Valley Partnership 2001: 3; Stenson 2000b; ACTVAR 2000).

Conclusion – dilemmas of democracy

I have tried to integrate some of the themes of political economy, currently, though not by necessity, the special interest of Marxist theorists, into a modified, realist, governmentality analysis of local crime control, emphasising the role of politics, governance and choice. It is important to stress that, even in this Middle England economic powerhouse and comfortable retreat for the rich and famous, the complex ingredients of demographically diverse, advanced democratic societies are present. They result in part from the political choices made about how to manage local economic restructuring. Here, a dominant neoliberal approach has allowed a rapid, Darwinian form of economic growth, with minimal help from central government or the EU for the inevitable losers in the game. At local policy levels, this has been associated with a significant shift away from universal, equitable service delivery in favour of attempts to target resources to people and areas representing high needs and risks. I have argued that reconstituting social government through a narrow form of targeting is fraught with tensions, not least because the affluent majority are also part of the problem and must be drawn into a shared, social strategy to manage it.

As much as in Middlesbrough or Bradford, the conditions of life in the Thames Valley manifest the results of both Tory and New Labour government policies as well as global trends. By contrast with our major neighbours in the EU, these administrations have favoured the needs of the City of London financial institutions and the new services and hi-tech sectors. This is in preference to the needs of the major public services, the core manufacturing industries and the citizens who rely on them. Let us hope that employment in Thames Valley's new sectors is not as ephemeral as some analysts predict, melting away like the snow in spring with the first major economic downturn. The consequences for community safety would be profound.

Already, the ingredients of diversity resulting from socio-economic change so far include a growing ethnic and religious complexity in urban areas and an undermining of older, received notions of shared, national and local identities (Modood *et al* 1997; Stenson *et al* 1999). Among these populations are significant proportions of disaffected, deprived young men. As public order disturbances nationally over the last decade have revealed, many of these young people are vulnerable to racist and class discrimination and criminal victimisation, and also involvement in illegal economies and criminal offending (Ousley 2001). Such demographic changes in the Thames Valley, as elsewhere, interact with the growth of non-nuclear family households. This can affect the homeless and travelling populations, the vulnerable elderly and mentally disturbed living in the so-called 'community', and single and single parent households. The volatile mixture of these groups can be manifested in anti-social behaviour and shifting, blurred boundaries between the categories of offender and victim (MacVean 2001).

These great social changes are also associated – for both the affluent and the poor – with less easy access to kin and settled neighbourhood networks. They also mean less access to and involvement in shared public spaces and services, and involvement in civic and altruistic voluntary work (Puttnam 2001). This perhaps has had particular impact on the more mobile middle class and deprived white populations, among which deep-rooted feelings of fear and insecurity have spread beyond the big cities and into the destinations of 'white flight', the affluent suburbs and countryside (Loader *et al* 1998; Stenson and Watt 1999b). These social changes also help to explain new patterns of vulnerability and criminal victimisation, and the retreat of the affluent majority into inward-looking, suburban, car-based, risk-averse, lifestyles and neighbourhoods.

However, our knowledge of these phenomena is patchy. It is doubtful if fluctuations in the official crime rate provide an accurate gauge of life in high-risk areas and journalistic reliance on these figures usually misleads the public. Even the proposed doubling of the national British Crime Survey sample to 40,000 will be spread thinly across the nation and will be unable to provide robust, local databases to measure changes in the lifestyles of and levels of criminal victimisation among the poor or marginalised. Robust data can only be provided by regular in-depth and geographically varied anthropological and statistical studies of life on the margins. The state and the social science community have shown precious little inclination to undertake such difficult and sometimes dangerous work on the required scale.

Responding to these challenges requires close relations between elected representatives, the academy, the regulatory professions and the full range of citizens' groups. However, the degree of discretionary space for policy and practice open to professionals and the voluntary sector may have diminished somewhat with the process of audit, crime strategies and the statutory requirement to undertake Best Value reviews of service delivery. These initiatives have provided councillors with greater involvement in crime control policy. As one community safety officer remarked to me, for a lot of councillors responsible in committee for community safety, 'it means little more than CCTV and more bobbies on the beat'. Greater democracy in the form of closer scrutiny and control over community safety budgets may jeopardise much of the broader work undertaken within a holistic philosophy, including the priority given to the physical security of poor and other vulnerable people. It is a truism of political philosophy that democracy that unleashes intolerance of minorities clashes with the values of liberalism in its broad rather than narrow sense. There is the possibility that without the protective shield of networks like the Thames Valley Partnership, the punitive pressures from the government, the media, elected representatives and vocal citizen groups may drive back the definition of community safety to a default position. In this position, community safety means defending the affluent majority, the local winners in the new global economy, from those defined as threatening, high-risk, outsiders and losers in the neoliberal game (Young 1999). This would provide a major threat to the possibility of social, inclusive, *liberal* democracy through strategies of crime control.

Acknowledgements

Though they are not responsible for my views I have benefited particularly from discussions with personnel in the Thames Valley local authorities, Thames Valley Police, the Thames Valley Partnership and the Association of Councils of the Thames Valley Region. In particular, I thank the following: Sue Raikes, Rob Beckley, Anne Smith, Geraldine White, Mike Petford, Rob Callow, Maggie Allan, Matthew Moore, Barry Deller and Barry Pember.

References

ACTVAR (Association of Councils of the Thames Valley Region) (2000) *Survey of Community Safety Partnerships*. High Wycombe: Association of Councils of the Thames Valley Region.

Audit Commission (1999) *Safety in Numbers: Promoting Community Safety*. London: Audit Commission.

Ball, M. and Awan, L. (2001) *Never Too Early: An Evaluation of Methods of Early Years Intervention*. Chilton: Thames Valley Partnership.

BBC2 (1998) *The Force – Castlefield*. 4 February.

Bourdieu, P. (1990) *The Logic of Practice*. Cambridge: Cambridge University Press.

Christie, N. (1993) *Crime Control as Industry: Towards Gulags Western Style?* London and New York: Routledge.

Cohen, S. (1985) *Visions of Social Control*. Cambridge: Polity.

Coleman, R. and Sim, J. (1998) 'From the Dockyards to the Disney Store:

Surveillance, Risk and Security in Liverpool City Centre', *International Review of Law Computers and Technology*, 12 (1), 27–45.

Countryside Agency (2001) *The State of the Countryside 2001 – An Introduction.* London: Countryside Agency.

Crawford, A. (1997) *The Local Governance of Crime: Appeals to Community and Partnership.* Oxford: Clarendon Press; London: Longman.

Cuneen, C. (2001) *Conflict, Politics and Crime: Aboriginal Communities and the Police.* Crows Nest, NSW: Allen & Unwin.

Davies, N. (1997) *Dark Heart.* London: Vintage.

Davis, M. (1992) *City of Quartz.* London: Vintage.

Dean, M. (1999) *Governmentality: Power and Rule in Modern Society.* London: Sage.

Dingwall, G. and Moody, S. (eds) (1999) *Crime and Conflict in the Countryside.* Cardiff: University of Wales Press.

Edwards, A. and Benyon, J. (2000) 'Community Governance, Crime Control and Local Diversity', *Crime Prevention and Community Safety: An International Journal*, 2 (3), 35–54.

Feely, M. and Simon, J. (1994) 'Actuarial Justice: the Emerging New Criminal Law', in D. Nelken (ed.), *The Futures of Criminology.* London: Sage.

Felson, M. (1998) *Crime and Everyday Life*, 2nd edn., Thousand Oaks, CA: Pine Forge.

Foucault, M. (1977) *Discipline and Punish.* Harmondsworth: Penguin.

Foucault, M. (1991/1979) 'Governmentality', in G. Burchell, C. Gordon and P. Miller (eds), *The Foucault Effect: Studies in Governmentality.* Hemel Hempstead: Harvester Wheatsheaf.

Galbraith, J.K. (1992) *The Culture of Contentment.* London: Sinclair-Stevenson.

Goldblatt, P. and Lewis, C. (eds) (1998) *Reducing Offending: an Assessment of Research Evidence on Ways of Dealing with Offending Behaviour*, Home Office Research Study 187. London: Home Office.

Gordon, C. (1991) 'Governmental Rationality: An Introduction', in G. Burchell, C. Gordon and P. Miller (eds), *The Foucault Effect: Studies in Governmentality.* Hemel Hempstead: Harvester Wheatsheaf.

Gordon, P. (1987) 'Community Policing', in P. Scraton (ed.), *Law, Order and the Authoritarian State.* Milton Keynes: Open University Press.

GO-SE (Government Office of the South East) (2000) *South East Regional Development Plan 2000–2006*, www.go-se.gov.uk.

Grimshaw, R. and Jefferson, T. (1987) *Interpreting Policework.* London: Allen & Unwin.

Hay, C. (1996) *Re-Stating Social and Political Change.* Buckingham: Open University Press.

Hetherington, K. (1998) 'Vanloads of Uproarious Humanity: New Age Travellers and the Utopics of the Countryside', in T. Skelton and G. Valentine (eds), *Cool Places, Geographies of Youth Cultures.* London: Routledge.

Hirst, P. and Thompson, G. (1995) *Globalization in Question.* Cambridge: Polity Press.

Hogg, R. and Brown, D. (1998) *Rethinking Law and Order*. Annandale: Pluto.

Home Office (1991) *Safer Communities: The Local Delivery of Crime Prevention Through the Partnership Approach (The Morgan Report)*. London: Home Office.

Hudson, B. (2001) 'Punishment, Rights and Difference: Defending Justice in the Risk Society', in K. Stenson and R.R. Sullivan (eds), *Crime Risk and Justice: The Politics of Crime Control in Liberal Democracies*. Cullompton: Willan.

Hughes, G. (1998) *Understanding Crime Prevention: Social Control, Risk and Late Modernity*. Buckingham: Open University Press.

Hutton, W. (1995) *The State We're In*. London: Cape.

Jessop, B. (2000) 'From the KWNS to the SWPR', in G. Lewis, J. Clarke and S. Gewirtz (eds), *Rethinking Social Policy*. London: Sage.

Jones, D. (2001) *A Report on the Work of SKIDZ, the Wycombe Motor Project, 1999–2000*, Report for Thames Valley Community Safety Trust. High Wycombe: Social Policy Research Group, Buckinghamshire Chilterns University College.

Kellner, P. (2001) 'Yes, We Still Need Meritocracy', *New Statesman*, 9 July, 25.

Loader, I., Girling, E. and Sparks, R. (1998) 'Narratives of Decline: Youth, Dis/order and Community in an English "Middletown" ', *British Journal of Criminology*, 38 (3), 388–403.

McLaughlin, E. and Murji, K. (2001) 'Lost Connections and New Directions: neo-liberalism, new public managerialism, and the "modernisation" of the British police', in K. Stenson and R.R. Sullivan (eds), *Crime Risk and Justice: The Politics of Crime Control in Liberal Democracies*. Cullompton: Willan.

MacVean, A. (2001) *A Report on the Chiltern Vale Anti-Social Behaviour Partnership*, report for Thames Valley Community Safety Trust. High Wycombe: Social Policy Research Group, Buckinghamshire Chilterns University College.

Modood, T., Barthoud, R., Lakey, J., Nazroo, J., Smith, P., Virdee, S. and Baishon, S. (eds) (1997) *Ethnic Minorities in Britain, Fourth National Survey: Diversity and Disadvantage*. London: Policy Studies Institute.

O'Malley, P. (2001) 'Risk, Crime and Prudentialism Revisited', in K. Stenson and R.R. Sullivan (eds), *Crime Risk and Justice: The Politics of Crime Control in Liberal Democracies*. Cullompton: Willan.

Ousley, H. (2001) *Community Pride, Not Prejudice: Making Diversity Work in Bradford*. Bradford: Bradford City Council.

Parenti, C. (1999) *Lockdown America: Police and Prisons in the Age of Crisis*. London/New York: Verso.

Pollard, C. (1997) 'Zero Tolerance: Short Term Fix, Long Term Liability', in N. Dennis (ed.), *Zero Tolerance: Policing a Free Society*. London: Institute of Economic Affairs.

Puttnam, R. (2001) *Bowling Alone*. New York: Simon & Schuster.

Rose, D. (1996) *In The Name of the Law: the Collapse of Criminal Justice*. London: Jonathan Cape.

Rose, D. (2001) 'Opium of the People', *The Observer*, 8 July.

Rose, N. (1996b) 'The Death of the Social? Re-figuring the Territory of Government', *Economy and Society*, 22 (2), 283–99.

Rose, N. (2000) 'Government and Control', *British Journal of Criminology*, 40 (2), 321–39.

Shearing, C. (1996) 'Public and Private Policing', in W. Saulsbury, J. Mott and T. Newburn (eds), *Themes in Contemporary Policing*. London: Policy Studies Institute.

Sparks, R. (1992) 'Reason and Unreason in "Left Realism": Some Problems in the Constitution of the Fear of Crime', in R. Matthews and J. Young (eds), *Issues in Realist Criminology*. London: Sage.

Stenson, K. (1991) 'Making Sense of Crime Control', in K. Stenson and D. Cowell (eds), *The Politics of Crime Control*. London: Sage.

Stenson, K. (1993) 'Community Policing as a Governmental Technology', *Economy and Society*, 22 (3), 373–89.

Stenson, K. (1996) 'Communal Security as Government – the British Experience', in W. Hammerschick *et al* (eds), *Jahrbuch für Rechts und Kriminalsoziologie*. Baden-Baden: Nomos.

Stenson, K. (1997) *Early Interventions to Prevent Crime in Thames Valley*, Report for Thames Valley Partnership and The Turners Court Youth Trust. High Wycombe: Social Policy Research Group, Buckinghamshire Chilterns University College.

Stenson, K. (1998) 'Beyond Histories of the Present', *Economy and Society*, 29 (4), 333–52.

Stenson, K. (1999) 'Crime Control, Governmentality and Sovereignty', in R. Smandych (ed.), *Governable Places: Readings in Governmentality and Crime Control*. Aldershot: Dartmouth.

Stenson, K. (2000a) 'Crime Control, Social Policy and Liberalism', in G. Lewis, S. Gewirtz and J. Clarke (eds), 'Rethinking Social Policy', London: Sage.

Stenson, K. (2000b) 'Someday Our Prince Will Come: Zero-Tolerance Policing and Liberal Government', in T. Hope and R. Sparks (eds), *Crime, Risk and Insecurity*. London: Routledge.

Stenson, K. (2000c) *Community Safety in the New Buckinghamshire, the Evidence Base*, Report for Buckinghamshire County Council and Chiltern District Council. High Wycombe: Social Policy Research Group, Buckinghamshire Chilterns University College.

Stenson, K. (2001) 'The New Politics of Crime Control', in K. Stenson and R.R. Sullivan (eds), *Crime Risk and Justice: The Politics of Crime Control in Liberal Democracies*. Cullompton: Willan.

Stenson, K. (2002 forthcoming) 'Reconstructing the Government of Crime', in G. Wickham and G. Pavlich (eds), *Rethinking Law, Society and Governance: Foucault's Bequest*. Oxford: Hart.

Stenson, K. and Edwards, A. (2001) 'Crime Control and Liberal Government: the "Third Way" and the Return to the Local', in K. Stenson and R.R. Sullivan (eds), *Crime Risk and Justice: The Politics of Crime Control in Liberal Democracies*. Cullompton: Willan.

Stenson, K. and Watt, P. (1999a) 'Governmentality and "the Death of the Social"? A Discourse Analysis of Local Government texts in South-East England', *Urban Studies*, 36 (1), 189–201.

Stenson, K. and Watt, P. (1999b) 'Crime, Risk and Governance in a Southern English Village', in G. Dingwall and S. Moody (eds), *Crime and Conflict in the Countryside*. Cardiff: University of Wales Press.

Stenson, K., Travers, M. and Crowther, C. (1999a) *The Police and Inter-Ethnic Conflict*, Report for the Metropolitan Police Service. High Wycombe: Social Policy Research Group, Buckinghamshire Chilterns University College.

Stenson, K., Watt, P., Kehoe, P. and Chappell, A. (1996) *Deprivation in High Wycombe*, Report for Wycombe District Council and the South Buckinghamshire Health Trust. High Wycombe: Social Policy Research Group, Buckinghamshire Chilterns University College.

Thames Valley Partnership (2001) *Community Safety and Social Exclusion, a Discussion Paper*. Chilton: Thames Valley Partnership.

Waddington, P.A.J. (1999) *Policing Citizens*. London: UCL Press.

Watt, P. and Jacob, K. (2000) 'Discourse of Social Exclusion: an Analysis of *Bringing Britain Together: a National Strategy for Neighbourhood Renewal*', *Housing, Theory and Society*, 17, 14–26.

Watt, P. and Stenson, K. (1996) 'Poverty Amidst Plenty', *Poverty*, 95, 13–16.

Watt, P. and Stenson, K. (1998) 'The Street: "It's a bit dodgy around there": Safety, Danger, Ethnicity and Young People's Use of Public Space', in T. Skelton and G. Valentine (eds), *Cool Places: Geographies of Youth Cultures*. London: Routledge.

Watt, P., Stenson, K. and Kehoe, P. (1997) *Deprivation in Lane End*, Report for Wycombe District Council. High Wycombe: Social Policy Research Group, Buckinghamshire Chilterns University College.

White, R. (1998) *Public Spaces for Young People: a Guide to Creative Projects and Positive Strategies*. Sydney: Australian Youth Foundation.

Winlow, S. (2001) *Badfellas: Crime, Tradition, and New Masculinities*. Oxford: Berg.

Young, J. (1999). *The Exclusive Society*. London: Sage.

Chapter 7

Learning from diversity: the strategic dilemmas of community-based crime control[1]

Adam Edwards

Introduction

I first became interested in community-based crime control during the early 1990s when, in the aftermath of the Morgan Report into local crime prevention (Home Office 1991), public-private partnerships gained an increasing influence over the conduct of local crime control policymaking. The growth of public-private partnerships across the social policy spectrum, in delivering housing, education, health and local economic development, in addition to crime control, was acknowledged by the UK Economic and Social Research Council, which funded a £2.3 million research programme into the implications of this emerging system of 'local governance' for the delivery and democratic accountability of public services (Stoker 1999). As part of this research programme I conducted a comparative case study of local partnerships for crime prevention in the East Midlands of England.[2]

Given the orientation of the ESRC's Local Governance Programme and my own background in political studies, my principal interest in the practice of crime prevention partnerships has been their effect on altering or reproducing relationships of political power in this area of public policymaking. This focus on the relations of political power has shaped my interest in the evolution of local partnerships in Britain: from the 'community safety' era of the post-Morgan Report/pre-Crime and Disorder Act 1998 through to the new statutory crime and disorder partnerships provided for in this Act.[3] My principal interest has therefore been in questioning the *process* of these partnerships rather than their *outcomes* in altering patterns of crime and disorder (cf Crawford 1998: 196–207).

This concern with process and political power has been reflected in other case studies of crime control in English localities in recent years (Coleman and Sim 1998; Crawford 1994, 1997; Gilling and Barton 1997; Loader *et al* 1998; Hughes 1997, 1998; Stenson and Watt 1999) and in the broader study of crime control at the national and international level (Stenson 1991, 1999; Smandych 1999; Garland 1996, 2001). It is in comparing the perspectives and findings from this critical mass of work with my own research in the East Midlands of England that I have become interested in the problem of drawing lessons about the diverse practices of crime control. This problem is neatly demonstrated in Lacey and Zedner's comparative work on community-based crime control in Britain and Germany, which identifies a broad variety of practices within, as well as between, each country and the consequent difficulties in 'reconciling this acuity to local difference with the generalising tendencies of the comparative' (1995: 319).

The revelation, through *cross*-national comparative research, that differences in governing practices within advanced liberal polities are often as great as those between such polities is one of the principal features of contemporary social scientific interest in localities as the most appropriate units of analysis for research into social change. Processes of 'globalisation', it is argued, accentuate the uneven development of political, economic and cultural relations throughout nation-states as different localities struggle to adapt to the threats and opportunities of an increasingly interconnected and interdependent world (Bottoms and Wiles 1996; Hirst and Thompson 1996). The, rather inelegant, concept of 'glocalisation' has been coined to capture this uneven effect of de-regulated international political and economic relations on particular localities given their specific political and economic histories and consequent ability to adapt (Swyngedouw 1992).

The concept of glocalisation suggests that social relations are now being stretched over new spatial scales and that an understanding of the causes and consequences of social change in national terms, such as 'Britain' compared with 'France' or the United States' etc., is insufficient. More determinate, and therefore insightful, accounts need to differentiate between social practices occurring at other, supranational and subnational scales. In terms of government the challenge of understanding political change is complicated further by the 'hollowing out' of nation-state capacities to govern through the upward transfer of powers to supranational organisations like the European Union, the downward transfer of powers to regional and local authorities and the outward transfer of governing responsibilities to private and voluntary organisations allied with an emphasis upon private citizens' responsibility for their own 'self-government' (Rhodes 1994; Jessop 1994).

As a consequence, to understand the process of governing complex social problems like crime and disorder is to examine how political action is practised at different, supranational, national, regional, local and sublocal/neighbourhood, *tiers* and across different, statutory, private and voluntary, *spheres* of governing (Baine *et al* 1991; Lowndes 1993). Advanced liberal government, in these terms, is the outcome of networks of intergovernmental relations (IGR) between actors organised at these different tiers and in the different spheres of a differentiated polity (Rhodes 1997: 7ff.). While even unitary liberal polities like Britain have always been characterised by IGR between national and subnational authorities, the increasing emphasis on 'community governance' represents a key shift in the quality of these relations. It forms part of a broader shift from the national-universal provision of public services toward the targeting of government interventions on highly specific populations and geographical areas (Stenson 2000). Current government policy on crime and social exclusion in Britain has intensified this shift to targeted provision by emphasising the centrality of sublocal areas of administration, in particular the enumeration units that make up neighbourhoods (Neighbourhood Renewal Unit 2001; Social Exclusion Unit 2000; Stenson and Edwards 2001). If local and sublocal tiers are now becoming a key focus for government, the 'responsibilisation' of voluntary and private actors also represents a major shift in the scope of IGR and related 'degovernmentalisation of the state' (Rose 1996; Garland 1996). The proliferation of public-private partnerships across the spectrum of government activity exemplifies this increasing exercise of political power beyond the state.

These trends in the scope and focus of IGR, toward the particularisation of government through targeting and the degovernmentalisation of the state through the formation of public-private partnerships, provoke crucial questions about the exercise and democratic accountability of government. It is argued that partnerships have the capacity to be more dynamic, innovative and democratic than either the 'first way' of 'old' (*sic*) social democratic, top-down, unresponsive and state-centred government or the 'second way' of neoliberal, exclusive, laissez-faire government through markets (Giddens 1998). Each of these ways of governing has a particular approach to the social contract between governors and governed. State bureaucracies demand 'loyalty' in exchange for guarantees about the public provision of basic goods and services. Neoliberal regimes model the relationship with their citizens on that between a business and its customers and offer them opportunities to 'exit', or take one's custom elsewhere, by privatising formerly public goods and services and creating quasi-market competition among providers of these goods and services. Whereas the first way is thought to disempower citizens by insulating public authorities from day-to-day accountability for their decisions, neoliberal strategies disempower citizens by excluding those 'customers' without the wealth and influence to effectively demand better quality services from non-elected and democratically unaccountable providers. Conversely the third way of public-private partnerships is thought to be more empowering: to offer the possibility of greater 'voice' to local citizens, by involving them in the everyday practice of governing through inter-organisational or 'multi-agency' networks (Stoker 1999; Burns *et al* 1994; cf. Hirschman 1970).

The generic claims made for the empowering qualities of partnerships in community governance have provided the focal point for arguments about the actual process of community-based crime control. Official accounts of the 'crime prevention process' have echoed these claims expressing a belief in the capacity of partnerships to enhance the policy response to problems of local crime and disorder, draw upon the resources and expertise of all relevant statutory, private and voluntary agencies and involve local citizens as active participants (Ekblom 1988; Home Office 1993; Home Office 1998: 3.1–5.23). This model of process has, however, been criticised for its 'naive pluralism' in so far as it assumes an equal and open dialogue of ideas about crime among those invited to participate in local partnerships and the wider public (Crawford 1994: 500). In place of any consideration of the protracted aetiological and normative arguments that have driven research into crime control, this official discourse is suffused with administrative platitudes on the need for 'better leadership', 'better coordination', 'more accurate information', 'sustainable interventions', 'more sophisticated evaluation and monitoring', etc. (Home Office 1990, 1993, 1998). Conversely, critics of the partnership approach have concentrated on the *political content* of this process: 'Who was involved? What decisions were taken? How were they arrived at? How did the various parties relate to each other? Did the parties do what was planned or did they do something else? Did any unforeseen events arise?' (Crawford 1998: 207). From this perspective the actual involvement of certain actors and not others and the interrelationships between those involved and those excluded is an open question for research into the substantive content of community-based crime control partnerships.

Case studies on the substantive political content, the real 'blood and guts', of local crime control processes suggest there is a significant diversity in the actual conduct of partnerships in particular localities in England. It has been variously argued that such conduct is an expression of: 'authoritarian corporatism' (Crawford 1994, 1997), a more effective way of dispersing 'authoritarian state' power over 'problematic' populations (Cohen 1985; Gordon 1987; Coleman and Sim 1998); and open-ended, inclusive, deliberation over controversial issues such as street prostitution and domestic violence (Hughes 1997; Stenson and Edwards 2001).

Such diversity is a key theme of this edited collection, not least because the more determinate a study of local crime control becomes, the harder it appears to be to reconcile an understanding of particular local political processes and institutions with the search for universal,'best' practices that can be transferred across very different social contexts. This dilemma has long been a concern of comparative public policy analysts who identify a common opposition between advocates of the 'total fungibility' or transferability of policy measures and those who claim such transfer is precluded by the 'total blockage' presented by the particular social, political and economic qualities of local governance (Rose 1993: 34–40). In criminological discourse this tension has been addressed *epistemologically* in terms of the need for more comparative research to ascertain the degree of similarity and difference among national and local contexts of crime control and, consequently, the applicability of alternative theories and practices of control (Nelken 1994; Lacey and Zedner 1995).

Conversely, I have argued that the tension between universality and particularity in lesson-drawing about governing processes cannot be resolved in terms of epistemological arguments over *how* such processes can be evaluated. Rather, this is fundamentally an ontological question of precisely *what* is being evaluated: what is the substance of inter-governmental relations between actors involved in community-based crime control? How do these relations shape the actual practice of particular partnerships? How, nonetheless, could partnerships act given their real powers and liabilities? (Edwards 2001). Switching the focus of research away from comparisons of the formal similarities and differences among local crime control partnerships toward a concern with the substantive relations of connection among actors involved in these partnerships implies a very different approach to lesson-drawing. Whether governmental activities appear similar or different is less important than whether they can be understood as 'necessary' or 'contingent' by virtue of their real powers and liabilities (Sayer 1992: 88ff., 2000). Necessary relations are those which have to occur between actors for those actors to exist; for example, one cannot be a husband without having a wife or be in a 'partnership' without partners. Contingent relations refer to connections between objects that can exist without one another and where their relationship is neither necessary nor impossible; for example, it is possible but not necessary that partnerships occur between people of different ethnic, religious and class backgrounds, etc. The identification of necessary and contingent relations provides a rationale for research into diverse practices of local crime control processes and a framework for lesson-drawing. Necessary relations are, by definitional fiat, generic and the lessons drawn from them are more likely to withstand transfer across very different social contexts. Contingent relations provide an insight into the qualities of the particular social contexts in which governing processes occur and therefore enable a more determinate account of how and why what actually happened, happened. Through comparative research into the identification of how necessary and contingent relations combine in any one 'concrete' instance, it is possible to draw lessons about how governing processes could be different, given their powers and liabilities (Sayer 1992: 140ff.).

The remainder of this chapter discusses the identification of certain 'strategic dilemmas' that are necessarily generated by public partnerships by virtue of their powers and liabilities, the possible ways of acting, possessed by these partnerships. A concrete analysis is then provided of the experience of these dilemmas in community-based crime control partnerships in two cities, Leicester and Nottingham, in the East Midlands of England and the lessons that can be drawn from this experience for the prospective practice of community-based crime control.

The strategic dilemmas of community-based crime control

Research into the practice of governing through partnerships has argued that while networking may offer a means of transcending the disempowering effects of hierarchical state-centred approaches on the one hand and quasi-markets on the other, it generates its own tendencies toward governing failure and, therefore, new 'strategic dilemmas' for those political actors involved (Jessop 1997). Strategic dilemmas have been defined as situations in which 'agents are faced with choices such that any action undermines key conditions of their existence and/or their capacities to realise some overall interest' (Jessop 1997: n. 18). Four strategic dilemmas have been associated with governing through partnerships: *cooperation versus competition; openness versus closure; governability versus flexibility;* and *accountability versus efficiency* (Jessop 1997).

Competition versus cooperation

Partnerships can provide opportunities for building stable, long-term, exchange relationships based on trust and cooperation, yet they also create opportunities for destabilising, short-term, self-interested competitive behaviour. This dilemma was manifest in the dependence of the post-Morgan partnerships on competitive grant-aid regimes for scarce financial resources. The grant regimes open to these partnerships, in particular the Safer Cities, City Challenge and Single Regeneration Budget programmes, generated specific forms of competition.

Within local partnerships the successful competition for funds was acknowledged by local partners in Leicester and Nottingham as a key factor in the formulation and sustainability of partnerships, especially among the statutory agencies as the capture of external funding meant there could be an equitable ownership of a partnership. Unsuccessful competition, however, eroded the trust, and therefore cooperation, between these agencies and, especially, between the partnership and local citizens whose expectations of investment had been raised through their consultation/participation in the bidding process. There are significant opportunity costs associated with investing time and effort in bidding for resources in order to expand governing capacity as opposed to governing with an existing level of resources.

Competition for resources can also erode trust *between local partnerships within an administrative district.* This form of competition is, potentially, the most virulent threat to the partnership approach as there is a clear incentive for statutory, voluntary and business actors with an interest in a particular sublocal neighbourhood and/or population to amplify their claim on scarce resources at the expense of other neighbourhoods and populations. In Nottingham and Leicester this form of competition was manifest in claims made by partnerships on municipal housing estates on the outer ring of these cities for prioritisation over those inner-city neighbourhoods that had, historically, been the main beneficiaries of grant aid for urban regeneration (Chapman 1994). Irrespective of the intentions of particular partnerships, this intra-district/inter-neighbourhood competition for resources has the real liability of exacerbating tensions between different communities, particularly where there is an ethnic dimension to the inner-city/outer-estate concentration of populations. Conversely, however, actors at the district level, responsible for the generation and coordination of crime control partnerships, acknowledged the effect of the bidding process in galvanising local actors to think more imaginatively about the problems of, and responses to, crime, disorder and social exclusion faced by particular neighbourhoods and communities. This competition also has the potential to drive intra-national/inter-local policy change and learning in so far as innovations at the local level can be transferred to other localities.

Openness versus closure

The capacity of partnerships to promote innovative responses to apparently intractable problems such as crime and disorder generates another key dilemma. To enable such innovation partnerships must be open to the ideas and resources of a broad repertoire of interest groups. For partnerships to actually intervene in these problems they must, however, place limits on the scope of participation and balance deliberation with action. Failure to do so in certain partnerships has led to the criticism that they are merely 'talking shops' that alienate both those actors who participate and the broader public by not delivering tangible improvements (Liddle and Gelsthorpe 1994). The dilemma is that closure on participation may lock-in members whose exit would be beneficial and block the recruitment of new partners, resources and ideas that enable partnerships to learn, innovate and adapt to their changing circumstances. The Morgan Report argued that by defining their work in the relatively narrow terms of 'crime prevention' partnerships had reinforced the perception that community-based crime control was a police-based practice, whereas the Report's preferred concept of 'community safety' broadened the appeal of this practice to 'all sections of the community' (Home Office 1991: 3.6). The idea of community safety also encourages experimentation with 'a broad spectrum of activities, ranging from the prevention of opportunity through deterrence to more social aspects of crime prevention' (Home Office 1991: 3.5).

Conversely, openness can undermine partners' collective acceptance of long-term time horizons while enabling opportunistic actors to pursue their short-term self-interested reasons for participating. The openness of community safety strategies to a broad range of actors and a wide portfolio of activities, from reducing the opportunities for crime through to local economic regeneration projects, has been criticised for its 'extreme vagueness' and unmanageable 'focus' (Pease 1994: n. 11). Both the Leicester and Nottingham partnerships encountered problems of coordinating their strategies as the scope of activity was broadened beyond situational measures against specific instances of crime and disorder to encompass more ambitious social projects, such as the medium- to long-term regeneration of local labour and housing markets and educational attainment levels. Leaders of these partnerships referred to this problem as the 'project effect', in which the strategies envisaged in their 'action plans' collapsed into a collection of tenuously related projects as financial resources were only made available by non-local funding bodies on a project-by-project basis and as the very breadth of these strategies soon outflanked the organisational capacities of those actors involved. The project effect was also driven by the short-term time-horizons of statutory, voluntary and business actors used to expecting 'early wins' and immediately demonstrable gains for the interests they represent rather than the less tangible idea of long-term regeneration in the collective interests of the partnership.

The openness of community safety partnerships has also been criticised for subverting social policy goals, such as improving educational attainment, housing blight and employment opportunities, etc., by justifying them as an effective means of crime control rather than as important ends in themselves (Pease 1997). In this way community safety partnerships may further the 'criminalisation of social policy' in which the scope of government intervention in social problems is limited by the demands of crime control rather than the need for increased public investment in education, housing and employment, etc. (Crawford 1998; Stenson 1998). Conversely, closing the remit of crime control partnerships around highly specific interventions against particular types of crime, offending and victimisation ignores the effect of social contexts in generating these problems. If it is accepted that social contexts in which populations are excluded from better educational, housing and employment opportunities generate crime, then it can be argued that community safety strategies provide a vital 'socialisation of crime control'.

Governability versus flexibility

Partnerships are seen as superior to bureaucratic hierarchies and quasi-markets as a means of governing complex problems because they enable the kind of strategic guidance (governability) that is subverted by markets while providing the flexibility to adapt to rapidly changing circumstances that is precluded by relatively inert bureaucracies. In practice, however, the flexibility of the Leicester and Nottingham partnerships to adapt their crime control strategies to the conditions of the particular populations they were dealing with was constrained by the methods of performance evaluation and monitoring to which they were subjected by non-local funding bodies. Key statutory agencies such as the police, probation and social services are subject to nationally set performance criteria that, local actors argued, compelled them to prioritise the objectives of their home organisations above those of the partnership.

The capacity of partnerships to exercise strategic guidance by co-ordinating a range of agencies and projects over the medium to long term was also constrained by the criteria attached to non-local funding. In particular, national government grant aid, such as that provided by the Single Regeneration Budget, is often released to local partnerships on a quarterly basis and on the proviso that these partnerships demonstrate that outputs are being met across these three-monthly timescales. Some local actors felt that these timescales compelled the partnerships to prioritise easily demonstrable interventions, such as reducing the situational opportunities for burglary, over medium- to long-term work with offenders or on the conditions thought to generate offending behaviour. In this way some local partners felt the social dimension of crime control advocated by the Morgan Report was precluded by their dependence on funding provided in short episodes and in accordance with highly directive performance criteria by national bodies who lacked an appreciation of the local qualities of crime, disorder and social exclusion.

Accountability versus efficiency

In addition to the claims made for the efficiency of public-private partnerships as governing techniques, it is argued that they have the power to revitalise democratic decisionmaking by enabling the direct participation of local communities. Relative to markets, which exclude those actors without the resources to effectively demand services and which inscribe severe inequalities into political representation, and bureaucracies, which are renowned for their inertia and lack of responsiveness, networks of relations among actors in partnerships are regarded as a means of enabling innovations in participatory 'associative' democracy (Hirst 1994, 1997).

In turn, however, partnerships present significant problems for attributing political responsibility. If partnerships have the power to distribute 'ownership' of the decisionmaking process equally, they also have the liability of removing clear lines of accountability and enabling partners to 'pass the buck'. Whereas the post-Morgan partnerships were subject to clear lines of financial accountability to their non-local funding bodies, their political accountability to local populations for the decisions they made about prioritising certain types of crime, offending and victimisation was not at all clear (Edwards and Benyon 2000).

In the context of this opaque political accountability, 'public-private arrangements run the risk of privatizing politics and/or promoting the statization of the private sphere' (Jessop 1997: 23). The direct participation of local communities in the decisionmaking process, especially in such an emotionally charged policy field as crime control, has the liability of a dangerous privatisation of politics ranging from bigoted constructions of community to outright vigilantism and punishment beatings of suspected offenders (Davis 1990; Johnston 1996). The potential for this was clearly demonstrated in Britain during the summer of 2000 when, after the horrific abduction, sexual assault and murder of a young girl, the *News of the World* (a national tabloid newspaper), launched a 'name and shame' campaign against known paedophiles by publishing their pictures and details of their offences (*News of the World*, 23 and 30 July, 6 August 2000). As a consequence of this, innocent citizens resembling those named and photographed were assaulted, including an attack upon a *paediatrician*, and the homes of offenders on release were fire-bombed.

Other commentaries have identified the potential of community-based partnerships to exclude individuals, perceived to be a part of dangerous, anti-social populations, from reintegration back into community life (Coleman and Sim 1998). Representatives of the youth and social services involved in the Leicester and Nottingham partnerships acknowledged that community safety strategies provided them with hitherto unimaginable opportunities to influence the character of local crime control away from punishment and exclusion towards reintegration and welfare. Nonetheless, they acknowledged that their very involvement had the potential to jeopardise their relationship with their clients, especially given the emphasis in partnerships on exchanging sensitive intelligence with the police, probation service, local authority housing department and other organisations whose essential purpose is perceived, among these clients, to be punitive.

Strategic dilemmas in the post-Crime and Disorder Act partnerships

As the first cycle of the post-Crime and Disorder Act 1998 partnerships will not be completed until April 2002 observations on the effect of the new statutory duty on these dilemmas are tentative. Nonetheless it is possible to identify certain trends. Preliminary findings from an ethnographic study of the Leicester Crime and Disorder Partnership suggest that the funding opportunities open to the new statutory partnerships have exacerbated the problems associated with competition. Local representatives of the two leading agencies, Leicestershire Constabulary and Leicester City Council, have argued that the additional resources required to fulfil the statutory duty have not been accounted for in the mainstream funding provided by the Treasury in its annual spending rounds since April 1999. This constraint on finance was also exacerbated by the knock-on effect of the New Labour national government's decision to fix public expenditure at levels set by the outgoing Conservative administration for the first two years of its first term (1997–99). In keeping with the emphasis of New Labour on targeting public resources at highly concentrated problem populations, resources have been made available through a raft of grant-aid programmes that continue to be delivered through competitive bidding processes in which local partnerships have to demonstrate the need for support by identifying 'hotspots' of crime and disorder often at the sub-ward level of enumeration units. This has exacerbated competition both within and between neighbourhoods given that those populations and neighbourhoods that do not quite qualify as a 'hotspot', yet still experience significant problems of crime and disorder, effectively lose out twice: first for not being selected and second for having what resources are currently deployed in their neighbourhoods siphoned off to ensure that statutory duties are met in the selected areas.

The logic of targeting also produces severe competition among neighbourhood partnerships with regard to those public finances that are provided to local authorities directly. For example, the Leicestershire probation service has received an annual allocation of £300,000 to fund individual Drug Treatment Orders, as legislated for in the Crime and Disorder Act. As one local community safety officer remarked, this funds a maximum of 100 orders county-wide when there are easily that many addicts in inner-city Leicester alone. The partnership had identified the growth of heroin use in inner-city Leicester as a priority for action in the aftermath of intelligence on the oversupply of this drug – reports suggested that a 'wrap' of heroin (30 mg) is cheaper to purchase than a pint of beer (*Leicester Mercury*, 26 March 2001). The options for adopting the kind of balanced portfolio of law enforcement and social and situational prevention measures, advocated in the Morgan Report, in response to locally specific problems such as this have been severely restricted by the parsimony of highly targeted grant aid and by national government strictures on where to target those funds that are made available – hence funds made available through the new Crime Reduction Programme have had to be targeted on the national government priority of reducing opportunities for burglary. As a consequence the primary measures taken against the problem of heroin-use and associated problems of anti-social behaviour, the detritus of drug use in public places and the threat of robbery, etc., have been restricted to episodic law enforcement raids on dealers and further investment in stationary and mobile CCTV surveillance.

The regression of the statutory crime and disorder partnerships back to pre-Morgan Report strategies of crime control has been further encouraged by the explicit focus on 'crime and disorder' rather than the broader notion of community safety. In Leicester this has been reflected in the statutory partnership's crime and disorder action plan which is exclusively concerned with police categories of offending and victimisation (Leicester Partnership Against Crime and Disorder 1999: 11–12) and is starkly contrasted with the City Council's former community safety strategy, which encompassed the creation of employment opportunities, work with the homeless and harm minimisation approaches to substance misuse (Leicester City Council 1995: 9). This potential closure of partnership work around a mixture of law enforcement and opportunity reduction has also been exacerbated by the conflicting messages on crime control and social exclusion sent out by the Crime and Disorder Act and by other national government initiatives. It must be acknowledged that New Labour established a national government organisation, the Social Exclusion Unit, dedicated to developing 'joined-up', 'integrated and sustainable approaches to the problems of the worst housing estates, including crime, drugs, unemployment, community breakdown, and bad schools etc.' (Social Exclusion Unit 1998). Yet this more imaginative strategy for 'neighbourhood renewal' is counter-balanced by more punitive measures in the Crime and Disorder Act, such as anti-social behaviour orders and child curfews, the consequence of which has been to generate expectations among local citizens that complex and multi-faceted problems, such as substance abuse, street prostitution and the use of public space by young people, can and will be tackled through punitive interventions by local authorities and the police (Stenson and Edwards 2001: 79–80).

The proliferation of partnership-based initiatives under New Labour has also exacerbated the governability of complex social problems at the local level. It is an irony that as New Labour has emphasised the importance of 'joining-up' the government of 'wicked issues' like crime and disorder it has also established a cornucopia of parallel organisations that compete for the limited organisational resources of local actors. In addition to statutory crime and disorder partnerships local actors have to divide their time and effort between, *inter alia*, single regeneration budget partnerships, health and education action zones, new deal for communities, drug action teams, surestart initiatives, the connexions programme and neighbourhood renewal partnerships. The coordination of these government initiatives has been further complicated by their administrative division between departments in Whitehall, the recently established Regional Development Agencies and the Integrated Regional Offices inherited from the former Conservative national government.

To clarify the political accountability of the crime and disorder partnerships to their local populations, the statutory duty placed an obligation on all partnerships to conduct local audits of crime and disorder and circulate a report on the findings of the audit for public scrutiny and comment. Notwithstanding the political decisions implicit in the sampling frames, foci and categories employed in these audits, such consultation is only episodic, happening once at the outset of each three yearly cycle of the statutory partnerships. In addition, the use of such audits as the 'objective' basis for identifying and targeting 'hotspots' of crime and social exclusion has been particularly controversial in Leicester, where the City Council's *Atlas of Social and Economic Conditions in Leicester* (Thomas and Robertson 1998) was contested by voluntary sector actors in neighbourhoods not identified as a priority for regeneration. These actors were successful in employing a social scientist to deconstruct the atlas and conduct more intensive, qualitative as well as quantitative, research demonstrating equally high levels of exclusion and need in non-prioritised areas (Loughborough University 2000). While arguments over the veracity and appropriateness of these competing approaches to 'mapping' and interpreting crime and social exclusion are unresolved, this exercise demonstrates the limits to, if not counter-productive effects of, using audits as a principal vehicle for the political accountability of non-elected authorities such as public-private partnerships.

Beyond the politics of audit, arrangements for the day-to-day accountability of the crime and disorder partnerships have been left to the discretion of each partnership. As a consequence there is, at present, an experimental attitude towards degrees of citizen involvement in the decision-making process that can range from 'consultation' through to citizen participation and citizen control (cf. Burns *et al* 1994: 162–3). Whereas episodic consultation exercises do not fulfil the real potential of partnerships to revitalise local democracy, and may well exacerbate local tensions, empowering local citizens to actively participate, even control, the decisionmaking process has certain liabilities. The potential 'statization of the private sphere' was evident in one of the inner-city action teams of the Leicester Crime and Disorder Partnership where local tenants and residents associations were used by the police and housing officers for intelligence on the residential locations of drug pushers as a prelude to law enforcement raids and the siting of CCTV surveillance. Conversely the active participation of local citizens in this same action team had the potential of privatising politics through demands made by a coalition of local residents for the use of anti-social behaviour orders and 'zero tolerance' policing strategies against street prostitutes in the neighbourhood. In opposition to this another coalition of interests, including the police and welfare professionals, argued that such strategies were highly costly and ineffective as either prosecuted individuals simply broke exclusion orders or else displaced their activities to other parts of the neighbourhood. Conversely this other coalition argued for an alternative problematisation of street vice as an issue of welfare rather than punishment, in which individual prostitutes should be referred to employment, housing and drug advice agencies.

These examples suggest that the opportunities for deliberative democracy offered by active citizen participation in local partnerships outweigh the potential exclusivity associated with the privatisation of politics and/or the statisation of the private sphere. Partnerships offer the potential for ongoing dialogue which is, surely, the necessary democratic mechanism for educating and engaging citizens about social problems that are not only complex but, like crime and disorder, are also laden with volatile emotions manipulated, in turn, by a vicarious mass media. These examples also suggest a broader point about the actual practice of concrete partnerships as opposed to the potential realisation of their powers and liabilities. The strategic dilemmas of this governing technique are an expression of the structural relations between statutory, voluntary and business actors at different tiers of government. Through a comparative examination of their manifestation in concrete partnerships and localities it has, nonetheless, been possible to identify diversity in the actual and thus *potential* practice of partnerships. A more determinate account of partnerships requires a conception of *political agency* to understand how strategic dilemmas are apprehended in the way they are and, subsequently, how they could be apprehended differently.

Political agency and the apprehension of strategic dilemmas

A concrete analysis of partnership in practice implies an understanding of the dispositional qualities of actors and how these interact with the specific contexts that shape their action. The predominant tradition, certainly in official discourse on crime control, has been to reduce dispositions to the rational choices that actors can make about the costs and benefits of action (Clarke and Felson 1998; Roshier 1989). Rational choice theory has, however, been criticised by more anthropological approaches for precluding an understanding of the institutional dispositions and collective consciousness that shape the reception, acceptance or rejection of competing discourses about crime control and community in diverse social contexts (Loader *et al* 1998; Taylor *et al* 1996). These anthropological studies emphasise the centrality of emotion and affective sensibilities toward the perceived risks, threats to and means of security in particular localities. In these terms 'irrational' fears about crime and the resonance of competing appeals for punitive or welfare-oriented strategies are placed at the core of explanations for the actual practice of crime control. As a consequence of this, however, the debate over agency in crime control has polarised around the 'Cartesian' dichotomy of *either* rationality *or* emotion.

Alternatively, research into the actual dynamics of policy change and learning suggests that political action is driven more by the *habitual* apprehension of problems in terms of belief systems constituted by a combination of instrumental rationality and emotional attachment (Sabatier 1993). Actors coalesce around the normative core principles of a belief system, for example the axiomatic principles of different communitarian philosophies that attribute crime to problems of social inequality or moral turpitude (cf. Hughes 1998). These coalitions adopt fundamental positions on policies in so far as these are thought to translate core principles into practice, for example the use of universal welfare programmes to reduce inequalities through income re-distribution or the reassertion of moral authority through controls on 'anti-social behaviour'. Whereas coalitions are more open to persuasion about changes in the 'secondary' aspects of policy, such as the dynamics of implementation, the administration of budgets and so on, their attachment to core principles and fundamental policy positions means that major shifts in governmental practice entail external shocks to a policy field and the related redistribution of resources among actors.

In these terms the 'recurring ambivalence', in advanced liberal governmentality, between 'adaptive' crime control strategies, such as the reduction of opportunities for law-breaking, and strategies of 'denial', such as the resilient commitment to law enforcement and imprisonment, only leads to 'volatile and contradictory' policies from the perspective of rational critique (Garland 1996). From the perspective of coalitions formed around habitual ways of thinking, the advocacy of strategies of opportunity reduction and imprisonment is coherent and sensible in so far as a particular advocacy coalition believes these strategies will reduce crime by, for instance, restoring moral authority. Similarly, advocates of community safety routinely combine situational and social crime prevention measures in the belief that these are complementary rather than mutually exclusive (Home Office 1991: 32). For example, from the perspective of coalitions that believe in reducing crime by reducing social inequality, it is plausible that opportunity reduction measures that 'deflect' risks of victimisation away from the most vulnerable can complement other egalitarian social policy interventions.

As broader commentaries on social and political change have noted, it is not the internal contradictions of a governing programme that matter so much as the effectiveness and acumen of competing coalitions in translating policy in terms of their particular interests (Bourdieu 1977, 1990; Callon 1986; Latour 1986). Here the notion of translation refers to the process by which coalitions win political arguments and define policy by successfully articulating the identities, interests and appropriate actions of others. Four key moments in this process have been identified (Callon 1986: 203–19).

Firstly coalitions problematise an issue in such a way as to establish their own role as indispensable for its resolution. For example, the construction of crime and disorder audits around specific categories of 'street' crime, as distinct from audits encompassing broader categories of health, safety and environmental hazards, establishes the police and probation services at the centre of control strategies rather than the Health and Safety Executive or Environment Agency.

Secondly, effective coalitions employ various devices for interesting allies to their cause, such as social scientific findings on the nature and distribution of threats to security. Such devices are used both as a means of corroborating and legitimising the problematisation offered by a particular coalition while discrediting those offered by other coalitions. For example advocates of situational crime prevention have proselytised their cause by citing findings from 'successful case studies' while questioning the evidence for successful social crime prevention initiatives (Clarke 1997; Pease 1997).

Thirdly, potential allies are actually enrolled in a coalition through various devices of negotiation and bargaining, such as the offer of financial, organisational-informational and political resources and emotional appeals to the righteousness of their cause. This has been a particularly prominent feature of debates among crime control partnerships and civil libertarians over the use of eviction notices to control 'anti-social' families on municipal housing estates. Advocates of this measure argue that the immediate rights of neighbours to peaceful coexistence are superior to the accommodation, counselling, income-support and other needs of 'problem' families.

Finally, the successful mobilisation of an advocacy coalition entails the discrediting and disorganising of competing coalitions, the displacement of actors from these coalitions and then the reassembling of these actors into new alliances. Central to this process is the acumen, the accomplished agency, of 'spokespersons' and the according of credibility and authenticity to their claims for support. For example, representatives of the local authority housing department and police may use their organisational-informational resources about the location and activities of 'problem families' and employ the depositions of victims and witnesses of anti-social behaviour in mobilising support for a strategy that closes responses around the use of anti-social behaviour orders and/or eviction notices. Conversely, representatives of the social and youth services and citizens' advice bureau may deploy their specialist knowledge about the pressures on these families in mobilising support for an alternative strategy open to measures such as intensive social work, counselling, advice on parenting skills, the diversion of children into directed youth activities and/or the involvement of a mediation agency to provide neutral arbitration between neighbours, etc.

The actual practice of partnerships can, therefore, be understood as a contingent outcome of these struggles to translate problems of crime control and the quintessential role of key actors who are capable of apprehending strategic dilemmas and acting as spokespersons for an imaginative repertoire of responses to these dilemmas. These contingencies were illustrated in the response of partnerships in Leicester and Nottingham to the dilemmas of controlling young people's use of public space.

Translating community-based crime control: struggles over youth and disorder

Leicester and Nottingham share certain political-economic qualities. Historically the economic base in both cities has been dependent on the textile industry and both have encountered increasing difficulties in maintaining this economic base as production has shifted to the lower unit cost producers in the developing economies of South East Asia and as economic regeneration has produced service sector employment opportunities that have bypassed those communities that evolved as labour supply to the textile industry. Both cities share a similar political history, with long-standing majority Labour Party control of elected local government, and both are subject to the same regional governing structures of the Government Office of the East Midlands (GOEM) and the East Midlands Development Agency (EMDA). Finally, both cities have been affected by successive waves of postwar immigration from the former colonies of the British Empire and by the more recent resettlement of refugees and asylum seekers from civil wars in the Balkans and the Horn of Africa, which have introduced a further complexity into the demographic mix of these cities and the consequent milieu of local political struggles for resources.

Notwithstanding these formal similarities, however, there has been a substantive difference in relations between district-wide governing regimes and the communities targeted by partnerships for crime control and neighbourhood renewal in both cities. In Leicester the political orientation of partnerships has been 'upwards' to the interests of non-local funding bodies and corporate business whereas in Nottingham governing authorities have endeavoured to combine the appeal for inward investment with a 'downwards' orientation toward the priorities and interests of socially excluded communities. In Nottingham authorities have emphasised the active participation of these communities in strategies for renewal from 'the bottom up'. A key innovation here has been the piloting of neighbourhood trust funds in which area forums are given a charitable status and, therefore, the legal rights to lever in financial resources which they can then use to support interventions tailored to the specific needs and priorities of local citizens.

These alternative governing cultures have been crystallised in the habitual apprehension of the strategic dilemmas encountered by partnerships working on outer-housing estates in the two cities. Again, these outer-housing estates shared formal similarities in so far as both contained high levels of structural unemployment due to the shrinkage and mechanisation of textiles production, their geographical isolation from growing service sector employment opportunities in the cities' commercial districts, the erratic and expensive nature of the deregulated public transport systems and the absence of local public amenities and limited service provision for young people. On both estates the overwhelming proportion of the population are white and the key tensions are between the elderly retired population on the one hand and young families on the other. In this context a key dilemma for the partnerships has been over the response to the 'anti-social' use of public space by young males and here it is possible to identify substantive differences in the strategies adopted.

The catalyst for the establishment of partnerships on both estates was similar, a series of major disturbances following police operations against acts of burglary, vandalism, arson and 'TWOCing' (Taking automoblies WithOut the Consent of their owners and 'joyriding' (*sic*) these stolen vehicles around the estates at high speed before dumping and burning them) committed by gangs of young males. The response, however, was significantly different. In Leicester a coalition of representatives from the residents and tenants association, housing department and local constabulary pressed the partnership to prioritise investment in high-profile police patrols, CCTV surveillance and the target-hardening of domestic dwellings to more effectively exclude the threat of young male activity. An alternative coalition of parents, school teachers and youth workers defined the problem in terms of an absence of facilities for young people, particularly in the evenings, at weekends and during school vacations. The former, 'exclusionist', coalition was successful in recruiting the city council officers who led the partnership and controlled access to resources available through grant aid dispensed by the national government's regional office to their cause. The spokespersons of this coalition cited evidence on the effectiveness of opportunity-reducing techniques and complemented this with an argument about the legitimate rights of peaceful residents to gain immediate relief from anti-social behaviour of young males. While the competing, 'reintegrative', coalition presented an equally emotive argument for prioritising investment in activities for young people, the political culture of the city council inscribed a bias or 'strategic selectivity' (cf. Jessop 1990: 9–10) into this struggle in favour of the exclusionist coalition. The orientation of the city council toward the funding priorities and performance measurement criteria of non-local agencies geared it towards arguments over the efficacy and demonstrability of short-term opportunity-reducing controls advanced by the exclusionist coalition.

On the Nottingham estate the reintegrative coalition was more successful in winning support from the city council gatekeepers for their translation of the problem of crime, disorder and young people. Spokespersons for this coalition were more imaginative in complementing emotional arguments about the rights and needs of young people with evidence on the local demand for, and practicability of, social crime prevention strategies. They conducted a sample survey of young families about these needs and convened a series of public meetings bringing young and elderly people together to discuss the use of public space on the estate. In addition they referred to evidence on the impact of youth outreach work and youth activities organised in centres with flexible opening hours in other localities. On the basis of this portfolio of consultation and comparative analysis, the reintegrative coalition succeeded in securing additional resources for young people. While the exclusionist coalition was also successful in securing resources for opportunity-reducing measures and law enforcement strategies (the use of eviction notices was actually piloted nationally by Nottingham City Council on this estate), these were regarded as a compliment to, rather than a substitute for, a more reintegrative approach. In turn this reflected the openness of the city council to experiments in neighbourhood renewal from the bottom up, not least through innovations in the generation of locally controlled resources such as charitable trusts.

Conclusion: learning from diversity

These struggles over partnership responses to youth crime and disorder in Leicester and Nottingham exemplify the challenges of drawing lessons from community-based crime control. Through building a progressively concrete and complex account of their practices it is possible to clarify how each *actually* acted and, consequently, how each *could* have acted, given the *real* powers and liabilities of governing through partnership arrangements in the conditions of advanced liberal polities such as Britain. It has been argued that these arrangements provide opportunities for more innovative, dynamic and democratic government but also generate their own strategic dilemmas. In extending 'voice' to actors hitherto excluded from public authority, partnerships have altered the nature of intergovernmental relations among organisations in different spheres and at different tiers of government.

The outcome of these intergovermental relations is 'contingently necessary' because although it is possible to identify necessary causes of partnership activity, such as the dependence of local actors on non-local resources and other relations of power dependence, the apprehension and manipulation of these relations is a contingent facet of political agency, as demonstrated by the diverse experiences of the 'reintegrative' and 'exclusionary' advocacy coalitions in Leicester and Nottingham. Through systematic comparative analysis of local crime control processes it is possible for coalitions to draw lessons from the successes and failures of like-minded actors elsewhere in manipulating the resources available to them.

Central to this process of learning is an understanding of the possibilities for political action open to actors at different tiers of government. To identify the scope for action that residents on outer-estates in Leicester and Nottingham have is not to imply a naive pluralism. Clearly there are major inequalities in the distribution of governing capital between voluntary sector organisations on the one hand and businesses and statutory agencies on the other. A more critical pluralist approach seeks to identify the kinds of intervention that are necessary at different tiers of government in order to enhance the governing capacities of, for example, voluntary organisations of local citizens *relative to* statutory agencies and of statutory agencies *relative to* corporate business etc. It can be argued, for example, that to genuinely enhance the capacity of local citizens to actively participate in local crime control and other governing processes, it is necessary to restructure the access which voluntary sector organisations have to public finances and other sources of support.

Devolving control over public finances from national government's regional offices to local authorities and then from these authorities into local 'strategic partnerships' containing voluntary sector organisations is currently being explored through the national government's 'Neighbourhood Renewal' and 'Community Empowerment' funds (Neighbourhood Renewal Unit 2001). The idea behind such strategic partnerships is that they should inform the targeting of all the public finances that come into a locality, whether through mainstream funding to statutory bodies such as the police and elected local government or through the plethora of grant-aid programmes and quangos (quasi non-governmental organisations). Whether or not these partnerships will actually control the targeting of these resources or be restricted to 'advising' existing budget holders will be the subject of a crucial political battle. The key point is that this battle is there to be had but must be conducted at different tiers, through local struggles over the constitution of strategic partnerships and through representations to regional and national government. Central to these struggles will be the capacity of competing advocacy coalitions to translate their instrumental and emotional arguments over the 'just' exercise of sovereignty.

In addition to clarifying the foci and key sites of political battles over sovereignty, critical pluralism also provides a core set of normative principles around which advocates of community empowerment can coalesce. The belief that complex and emotionally charged issues like crime and disorder need to be subject to open and inclusive democratic deliberation is the basis for contesting dilemmas over the openness and accountability of new governmental powers such as public-private partnerships. The stakes in current struggles over sovereignty in advanced liberal polities, especially over issues of crime and disorder, could not be higher as recent instances of vigilante action and rioting in English cities have demonstrated. Yet clearly there are serious risks associated with community empowerment in this area of policy as the devolution of decisionmaking powers has the liability of privatising government around bigoted and exclusionary constructions of crime control and community. A key challenge for critical pluralists is to develop innovations in participative forms of democracy that enable local citizens to voice their anxieties while avoiding the liability of actually exacerbating tensions among different sections of the local citizenry. Learning from the experiences of experiments in participative democracy ought to be at the epicentre of comparative action research on community engagement in crime control processes.

Notes

1 An earlier and longer version of this chapter was presented to the Centre for Criminal Justice Research Seminar Series, Liverpool John Moore's University, 6 June 2001 as a paper entitled, 'Learning from Diversity: A Critical Realist Approach to Crime Control and Community'. The author would like to acknowledge the following for their critical feedback in preparing this chapter: Roy Coleman, Pete Gill, Simon Hallsworth, Joe Sim, Kevin Stenson and Steve Toombs.
2 The author would like to acknowledge the support of the UK Economic and Social Research Council for their support for this research (Grant No. L31125035). Findings from this research have, hitherto, been published in co-authored work (Benyon and Edwards 1999; Edwards and Benyon 2000; Stenson and Edwards 2001).
3 I have been conducting an ethnography of the Leicester Partnership Against Crime and Disorder's *Crime and Disorder Strategy, 1999–2002*, since its establishment as part of the new statutory duty of the Crime and Disorder Act 1998, in my capacity as chair of one of the Partnership's 'Local Action Teams' in inner-city Leicester.

References

Baine, S., Bennington, J. and Russell, J. (1991) *Changing Europe: Challenges Facing the Voluntary and Community Sectors in the 1990s*. London: National Council of Voluntary Organisations.

Benyon, J. and Edwards, A. (1999) 'Community Governance of Crime Control', in G. Stoker (ed.), *The New Management of British Local Governance*. London: Macmillan.

Bottoms, A. and Wiles, P. (1996) 'Understanding Crime Prevention in Late Modern Societies', in T. Bennett (ed.), *Preventing Crime and Disorder*. Cambridge: Cambridge Cropwood Series.

Bourdieu, P. (1977) *Outline of a Theory of Practice*. Cambridge: Cambridge University Press.

Bourdieu, P. (1990) *The Logic of Practice*. Cambridge: Cambridge University Press.

Burns, D. *et al* (1994) *The Politics of Decentralization*. London: Macmillan.

Callon, M. (1986) 'Some Elements of a Sociology of Translation: Domestication of the Scallops and the Fishermen of St Brieuc Bay', in J. Law (ed.), *Power, Action and Belief*. London: Routledge & Kegan Paul.

Campbell, B. (1993) *Goliath: Britain's Dangerous Places*. London: Methuen.

Chapman, G. (1994) 'They Are Not Working Now', *Guardian Newspaper*, 23 November.

Clarke, R. (ed.) (1997) *Situational Crime Prevention: Successful Case Studies*, 2nd edn. Albany, NY: Harrow & Heston Publishers.

Clarke, R. and Felson, M. (1998) *Opportunity Makes the Thief*. London: Home Office.

Cohen, S. (1985) *Visions of Social Control*. Cambridge: Polity.

Coleman, R. and Sim, J. (1998) 'From the Dockyards to the Disney Store: Surveillance, Risk and Security in Liverpool City Centre', *International Review of Law Computers and Technology*, 12 (1), 27–45.

Crawford, A. (1994) 'The Partnership Approach to Community Crime Prevention: Corporatism at the Local Level?', *Social and Legal Studies*, 3, 497–519.

Crawford, A. (1997) *The Local Governance of Crime*. Oxford: Clarendon Press.

Crawford, A. (1998) *Crime Prevention and Community Safety: Politics, Policies and Practices*. London: Longman.

Davis, M. (1990) *City of Quartz*. London: Vintage.

Edwards, A. (2001) *Learning from Diversity: A Critical Realist Approach to Crime Control and Community*. Paper presented to Centre for Criminal Justice Seminar Series, Liverpool John Moore's University, 6 June.

Edwards, A. and Benyon, J. (2000) 'Community Governance, Crime Control and Local Diversity', *Crime Prevention and Community Safety: An International Journal*, 2 (3), 35–54.

Ekblom, P. (1988) *Getting the Best Out of Crime Pattern Analysis*. London: Home Office.

Etzioni, A. (1995) *The Spirit of Community*. London: Fontana.

Garland, D. (1996) 'The Limits of the Sovereign State: Strategies of Crime Control in Contemporary Society', *British Journal of Criminology*, 36 (4), 445–71.

Garland, D. (2001) *The Culture of Control: Crime and Social Order in Contemporary Society*. Oxford: Oxford University Press.

Giddens, A. (1998) *The Third Way: The Renewal of Social Democracy*. Cambridge: Polity.

Gilling, D. and Barton, A. (1997) 'Crime Prevention and Community Safety: A New Home for Social Policy?', *Critical Social Policy*, 17 (3), 63–83.

Gordon, P. (1987) 'Community Policing: Towards the Local Police State?', in P. Scraton (ed.), *Law, Order and the Authoritarian State*. Buckingham: Open University Press.

Hay, C. (1996) *Re-Stating Social and Political Change*. Buckingham: Open University Press.

Hirschman, A.O. (1970) *Exit, Voice and Loyalty*. Cambridge, MA: Harvard University Press.

Hirst, P. (1994) *Associative Democracy*. Cambridge: Polity.

Hirst, P. (1997) *From Statism to Pluralism*. London: UCL Press.

Hirst, P. and Thompson, G. (1996) *Globalization in Question*. Cambridge: Polity.

Home Office (1990) *Partnership in Crime Prevention*. London: Home Office.

Home Office (1991) *Safer Communities: The Local Delivery of Crime Prevention Through the Partnership Approach ('The Morgan Report')*. London: Home Office.

Home Office (1993) *A Practical Guide to Crime Prevention for Local Partnerships*. London: Home Office.

Home Office (1998) *Guidance on Statutory Crime and Disorder Partnerships*. London: Home Office.

Hughes, G. (1996) 'Communitarianism and Law and Order', *Critical Social Policy*, 16, 17–41.

Hughes, G. (1997) 'Policing Late Modernity: Changing Strategies of Crime Management in Contemporary Britain', in N. Jewson and S. MacGregor (eds), *Transforming Cities*. London: Routledge.

Hughes, G. (1998) *Understanding Crime Prevention: Social Control, Risk and Late Modernity*. Buckingham: Open University Press.

Jessop, B. (1990) *State Theory*. Cambridge: Polity.

Jessop, B. (1994) 'Post-Fordism and the State', in A. Amin (ed.), *Post-Fordism: A Reader*. Oxford: Blackwell.

Jessop, B. (1997) 'The Governance of Complexity and the Complexity of Governance: Preliminary Remarks on Some Problems and Limits of Economic Guidance', in A. Amin and J. Hausner (eds), *Beyond Market and Hierarchy*. Aldershot: Edward Elgar.

Jessop, B. (2000) 'From the KNWS to the SWPR', in G. Lewis *et al* (eds), *Rethinking Social Policy*. London: Sage.

Johnston, L. (1996) 'What is Vigilantism?', *British Journal of Criminology*, 36 (2), 220–36.

Johnston, L. (2000) *Policing Britain: Risk, Security and Governance*. London: Longman.

Keith, M. (1993) *Race, Riots and Policing: Lore and Disorder in a Multi-Racist Society*. London: UCL Press.

Lacey, N. and Zedner, L. (1995) 'Discourses of Community in Criminal Justice', *Journal of Law and Society*, 22 (3), 301–25.

Latour, B. (1986) 'The Powers of Association', in J. Law (ed.), *Power, Action and Belief*. London: Routledge & Kegan Paul.

Lazare, D. (1998) 'America the Undemocratic', *New Left Review*, 232, 3–40.

Leicester City Council (1995) *Leicester City Council Community Safety Strategy 1995–6*. Leicester: Leicester City Council.

Leicester Partnership Against Crime and Disorder (1999) *Crime and Disorder Strategy, 1999–2002*. Leicester: LPCD.

Liddle, A.M. and Gelsthorpe, L.R. (1994) *Inter-Agency Crime Prevention: Organising Local Delivery*, Crime Prevention Unit Paper 52. London: Home Office.

Loader, I., Girling, E. and Sparks, R. (1998) 'Narratives of Decline: Youth, Dis/order and Community in an English "Middletown" ', *British Journal of Criminology*, 38 (3), 388–403.

Loughborough University (2000) *SRB (Single Regeneration Budget) Round 2 Research and Evaluation Project*. Department of Social Sciences, Loughborough University.

Lowndes, V. (1993) 'The Other Governments of Britain: Local Politics and Delegated Administrations', in I. Budge and D. McKay (eds), *The Developing British Political System: the 1990s*, 3rd edn. London: Longman.

Neighbourhood Renewal Unit (2001) *Community Empowerment Fund: Preliminary Guidance*. London: Department for Transport, Local Government and the Regions.

Nelken, D. (1994) 'The Future of Comparative Criminology', in D. Nelken (ed.), *The Futures of Criminology*. London: Sage.

News of the World, 30 July, 6 August.

Ousley, H. (2001) *Community Pride, Not Prejudice: Making Diversity Work in Bradford*. Bradford: Bradford City Council.

Pease, K. (1994) 'Crime Prevention', in M. Maguire *et al* (eds), *The Oxford Handbook of Criminology*. Oxford: Oxford University Press.

Pease, K. (1997) 'Crime Prevention', in M. Maguire *et al* (eds), *The Oxford Handbook of Criminology*, 2nd edn. Oxford: Oxford University Press.

Pollard, C. (1997) 'Zero Tolerance: Short-term Fix, Long-term Liability?', in N. Dennis (ed.), *Zero Tolerance: Policing a Free Society*. London: Institute for Economic Affairs.

Rhodes, R.A.W. (1994) 'The Hollowing Out of the State', *Political Quarterly*, 65, 138–51.

Rhodes, R.A.W. (1997) *Understanding Governance*. Buckingham: Open University Press.

Rose, N. (1996) 'The Death of the Social? Refiguring the Territory of Government', *Economy and Society*, 22 (2), 283–99.

Rose, N. and Miller, P. (1992) 'Political Power Beyond the State: Problematics of Government', *British Journal of Sociology*, 43 (2), 173–205.

Rose, R. (1993) *Lesson-Drawing in Public Policy: A Guide to Learning Across Time and Space*. Chatham, NJ: Chatham House.

Roshier, B. (1989) *Controlling Crime: The Classical Perspective in Criminology*. Buckingham: Open University Press

Sabatier, P. (1993) 'Policy Change Over a Decade or More', in P. Sabatier and H. Jenkins-Smith (eds), *Policy Change and Learning*. San Francisco, CA: Westview Press.

Sayer, A. (1992) *Method in Social Science: A Realist Approach*, 2nd edn. London: Routledge.

Sayer, A. (2000) *Realism and Social Science*. London: Sage.

Smandych, R. (ed.) (1999) *Governable Places: Readings in Governmentality and Crime Control*. Aldershot: Dartmouth.

Social Exclusion Unit (1998) *Bringing Britain Together: A National Strategy for Neighbourhood Renewal*. London: HMSO.

Social Exclusion Unit (2000) *National Strategy for Neighbourhood Renewal: A Framework for Consultation*. London: Cabinet Office.

Stenson, K. (1991) 'Making Sense of Crime Control', in K. Stenson and D. Cowell (eds), *The Politics of Crime Control*. London: Sage.

Stenson, K. (1993) 'Community Policing as a Governmental Technology', *Economy and Society*, 22 (3), 373–89.

Stenson, K. (1998) 'Displacing Social Policy through Crime Control', in S. Hanninen (ed.), *Displacement of Social Policies*. SoPhi: University of Jyvaskyla.

Stenson, K. (1999) 'Crime Control, Governmentality and Sovereignty', in R. Smandych (ed.), *Governable Places: Readings in Governmentality and Crime Control*. Aldershot: Dartmouth.

Stenson, K. (2000) 'Crime Control, Social Policy and Liberalism', in G. Lewis *et al* (eds), *Rethinking Social Policy*. London: Sage.

Stenson, K. and Edwards, A. (2001) 'Crime Control and Liberal Government: The Third Way and the Return to the Local', in K. Stenson and R. Sullivan (eds), *Crime, Risk and Justice: The Politics of Crime Control in Liberal Democracies*. Cullompton: Willan Publishing.

Stenson, K. and Watt, P. (1999) 'Governmentality and "the Death of the Social"? A Discourse Analysis of Local Government texts in South-East England', *Urban Studies*, 36 (1), 189–201.

Stoker, G. (ed.) (1999) *The New Management of British Local Governance*. London: Macmillan.

Swyngedouw, E. (1992) 'The Mammon Quest. "Glocalisation", Interspatial Competition and the Monetary Order: the Construction of New Spatial Scales', in M. Dunford and G. Kafkalas (eds), *Cities and Regions in the New Europe: the Global-Local Interplay and Spatial Development Strategies*. London: Belhaven.

Taylor, I. *et al* (1996) *A Tale of Two Cities*. London: Routledge.

Thomas, A. and Robertson, I. (1998) *Atlas of Social and Economic Conditions in Leicester*. Leicester: Leicester City Council.

Chapter 8

'People pieces': the neglected but essential elements of community crime prevention

Janet Foster

Introduction

The people who live in high crime neighbourhoods have often been incidental rather than central to crime prevention effort. Yet, in a diverse range of ways they are an essential element of the jigsaw. In this chapter I explore some of the problems with ignoring the 'people pieces' and thread my reflections of researching some of Britain's poorest communities with the theory, politics, methods and practice of community crime prevention.

I was tempted to begin this chapter in a conventional manner with the theoretical foundations of community crime prevention, the political pressures which have driven the debate and responses to it. However, it seemed more important to start with where I am coming from, since my selection and critique of this material is fundamentally shaped by a belief that despite the now acknowledged importance of 'bottom-up' strategies to tackle crime and a range of other social issues these have been far too readily ignored. Lack of creativity, the relative ease of situational crime prevention, the growth of managerialism and crude performance indicators have all led agencies to focus on 'quick' and visible fixes often with little discussion or appreciation of their likely impact (witness the proliferation of CCTV). Criminologists meanwhile, though frequently expressing fears about the dominance of situational prevention, have rarely undertaken in-depth empirical research in communities plagued by crime. Indeed in recent years fear of crime, and the safer, affluent environs, have had a much higher profile.

I understand the reluctance. Ethnography is not easy especially in high crime neighbourhoods. It can be stressful and difficult (something Gans (1982) delightfully captures) and occasionally very scary. But it is also a privilege. The opportunity to glimpse other people's worlds, to listen to their experiences as offenders, victims, residents, housing managers and police officers; to observe the complex social processes which exist in neighbourhoods (though never feeling it is possible to properly convey these in words to a reader); to look at the interaction between communities and crime, their impact on criminal opportunities, traditions, networks and informal social control (Foster 1990; Foster and Hope 1993; Foster 1995, 1997); and to examine the impact of urban change and conflict (Foster 1992, 1996, 1999a) – have influenced my thinking in very fundamental ways. It has made the issues which touch people's lives very immediate; it has fuelled my sense of injustice about the ways that people with so little are pathologised by those with so much; and has left me frustrated that those who could usefully intervene, for a variety of reasons, either do not take action or do so inappropriately.

All too frequently high crime communities are perceived to be full of 'problem people', not people who *may* have problems. Even in the highest crime neighbourhoods it is estimated that only 1 per cent of the residential population can give an estate the appearance of being out of control. Many agencies have at best ambivalent attitudes, and at worst prejudicial views about some of the most needy with whom they come into contact. Yet:

> Those whom housing officers and other local tenants call 'problem families' (and understood in terms of the 'presenting symptoms' of their personal inadequacies) can also be understood as individuals, families and households who have fallen foul of the competitive struggle for employment in Post-Fordist society, the competitive struggle for housing shelter, and indeed, the increasingly difficult struggle which faces those without saleable skills, personal advantages or connection for some kind of secure position 'on the bottom rung' of a market society.
>
> (Taylor 1999: 117)

It is impossible to understand crime and offending in our poorest communities without taking this into account. In addition to examining the dynamics of community crime prevention in this chapter, drawing where appropriate from my own research in predominantly high crime areas as well as the broader theoretical and substantive literature, I also want to highlight what I regard to be some key methodological points about the ways in which communities and crime are researched. If in my enthusiasm I appear to be arguing for methodological purism I apologise in advance. I am not suggesting that I, or ethnographers in general, by dint of detailed observational material possess *the* authentic voice (there are always multiple voices), nor do I claim a special insight to *understand* these neighbourhoods. In fact the more one observes the more complex and ethereal they become (see Cohen 1989). Neither do I suggest that other methods do not have their worth. I simply want to highlight that the opportunity to observe communities and the complex interactions within them changes one's perspective and fundamentally influences approaches to tackling crime *because* of the 'people pieces'. The experiences of individuals, their life histories and interactions with one another, and the context of the locality and the way this is perceived and influences people's opportunities, activities and behaviour – all this produces a multi-layered experience. The 'deviant others' to the detached outsider are simply people to the ethnographer whose lives, including their offending, occurs within an important context. These lives frequently evoke emotions of sadness rather than condemnation, a desire to understand rather than judge. I will never forget as a young and inexperienced researcher encountering a toddler who began smashing his head repeatedly against a wall as I was chatting with his mother. I picked him up and sat him on my lap, where he remained totally silent, rigid and lifeless for more than half an hour. At the time I had no frame of reference for understanding his behaviour but it never occurred to me to 'blame' his mother.

My feelings could not contrast more starkly with prevailing attitudinal and political trends in crime control and criminal justice. As Garland argues those who 'slight free choice and stress social determinants now lack the kind of resonance and ideological appeal that they exerted in the heyday of the welfare state' because the 'message' is altogether much 'darker and less tolerant' (Garland 2001: 198–9). Of course this does not mean that justice and welfare are any less important, not least as Taylor (1999: 225) reminds us because 'market society' can be an 'alien and disorienting social reality' dominated by 'a set of social arrangements "not of the actor's own making or choosing" '. Yet, despite the manifold social influences on crime and the plight of the poor more generally, the prevailing ideology is one in which the needy are viewed as 'social parasites, rather than truly helpless' and that 'the destruction of welfare nets and entitlements is … justified as freeing the political economy to behave more flexibly, as if the parasites were dragging down the more dynamic members of society' (Sennett 1998: 139).

Perspectives on community crime prevention

Community crime prevention, which Hope (1995: 21) defines as 'actions intended to change the social conditions that are believed to sustain crime in residential communities' is bedevilled by complexity – a crucial but frequently neglected starting point. Figure 1 attempts to draw together some of the key factors in the community crime prevention process. This is by no means exhaustive, but provides an organising framework for discussion and a vehicle for moving between different levels (i.e. structural, theoretical, practical, methodological and political).

Philosophies, people and processes: the broader context

David Smith (2000: 151–2) suggests that 'Sociologists and criminologists have tended to get stuck in profound and possibly intractable philosophical debates concerning free will and determinism' when 'this supposed opposition is a nonsense' they are in fact integrally related. 'The central problem ... must be to understand how persons and situations mutually influence one another' (p.148) which means that 'any coherent account of thought and action must be interactionist' (Smith 2000: 157).

This interactionist context needs to embrace broader structural and social processes that influence the fate of countries, localities and individuals. Giddens (1990, in Hughes 1998: 132) likened late modernity to 'riding a juggernaut' and its impact affects not simply the poor and deprived but the advantaged too (albeit the latter are in a much better position to respond to it). David Garland (2001: 194) eloquently summarised the situation:

> Over time, our practices of controlling crime and doing justice have had to adapt to an increasingly insecure economy that marginalizes substantial sections of the population; to a hedonistic consumer culture that combines extensive personal freedoms with relaxed social controls; to a pluralistic moral order that struggles to create trust relations between strangers who have little in common; to a 'sovereign' state that is increasingly incapable of regulating a society of individuated citizens and differentiated social groups; and to chronically high crime rates that co-exist with low levels of family cohesion and community solidarity.

Despite the fears which permeate middle-class environs it is important

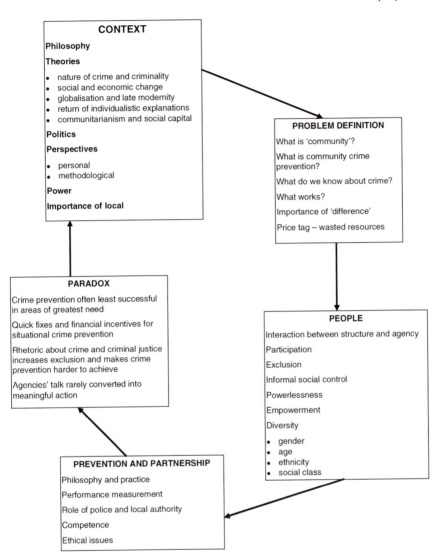

CONTEXT

Philosophy

Theories

- nature of crime and criminality
- social and economic change
- globalisation and late modernity
- return of individualistic explanations
- communitarianism and social capital

Politics

Perspectives

- personal
- methodological

Power

Importance of local

PROBLEM DEFINITION

What is 'community'?

What is community crime prevention?

What do we know about crime?

What works?

Importance of 'difference'

Price tag – wasted resources

PARADOX

Crime prevention often least successful in areas of greatest need

Quick fixes and financial incentives for situational crime prevention

Rhetoric about crime and criminal justice increases exclusion and makes crime prevention harder to achieve

Agencies' talk rarely converted into meaningful action

PEOPLE

Interaction between structure and agency

Participation

Exclusion

Informal social control

Powerlessness

Empowerment

Diversity

- gender
- age
- ethnicity
- social class

PREVENTION AND PARTNERSHIP

Philosophy and practice

Performance measurement

Role of police and local authority

Competence

Ethical issues

Figure 1 *Perspectives on community crime prevention*

to remind ourselves that property and violent crime is disproportionately concentrated (both in terms of victimisation and recorded offending) in the poorest and most deprived neighbourhoods (Mirrlees-Black *et al* 1998). Over the last two decades Britain has become 'ever more fragmented, economically divided and socially stretched' (Crawford 1998b: 246) with these patterns reflected in the geographies of exclusion (Sibley 1995) in which the 'haves' reside in communities of 'choice' and the 'have-nots' are locked in communities of 'fate' (Hirst 1994, cited in Hughes 1998: 116). In the latter are 'several thousand neighbourhoods and estates whose condition is critical, or soon could be' (Social Exclusion Unit 1998: 1). Yet even in these most desperate of circumstances, and despite the 'juggernaut' of globalisation that has devastated them, *difference* is evident: in levels of unemployment; in levels and types of crime across areas but also *within* them; and whether crime is tolerated, contained or spirals out of control. It is one of the major failings of policy responses to crime within communities that this diversity and difference has not been properly understood or integrated into attempts to tackle it.

Furthermore, the only way to uncover and understand this *difference* is by detailed research much of which *needs* to be qualitative in order to capture the diversity of perspectives because different groups and individuals 'define the "same" behaviour' in different ways, for example 'what is violence to one person is of little or no consequence to another' (Young 1999: 135).

Globalisation can very easily engender powerlessness and evoke a response that, since the impact of social and economic change is so vast and complex, what individuals do is unimportant. However, individuals are pivotal and important. Despite all the talk about partnership crime prevention policies are shaped and determined by quite 'literally one handful of individuals' (Koch 1998: 173) from the Home Office, the police and Crime Concern (which raises some important questions about the legitimacy of different voices (Koch 1999: 186) and the relative powerlessness of others to be heard). What was crucial to the success of the Priority Estates Project[1] was not only the structures (for example, estate-based management and tenant consultation) but the quality and commitment of the people who implemented them (see Foster and Hope 1993). Similarly the dedication of a tiny number of residents can be pivotal to turning an estate around. Yet, for a variety of reasons which I discuss later in this chapter it is very easy to lose sight of these vital 'people pieces'.

Problem definition

Specificity is crucial to successful crime prevention and the need to know *where* the problem is and *what* the problem is (which often differs from what it appears to be at superficial glance) is crucial. Furthermore, it is important to acknowledge that 'preventing crime is difficult: ... there is no agreement about how to prevent it; crime prevention is not the responsibility of any one agency; local effects are constrained by national policies ... (and) co-ordinating the input of agencies in high crime areas can be difficult to organise' (Bright 1997: 81).

These difficulties of course shape agency preferences for certain types of crime prevention (i.e. those that are relatively straightforward). Yet in order to be effective crime prevention programmes need to acknowledge and understand the complexity which exists. This process begins with properly defining 'community' and the role of communities in crime prevention.

'Community' is a much overused and little understood phrase, which 'does not have one single meaning, but many' (Crow and Allan 1994: 3). Although communities are often defined by territory or place, which is the approach I take here, 'communities of interest' are equally important and need not be geographically defined (Willmott 1986). Simply because people share a given geographic space does not mean they have similar sentiments or investment in a particular neighbourhood (indeed, as I observed in the battle over public housing on the Isle of Dogs, there may be a series of competing and conflicting interests (Foster 1996, 1999a). Gender, ethnicity, age, social class, length of residence and a broad range of other factors influence the sense of attachment or commitment people have (Willmott, 1986). Understanding and exploiting these attachments are crucial in terms of community crime prevention and community development more generally.

'Community' is 'a "feelgood" word', deeply embedded in our psyches, with an in-built assumption that it is 'a "good thing" ' (Hughes 1998: 105). Perhaps because of our fondness for it, community has become a convenient political and rhetorical device used like 'an aerosol can, to be sprayed on to any social programme, giving it a more progressive and sympathetic cachet' (Cochrane 1986: 51). This 'imprecise aura of vacuous virtue' (Reiner and Cross 1991: 10) is precisely why many academics are deeply antithetical to notions of community (Hughes 1998).

In terms of its value for tackling crime 'there are a number of fundamental confusions about the role and nature of "community" ' including 'an assumption that *more community equals less crime*' (Crawford 1998b: 243). Bright (1997: 34) suggests that while communities 'certainly have a vital and important role' and that there are examples where 'some community organisations have struggled impressively and sometimes successfully against overwhelming problems ... ten years of research in the UK and the United States suggests that their capacity to resolve crime and disorder problems is often overstated'. Furthermore, the extent of the 'polarisation' in some of

173

Britain's most deprived estates makes 'self-sustaining improvements unlikely or impossible' without ongoing 'intervention and special support' (Power and Tunstall 1995: 67).

I have often been struck by the stark contrast between the taken for granted world that ethnographers explore and the assumed and perhaps oversimplified world that practitioners and politicians sometimes construct. This is not necessarily their 'fault' – it is in part the result of the nature and organisation of their own social worlds and limited 'windows' they have into those of others, particularly the desperate and needy. This was ably illustrated during an interview with an executive from the Docklands Development Corporation. I had asked her about the local 'community'.

> 'I think we have this sort of romantic notion put around by things like *The Archers* and *Coronation Street* and we say, ah that's the community – but you tell me anywhere real nowadays, anywhere in Britain, including in villages, that lives like *The Archers* or *Coronation Street*. That's a romantic notion of community. You tell me what you mean by community and I'll tell you whether there's any sense of it round here.' I suggested a sense of belonging, an interrelatedness, particularly prevalent among those who had lived in an area for a long time and had extended family. 'There is heaps of that' she replied: 'To that extent the East End because of its traditional deprivation is still sort of many years behind the rest of Britain. Where in the rest of Britain do you have extended family patterns? Nowhere ... people don't have extended families anymore and that's becoming true here as well. However, having said that, I do think the Island is one of the last bastions of it.'
>
> (Foster 1999a: 294)

The notion that 'community' can only be discovered in fictional radio and television programmes rather than anything which relates to lived experience would surprise not simply established Isle of Dogs residents but many people up and down the country where disadvantage limits geographical mobility and where local networks (particularly among women) are vital sources of support. Stereotypical views also existed among staff on a London housing estate (Riverside) which was described by the housing manager as a ' "cesspool" where it was not "so much the problems of the estate as the problem people" '. His colleague said 'I think the overall consensus is that Riverside is a hostile place'. (Foster 1995: 567–8) These descriptions contrasted significantly with residents' perceptions:

'I don't think it's a particularly unpleasant estate ... You get the sort of odd people but I must say there's not a lot of animosity ... I think in some ways it's quite a family estate ... lots of grandparents and grandchildren living in the estate as well ... It just seems that most people know most of the people on the estate, if not to talk to, to nod to ... and I never get the feeling that there's a lot of ... bad feeling.'

(Foster 1995: 567–8)

One of the key assumptions made about high crime communities is that they are defeated, lack cohesion and are highly disorganised. However, what appears disorganised to an outsider may in fact have quite structured and well understood criminal hierarchies, and sometimes well established organised crime networks, within it. This was aptly demonstrated by Walklate's (1998: 558) research on a Salford estate and expressed as: 'I can't name any names but what's his face up the road will sort it out'. Taylor (1999: 168) argues that it is precisely in areas of long-term economic disadvantage and decline that 'new organized crime "syndicates" have developed'. For obvious reasons then crime may not be a good organising vehicle for community development (Crawford 1998a: 159; Gilling 1997: 195) in these neighbourhoods. There is also an assumption made by agencies and politicians that victims and offenders are two distinct groups (which they are not) and to assume that offenders are committed to lawlessness *per se* and cannot act in the public 'good'. At a local level these kinds of stereotypes are unhelpful (given the concentration of offenders often residing within high crime neighbourhoods, and the patterns of victimisation within them) and ignore the complexity (for example, in both the estates I observed for the PEP evaluation there were high-profile individuals seeking to make their estates safer places who had criminal records).

The need to 'define' or 'profile' communities is often regarded by practitioners to be a luxury which has little relevance to doing their jobs. Yet, many efforts to galvanise, develop and work with 'the community' end in failure precisely because this has not been done. The challenges facing high crime neighbourhoods, their connections with globalisation and other broader socio-economic change (for example with increasing individualism and changing patterns of trust), the competing interests and demands among different groups of people, the fact that different localities have different 'community careers' (Bottoms and Wiles 1986) and characteristics, and diverse, different and often competing needs which eschew the often formulaic and standardised agency approaches – is rarely understood by practitioners. Indeed, as Smith notes, 'in practice hasty and superficial judgements have often been made about what can be changed most easily' and such decisions are largely decontextualised without the 'people pieces' being properly considered. Yet, as Walklate (1998), in a study of two high crime neighbourhoods, notes, it is vital to understand

> the processes which differently place different communities and different sections of communities in relation [to] crime and their routine management of crime related problems. A facet of what Massey (1995) has referred to as the layering of communities. Such an understanding renders universal policy responses highly problematic, politically difficult to manage, yet nevertheless a real issue, *if* the purpose of such processes is still to make a difference. This implies, at a minimum, the need for a much more carefully and locally nuanced approach to the policy process.
>
> (Walklate 1998: 567–8, emphasis in the original)

As my research on Riverside demonstrated these differences may even involve different solutions *within* particular sections or housing blocks on a single estate (see Foster 1995). 'While the problems of such areas will not be resolved by prevention strategies alone' Bright (1997: 112) argues 'there is plenty of evidence that well-planned preventive measures can make a difference – sometimes a big difference. They can reduce the impact of crime on victims, improve the life chances of young people by halting their drift into offending and enhance the quality of life for everyone'.

People

In this section I want to focus on the 'people pieces' more significantly using two case studies from my own research in order to highlight the problems that structural disadvantage can promote and the ways in which the 'people pieces' can get left behind.

'The absence of future'

Although I have lived and researched in some of the poorest London Boroughs nothing prepared me for the desolation and hopelessness I encountered on Bladon, an estate on the outskirts of a Northern English city which ranks in the worst 5 per cent in the country on work poverty and 'breadline Britain' indicators (CASE 1998). In the three years we researched Bladon, despite what in many respects was a successful PEP initiative, crime and economic disadvantage intensified in some areas of the estate, and residents became increasingly polarised between a 'stable' group (some of whom were empowered by tenant consultation and saw the solution to the estate's problems as evicting 'problem' tenants and restricting access to the estate through allocations), and the increasingly stigmatised, but highly vulnerable subterranean culture, which included the young previously homeless, and families and individuals whose lives were often very chaotic and precarious. I am not going to discuss this research in any detail here as it has been published elsewhere (Foster and Hope 1993; Hope and Foster 1992), what I want to focus on is the impact that conducting this fieldwork had on me and my return to the estate a decade later, and to link these experiences into my broader argument about the need to understand and take account of the 'people pieces' more fully.

I was traumatised by the end of my fieldwork on Bladon. I had witnessed the emergence of an injecting drug problem almost overnight at the height of the AIDS epidemic. I had met an alcoholic agoraphobic who was a prisoner in his high-rise flat and who, perhaps as an act of pure frustration or 'because of the voices in his head' (his probation officer's explanation), eventually threw his only source of entertainment (the television) out of the window. Fortunately no one was on the ground several floors below when it landed. Even with my ethnographer's hat on I tried to avoid the drunks hanging around the shops (because I, like most of the residents, was scared of them and their abuse) and my stomach turned over when the caretaker described how a resident found a man 'laying on the doorstep with a cider bottle in his hand and … a gas canister in the doorway with the top off'. He told me: 'they do it, don't they, when they can't get the booze and what not'. 'There's so many queer people walking about' one of the residents explained, including, it turned out, a sex offender using the local telephone box to lure children to his flat (Foster and Hope 1993: 61).

Late one summer evening I saw a young child scale a high fence, jump onto the top of the porch, crawl up the drainpipe and climb into the house through a fan light window. The speed and agility with which he did this suggested it was not the first time. At a bus stop a young toddler sat in his buggy continuously repeating a series of swear words. His mother gave up after three attempts to stop him. I had never seen before, or indeed since, so many women who had been battered and bruised. Yet, despite all the problems around them, some residents seemed to insulate themselves from the manifold problems.

I never felt comfortable on Bladon (which I always attributed at the time to being so far away from home, now I wonder whether it was also due to the sheer intensity and nature of the problems which created such instability). Yet, people from all parts of the estate welcomed me, let me into their homes and were willing to help with the research. They were often astounded that I had come *all* the way from London *just* (as they put it) to talk to them about their experiences of living on the estate (and I lost count of the number of times people asked me if I'd had elocution lessons!). Most of all, though, despite all of the difficulties, there were still people who were willing to fight, who were committed to making the estate a better place to live.

When I left Bladon for the last time in 1990 I wondered how people would survive. I was also convinced that the frustrations, conflicts and tensions would eventually lead to a spontaneous riot. I was wrong. When I returned a decade later there had been no riot but this time the housing managers views that 'things' were 'very bad' and that 'the general situation on the estate' was causing 'alarm' chimed with my brief experience on returning (see Foster 2000: 320). Although the physical improvements, implemented in conjunction with the PEP initiative, had held up quite well (a real achievement over a ten-year process of sustained decline) there were 'hundreds of empty properties' and high tenant turnover (both elements which the PEP model suggests need to be tackled at an early stage to gain stability). The injecting drug culture which had just begun in the late 1980s (based largely on GP prescribed drugs) had become an endemic heroin culture. As if it did not have enough to deal with already Bladon was now being 'labelled the heroin capital [of the city] and [the city was] being labelled as the heroin capital of the North' (Foster 2000: 321). The tower blocks which had been a central focus of activity in the late 1980s were still 'big issues ... full of single, young people who have no support, no positive role models around them and the only thing they respond to is the peer group environment that they're thrust into' (Foster 2000: 321). This description was almost identical to ones uttered ten years earlier. Housing staff, still estate based, said that they 'felt under siege, reticent and sometimes fearful of encountering difficult and potentially volatile tenants, and of the risks associated with drugs paraphernalia' (Foster 2000: 322). What had once been a limited and isolated drug 'problem' (which was not very public) had now taken on a very different character.

McAuley (2000), in a compelling ethnography of drugs, crime and social exclusion on a poor housing estate in the Midlands, suggests that 'a social world with no control of its future' leaves 'crime and illicit drug-use as the only means of managing time and space', a view shared by the housing manager on Bladon who suggested that an 'escalating cycle of despondency' left 'drugs [to] fill the void'. 'They do it', he said, 'to make life bearable. They do it to feel normal' (Foster 2000: 322).

The impact of intergenerational unemployment had left people with no hope, or any

> '... expectation of a future ... partly because of what they've experienced, and what their parents have experienced, has been an absence of future. They have no concept of my idea [which] is to have a job, with a family, have a holiday twice a year ... All they can see is the very short-term future ... There don't appear to be any expanding job opportunities and so why should I conform? That's my rationale for it. What do I gain by conforming? All the horizons are short term and in the short term they gain by not conforming.'
> (Senior police officer, in Foster 2000: 322)

In these circumstances the rhetoric about communities and their potential to tackle crime seem rather problematic. As I will discuss later, bottom-up approaches which involve and work with communities are vital to successful crime prevention but these have to work alongside attempts to tackle structural disadvantage. As Crawford (1998b: 244) argues, the 'discourse' of community safety is highly problematic if it 'becomes the responsibility of the community' without proper thought being 'given to the place occupied by a community within a wider political economy and how this may sustain crime or undermine efforts at community crime prevention'. In Bladon, the police and local authority were acutely aware of the problems that long-term unemployment had wrought and voiced strong feelings of powerlessness (see Foster 2000) about the situation (another vital element in the 'people pieces').

Campbell's (1993: 244) analysis of the estates where riots occurred in the early 1990s suggested that angry young men 'admired and serviced' a 'criminalized brotherhood' while women strove to develop networks and generate 'solidarity and self-help' (pp.247, 319). There is perhaps little that is new in this. But what is more recent is the volume and longevity of 'status ZerO' (the young unemployed, not in education or training, Williamson 1997), its impact on young men's ability to make the transition into adulthood and the resulting absence of a 'stake or recognized role in their communities' (Power and Tunstall 1995). The process of being excluded and excluding is neatly summarised by Young (1998: 71) as a 'dialectic': 'They are excluded, they create an identity which is rejecting and exclusive, they exclude others by aggression and dismissal, and they are, in turn, excluded and dismissed by others.'

Sennett (1998: 146) argues that 'The indifference of the old class-bound capitalism was starkly material; the indifference which radiates out of flexible capitalism is more personal because the system itself is less starkly etched, less legible in form'. Drawing on the work of philosopher Paul Ricoeur, Sennett suggests that our stake in conformity is linked to feeling needed:

> 'Who needs me?' is a question of radical character which suffers a radical change in modern capitalism. The system radiates indifference. It does so in terms of the outcomes of human striving, as in winner-take-all markets, where there is little connection between risk and reward. It radiates indifference in the organization of absence of trust, where there is no reason to be needed. And it does so through re-egineering of institutions in which people are treated as disposable. Such practices obviously and brutally diminish the sense of mattering as a person, of being necessary to others.
>
> (Sennett 1998: 146)

Interestingly Komiya's (1999: 381–4) account of the role of informal social control and low crime rates in Japan mirrors Sennett's comments: 'The Japanese tolerate strong informal social control because in return they are supported and cared for by the (inner-circle) *uchi*-type group … what is important for crime prevention is not to care about others, but to be cared about by others'.

Shane Blackman's (1997: 120) ethnographic study of homeless youngsters in Brighton graphically conveys the sense of not being 'needed' and the 'emptiness' of their lives. Constantly faced with feelings of failure and being 'unable to meet people's expectations of them' one youngster described the experience as: 'It's almost as though you've died in your mind. There's nothing there at all' (p.120). Their bodies became the only 'personal capital' which remained and 'the last thing over which they can exercise control or choice' (p.118). The leap of faith required to move on from their situation was made all the harder by an 'aware[ness] of the futility of risking more, when their own experience of being told they are a failure led them to conclude that the outcome would be defeat' (Blackman 1997: 116–17).

The experience of exclusion may also have a fundamental influence on attitudes. Williamson's (1997: 77) research, for example, suggests that, unlike 'earlier studies of youth in transition, in which young people tended to blame themselves for their predicament', those he observed 'seemed to believe quite genuinely that they had been let down by others: politicians, professionals, parents'. My experiences in Bladon leave me with very similar emotions. It was obvious a decade ago that the housing allocation process needed to be tackled. It was self-evident that young people needed more supportive structures and it was obvious something needed to be done about drug misuse (indeed all of these issues were highlighted in our report). Yet more young people were housed there without adequate support, the drug problem was allowed to proliferate and intensify (with no intervention for many years) and somehow these problems were seen as simply inevitable rather than preventable. Even when Bladon's drug problems hit epidemic proportions in the late 1990s, the Health Authority did not introduce a needle exchange scheme or a methadone programme despite the improvement this might have produced (see Parker *et al* 1998) and police crackdown on drugs dealing in the area had some unintended and very negative consequences (see Foster 2000).

'This is where we go'

A very different, but none the less pernicious, exclusion occurred on the Isle of Dogs in London's Docklands. During two years of ethnographic research I sought to examine urban change and conflict from a variety of different perspectives – from the 'powerful' vested with regenerating the area; the previously well established (white) island families who had once worked in the docks and related industries (who perceived the Island to be 'theirs'); and a range of 'newcomers' (those who moved as a result of slum clearance in the 1960s, the predominantly Bengali house-holds forced there by a one-offer only housing policy and the affluent residents drawn to Docklands by the development itself).

The Docklands regeneration programme occurred at an unparalleled speed and scale. Yet for some time, especially for many of the poorer and more marginalised Island residents, the development was a very distant entity. As one put it: 'The thing is just so big that you can't relate to it' (Foster 1999a: 249). In its early phases little attempt was made to include pre-existing local residents in the development process. It was an archetypal 'top-down' approach. Excluded and unable to fight the actual and symbolic might of the powerful development machine was one thing, but when the neighbourhood councillors were seen to prioritise the housing of homeless families (predominantly Bengali) over the interests of 'local' and well established (white) Island families in 'their' housing (i.e. council housing) in 'their' part of the island (which was also being encroached upon by the erection of new owner occupied housing on vacant land and former industrial buildings) anger and frustration erupted and Bengali households, frequently forced to move to the Island against their will (because of its racist reputation), became scapegoats for 'local' white people's frustrations (Foster 1999a: 251). The result was frightening racial abuse and harassment. The battle for public housing and the racism which emanated from it has been published elsewhere (see Foster 1996, 1999a); my reason for mentioning it here is to demonstrate how important it is that agencies actually consider the impact of their policies on the 'people pieces' and seek to prevent harms resulting from them.

On the Isle of Dogs, the local authority and the Development Corporation refused to listen to the concerns of white Island families about the public housing crisis. Indeed a local councillor said 'they think because they have lived on the Island for a long time it gives them the God-given right to live here and have their sons and daughters living here. We can't work with them. That is the only explanation they have' (Foster 1999a: 277). Yet, as a former councillor observed: 'the con-frontational approach … is very counterproductive. It makes things worse to say to people: 'Get stuffed, we believe that homeless families should have priority. We don't care whether you get housing or not.' (Foster 1999a: 278). Furthermore, the Bengali families housed on the island were not satisfied either because they rightly felt that they had become 'pawns in many different games' (Foster 1999a: 278).

What was a very complex situation, and one which speaks volumes about the multi-faceted elements of powerlessness, was of course ripe for oversimplification. While the local authority, Development Corporation and councillors closed their ears, others, including the British National Party, were ready to listen (and exploit the situation) and in 1993 the Isle of Dogs became infamous for electing the first BNP councillor. These events ably demonstrate that a relatively small number of individuals *can* have a real (and in this case highly negative) impact.

Taylor (1999: 126) suggests that in market society 'issues of *difference* and widening *inequality*' result in 'tribalism' (Maffesoli 1995; Walzer 1992), not only expressed between nation-states but also *within* different elements of nation-states with groups desiring 'special status'. What I observed in the Isle of Dogs was a classic example of this. Sadly it was not an isolated case. As I write 12,000 people in Oldham voted for a British National Party candidate in the General Election of 2001.

Unsavoury as they are, these kinds of conflicts, tensions and divisions are perhaps inevitable in contested spaces. It is how they are managed which is crucial. If my experience in Docklands is anything to go by agencies rarely seem to be able to deal with them in anything other than inflexible and bureaucratic ways and rarely tackle the 'people pieces' head on.

The two case studies I have described in different ways exemplify the difficulties which have beset deprived neighbourhoods across Britain for decades because interventions have never 'succeeded in setting in motion a virtuous circle of regeneration, with improvements in jobs, crime, education, health and housing all reinforcing each other' (Social Exclusion Unit 1998: 1). This is precisely what the government hopes to achieve with a hugely ambitious agenda where the need for: 'investing in people, not just buildings; involving communities, not parachuting in solutions; developing integrated approaches with clear leadership; ensuring mainstream policies really work for the poorest neighbour-hoods; and making a long term commitment with sustained political priority' are all highlighted (Social Exclusion Unit 1998). For these to be realised another set of 'people pieces' need to be considered.

People and prevention

Shapland (1996: 355) argues that a great deal can, and has been, achieved at a *local* level to provide a positive basis for community crime prevention using bottom-up approaches. However, it is interesting that some of the most successful attempts to influence quality of life and reduce crime have not come from crime prevention initiatives *per se*. The Priority Estates Project, for example, sought to tackle poor housing management and encourage tenant consultation. A decade after the first PEP initiatives residents and housing staff in 15 of the 20 estates reported decreases in crime (Power and Tunstall 1995: 58). This is a significant achievement given the residualisation of public housing and that PEP tackles the most problematic estates and cannot get to the underlying structural problems (Power and Tunstall 1995: 57). The reasons for the success of PEPs is that their approach embraces people and processes.

> They act as facilitators within and between different groups of residents and act as a bridge between residents and the local authority. Their approach was also *local*: the estate bases provided hands-on control, direct contact with problems and the ability to respond to pressure. *Estates with a local office were easier to manage and better for residents.*
>
> (Power and Tunstall, 1995: 69)

The PEP approach also generates hope by demonstrating that change *is* possible and that by reforming structures and improving housing management, service delivery improves. As a resident on Bladon put it: 'I think PEP have brought the people together'. Another said: 'they rekindled the spirit of the people ... the attitude of the people definitely got better' (Foster and Hope 1993: 55–6). Of course PEP had not 'rekindled' *all* the people (and indeed the future of the estate was premised on a belief that *some* people should be forcibly removed and excluded) but as the balance between withdrawal and participation can be a fine one these changing attitudes were important and crucial elements for informal social control.

Informal social control is arguably one of the most important but still illusory elements of community crime prevention. Criminologists have frequently hypothesised that crime occurs in the poorest and most vulnerable areas because of the absence of informal social control yet my research on Riverside challenged the idea that informal social control is always absent in high crime areas (Foster 1995), while Baumgartner's (1988) work in a US suburb suggested that it was not informal social control but 'moral minimalism' which held the key to 'peace' in suburbia.

Despite the recognised importance of the public both in terms of crime recording and in their capacity to act as 'capable guardians' the importance of people in the crime prevention process is still frequently overlooked. Indeed high crime communities are often simply dismissed as apathetic, chaotic, disorganised and demoralised (thus letting agencies conveniently 'off the hook'). Perhaps because of these perceptions local authorities have enthusiastically endorsed situational techniques like CCTV to tackle their high crime neighbourhoods but have been more reluctant to support schemes which use people as preventive tools, for example concierge schemes. The underlying assumption is that (a) the technology is enough and (b) that it is the most appropriate (or at least most convenient) mechanism to tackle crime and disorder. Yet a few years ago most of our public spaces did not have CCTV and were not completely lawless. In all public space, whether high or low crime, 'the peace' is preserved 'by an intricate, almost unconscious, network of voluntary controls and standards among the people themselves, and enforced by the people themselves' (Jacobs 1961: 41). People can intervene, they can watch *and* act, they can negotiate and influence, and have an impact even in high crime neighbourhoods. Furthermore there are important questions about CCTV's value as a social control mechanism. Farr and Osborn's (1997) evaluation of CCTV and concierge schemes in high-rise housing blocks, for example, suggested that as long as appropriate housing allocation policies and good management were in place, the most successful schemes were 'intensive concierge' schemes with people situated in individual tower blocks (cited in Crawford 1998a). Technology can facilitate not compensate for people. It can also have unintended consequences, as in the CCTV scheme in the high-rise blocks on Bladon that ended up facilitating crime rather than preventing it by providing offenders living in the tower blocks with visual access (through mini TV screens in their flats) revealing who was entering and leaving the building. The security measures were predicated on an assumption that offenders lived outside not inside the blocks (even though the problems caused by some young tenants were well known at the time).

If the statutory agencies continue to seek technological solutions at the expense of people solutions (which also have a number of benefits, not least providing employment) they are likely to make matters worse. It has become a truism that fear of crime and its associated withdrawal from the public sphere has had a profound impact on crime and disorder (Wilson and Kelling 1982; Kelling and Coles 1997). However, an over reliance on technology may, as Smith (2000: 160) argues, become counter-productive diminishing both 'self-controls and community controls on criminal behaviour':

> If there are systems that make it physically impossible to avoid paying the fare on a public transport system, or to drive a vehicle faster than the speed limit, then people might become less inclined to pay the proper fare or stay within the speed limit in situations outside the control of these systems, because automatic external regulation had, over time, led to the erosion of internal self-regulation.

Although the prevailing trend rests in situational solutions (they are straightforward, though not necessarily cheap) there is some recognition that the loss of a range of intermediary individuals and agencies that once had a social control function (for example park keepers and caretakers) has left a void. It is hoped that the range of public and, increasingly, private sector services, for example neighbourhood wardens and private security, can act as agents of social control (Crawford 1998a: 137). Ironically this introduces yet another layer between the statutory agencies and the communities their services are supposed to reach.

The relationship between informal and formal social controls needs to be investigated more fully. Currently the criminal justice system receives vast sums of money while preventive efforts receive very little (and the majority of this goes on CCTV (Koch 1998)). Surely it makes sense to prevent (and to understand the complex processes that contribute to this) rather than invest so heavily in cleaning up the mess (especially as the mess is so much more difficult to tackle once it has become established).

Empowerment

Empowerment like 'community' is a much used but little understood phrase. In their evaluation of the City Challenge Programme, Hart *et al* (1997) examine both the dynamics of empowerment and the barriers to its enactment in practice. Their work is worthy of some detailed discussion. Hart *et al* (1997: 181) begin by highlighting the 'ironic' nature of empowerment, its use as a 'political tool' and its unintended consequences. They describe a 'multiplicity of ironies' in the empowerment message, the levels at which empowerment is offered (usually at an operational 'service-level' when the decisions which count are 'the stratégic [long-term economic] or structural [governmental] levels of decision making') and how the agencies themselves 'balance the practice with the rhetoric'. The result:

> The prime stakeholder who will ultimately determine the success or failure of the project is the community. Yet, at the strategic level, they have little or no real say in what happens to the area. Whilst they were consulted at the beginning of the project to determine what they assessed to be the prime targets for regeneration, time and again they are thwarted in their effort to exercise real control. In the final analysis of the level of power-holding, the inter-dependent relationship between agencies and the citizen is still top-down.
>
> (Hart *et al* 1997: 193)

Hart *et al* (1997: 197) argue that what in effect happens is that the pro-cesses designed to empower actually disempower and ironically 'increase the power of the power holders because they are failing to relinquish power in any meaningful way'. Furthermore, 'local service providers cannot deliver the participation that local residents demand, because they do not have the power to do so, their real accountability is elsewhere' (p.200). Consequently, despite the 'espoused' importance of consultation 'decisions that were to involve local people are increasingly being framed by professional staff *prior* to the consultation process' thus producing a 'reconsolidation of professional power' (p.198). Hart *et al* (1997: 199) suggest: 'Individuals are making decisions on behalf of the organisation in order that decision making is seen to be being done' to (a) 'get the job done' and (b) 'be managerially accountable' to government departments. So at a time where empowerment and bottom-up strategies are crucial Hart *et al* suggest that 'an inverse relationship is developing, the less power people feel they have, the more power is being taken by professionals to compensate and fill potential vacuums in the decision-making process and structures'.

Tam (1995: 130) suggests that in order to empower agencies must believe in empowerment and empowered structures. 'Many local authorities', he argues, 'need to move on from looking after the needs of their customers as they perceive them, to working with their customers in determining what those needs are and how they are best met from the perspective of the customers themselves' (Tam 1995: 135). This was ably demonstrated by a resident on the London PEP where the housing manager was not receptive to their approach:

'I think PEP could perhaps educate estate management into liaising with people ... if they could perhaps educate them that we're trying to foster community relationships rather than destroy 'em and rather than try and get a "them" and "us" situation which it obviously is at the moment, they should be trying to say they [the tenants] are the customer and you should be working with them not against them.'

(Hope and Foster 1992: 32)

If this kind of empowerment does not occur the result is what Hart *et al* describe as the 'disempowerment process' (see Figure 2).

The reluctance to relinquish power is based on a belief 'that people outside government have neither the understanding nor the sense of responsibility to be entrusted with any significant share of governmental power'. Yet as Tam (1995: 135) continues, 'most people respond positively when given real responsibility to deal with important issues' while 'the experience of being entrusted with important matters affecting the whole community in turn strengthens the sense of civic responsibility'. Despite the importance of empowerment agencies still talk *at* people. As this senior figure from the Docklands Development Corporation reflected: 'Our communication really left a lot to be desired because we didn't talk, we didn't talk things through, which means we didn't talk to people. We tended to talk at them' (Foster 1999a: 348). Yet,

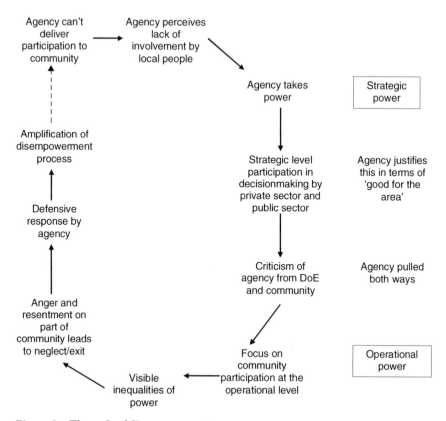

Figure 2   *The cycle of disempowerment*

Source: Hart *et al* (1997: 199)

as a senior police officer discovered, after being exposed to the community literature for the first time, it is important 'to listen and not just talk!' (Wing, forthcoming). Of course this is precisely what ethnographers do.

It is essential to work with and alongside not for or on behalf of communities because, as Hill (1994: 193) highlights: 'Local people have to feel that they are stakeholders in the process, and that they have something to contribute as well as receive'. However, this is difficult and needs to be acknowledged as such from the outset. As Hill argues: 'Balancing proactive urban initiatives between a multiplicity of local actors with the demands of community responsibility and responsiveness is a major task. So, too, is balancing social with economic objectives'. One of the keys to achieving this has to be linkages between the strategic and practical levels. The success of PEP is that it operates on the ground at a practical level but also seeks to influence strategic direction (e.g. by enforcing estate-based housing models in the areas where they operate).

Hart *et al*'s analysis of the City Challenge Programme has some depressing and uncomfortable resonance with the processes and practice of the Crime and Disorder Act 1998. Public consultation is now a mandatory requirement on the police and local authority but this has tended to be approached in an instrumental (i.e. 'let's get the job done if we *have* to do it') rather than in a creative or empowering manner. Recently focus groups and citizens panels have burgeoned as devices to ascertain public opinion. Yet there is little discussion about the representativeness of these panels or how reliable they are as a method for consultation or for formulating policy. Focus groups do have the advantage of being people focused but they tend to be short, de-contextualised snippets with no sense of being able to place these views into their broader framework.

To be fair it is difficult to do consultation well without detailed appreciation of individual localities and complex and competing communities within them (the first round of Crime and Disorder audits did not achieve this). Furthermore, in instrumental terms it is much easier for agencies to work with the highest-profile (though not necessarily representative) 'community members' and single-issue 'interest groups' or locally elected councillors and then to present these as 'the community' view. My research has made me very cynical about the abilities of local politicians and some 'community leaders' to 'represent' people. Perhaps because of the difference and diversity discussed earlier it is impossible to expect a few individuals to 'represent' a plethora of views, and for this reason alone perhaps we require a broader framework for consultation and representation than we currently possess. As Crawford (1998a: 268) argues: 'to ensure that security is perceived of as a "public good", rather than a "club good", the discourse of community safety should not be allowed to be captured by exclusionary politics or parochialism'. However, at present, as Bailey (1995: 220) notes:

[Partnerships] represent relatively closed institutions by which dominant local stakeholders collaborate in order to achieve partial definitions of the public interest. These definitions are largely determined by technocratic rather than democratic processes where dominant interests (which in some cases might include the local authority and sections of the local community) structure the boundaries of the debate in their own interests.

Partnerships: can they deliver?

> … rather than constituting an easy solution to the crime problem, crime prevention has opened up a new Pandora's box of questions about appropriate roles, responsibilities and legitimacy.
>
> (Crawford 1998a: 63)

Partnership may be an appealing philosophy but appears to be more about 'rhetoric' than reality (see Gilling 1997: 196), but one which is now so deeply embedded, rather like neighbourhood watch, that there is a political imperative to keep fuelling it despite its current inadequacies. The research literature suggests that partnership rarely 'works': there are deeply embedded cultural differences, power relationships and agendas between agencies which are rarely confronted and limit their ability to deliver in practice (Crawford 1997, 1998a, 1998b; Gilling 1997).

It is an interesting irony that while the inclusion of local authorities in the community safety framework was intended to broaden account-abilities, in practice the local authorities have generally allowed their community safety strategies to be directed by the police (who have presented themselves as the 'experts' and many of whom feel deeply defensive about the possibility of some of their responsibilities being wrested from them).

I am not convinced that local authorities were the right agency to share the community safety function. Although the assumptions were politically understandable and were intended to create 'greater long-term and strategic oversight, commitment and funding' and that 'local authorities would connect local community safety directly to the local democratic structure, and … enhance its legitimacy' (Crawford 1998a: 48), the massive failings of local authorities in relation to public housing and quality of life in high crime areas (Power 1987) made this decision practically highly questionable. Koch (1998: 185) suggests that local authorities' 'desire for statutory responsibility' may have been 'influenced by self-serving professional interests' especially at a time when there is a 'crisis in competence' and declining faith in the public sector (Lasch 1995).

The police have suffered a similar crisis of public confidence in recent years (see Morgan and Newburn 1997). Their role, while central to crime prevention, has been overestimated because 'in our concern over crime, we have mistakenly though understandably turned for help to the most visible and familiar part of the criminal justice system and thereby made the police both the object of our hopes and the target of our frustrations' (Wilson 1985: 74). The police have also been the most dominant group at the partnership table (and their action-oriented culture makes it likely this will continue), but like the rest of the public sector they do not have external 'customer'-driven focus or empowered management structures.

Far from being open and reflexive about the problems of partnership many statutory agencies, driven by managerialism and performance measures, have developed a 'culture of congratulation' (Young 1999: 136) rather than reflexive practice. Increasingly too there is simply denial (see Cohen 2001). These responses are shaped by pressures from government whose 'political obsession with management and efficiency has led to an assumption that many of the issues facing the country could be dealt with simply by reorganising the relevant public services to make them more efficient and effective' (Faulkner 1998: 4, cited in Crawford 1998b: 243). Garland suggest that this was 'the easy route' for politicians because 'segregation and punishment' was far easier than seeking 'to embed social controls, regulate economic life, and develop policies that will enhance social inclusion and integration' (Garland 2001: 203).

These trends suggest that if the 'people pieces' are to have greater prominence in crime prevention then an independent chair (or ombudsperson) is required in order for partnerships to deliver rather than simply talk, who can remind agencies *why* they are there (to solve joint problems, not to cynically meet performance targets), who can counteract tendencies towards outputs rather than outcomes, and who can provide stability in the face of ever changing personnel. This is vital because, as Crawford points out:

> The *intra*-organisational focus on 'outputs' can make agencies concentrate their energies upon their core tasks and activities at the expense of peripheral ones. Community safety, by its very nature, is precisely one such peripheral function of diverse agencies. Perversely, managerialist reforms may actually serve to push government departments and public sector agencies further into prioritising their own introspective needs at the expense of collaborative and inter-organisational commitments.
>
> (Crawford 1998b: 248)

Politicians, policymakers and practitioners must also recognise that there are *no* quick fixes. This is difficult in a culture where, as this LDDC official put it, 'Ministers and civil servants don't like to take decisions before they have to', where 'the emphasis is on trying to be just in time rather than prophetic', and where 'the cycle of parliamentary elections [and] civil servants whizzing about from job to job at huge speed' results in little continuity:

> 'There's nobody there who you agree the thing with [who] is gonna
> be there the following day. The civil service are extraordinary in
> this way, … and they do this I'm jolly sure deliberately … the
> politicians are electoral cycle and they're all playing their game of
> musical chairs and the civil servants know very well that they're
> not gonna be there when the consequences of their efforts are
> matured.'
>
> (Foster 1999a: 319–20)

Commitment and courage are required. Not withstanding the sustained
efforts of a few individuals these characteristics seem to be in rather
short supply!

Where do we go from here?

I believe we need to radically reform our public sector agencies to move
forward and we need to properly equip them with the tools to do their
difficult jobs. This view has been shaped most fundamentally through
my work with senior police officers. I was surprised by their limited
knowledge about the communities they policed, their reluctance to
embrace the complex dynamics which ought to have shaped their
response (because it made their role less clear-cut and more complex),
how little they know about crime and the criminological research which
could support their work, and how many failed even to ask what it was
they were seeking to achieve. This situation is typical of many agencies,
not just the police, and highlights the need for evidence-based practice
(Sherman 1998) and the role of a facilitator or intermediary who can
challenge inner-circle assumptions and encourage 'real' rather
than pseudo-partnership working. Why is this so crucial? Because it is
too important not to get it right. The millions of people in Britain who
live in poverty, many of them children growing up in deplorable
conditions with little hope and few opportunities, should expect
agencies to deliver a good service. Yet almost inexorably many of those
children will be cascading into the criminal justice system in just a few
years.

Criminologists have proved themselves to be good critics of what is
'wrong' with public attitudes to crime and criminal justice, politicians'
pronouncements and the management of crime. We have deconstructed
the multiple realities which operate behind the rhetoric and challenged

the simplistic knee-jerk and populist policies from ones which in principle might seem to have a chance of working on the ground. But perhaps we need to move one step further and try to have a more fundamental impact on practice. As Paul Ekblom (personal communication) wrote: 'converting the knowledge we create into practice is pretty vital to justifying our existence'.

We should not allow criminal justice policies to be driven by the whims of individual ministers and what is perceived to be 'popular' with '*Sun* readers' (Koch 1998: 175). We must not allow agencies to bury their heads in the sand and focus only on performance indicators. We must not forget the importance of the 'people pieces', because without these and the structural difficulties which shape them we can never hope to have any lasting impact on crime.

Note

1 The PEP initiative was set up to tackle some of the most difficult to let estates during the 1980s. The initiative, funded by the then Department of the Environment, had two central features: estate based housing management and tenant consultation. PEP consultants acted as facilitators encouraging the local authority to improve aspects of their service delivery (particularly tackling voids; the physical infrastructure; and other housing services like caretaking), and worked with tenants to improve consultation mechanisms, and the quality of life. The PEPs not only delivered improved housing management and a range of housing services alongside increased levels of tenant satisfaction but also appeared to have an impact on levels of crime.

References

Bailey, N. (1995) *Partnership Agencies in British Urban Policy*. London: UCL Press.

Baumgartner, M. (1988) *The Moral Order of the Suburb*. Oxford: Oxford University Press.

Blackman, S.J. (1997) 'Destructing a Giro': A Critical and Ethnographic Study of the Youth 'Underclass', in R. MacDonald (ed.), *Youth, the 'Underclass' and Social Exclusion*. London: Routledge, pp.113–29.

Bottoms, A. and Wiles, P. (1986) 'Housing Tenure and Residential Community Crime Careers in Britain', in A.J. Reiss and M. Tonry (eds), *Communities and Crime: Crime and Justice: A Review of Research*, Vol. 8. Chicago: University of Chicago Press, pp.101–62.

Bright, J. (1997) *Turning the Tide: Crime, Community and Prevention*. London: Demos.

Campbell, B. (1993) *Goliath: Britain's Dangerous Places*. London: Methuen.

Centre for the Analysis of Social Exclusion (CASE) (1998) Unpublished figures provided from data sets.

Cochrane, A. (1986) 'Community Politics and Democracy', in D. Held and C. Pollitt (eds), *New Forms of Democracy*. London: Sage.

Cohen, A. (1989) *The Symbolic Construction of Community*. London: Routledge (originally published 1985).

Cohen, S. (2001) *States of Denial: Knowing about Atrocities and Suffering*. Cambridge: Polity.

Crawford, A. (1997) *The Local Governance of Crime: Appeals to Community and Partnerships*. Oxford: Clarendon Press.

Crawford, A. (1998a) *Crime Prevention and Community Safety: Politics, Policies and Practices*. Harlow: Addison Wesley Longman.

Crawford, A. (1998b) 'Community Safety and the Quest for Security: Holding Back the Dynamics of Social Exclusion', *Policy Studies*, 19 (3/4), 237–53.

Crow, G. and Allan, G. (1994) *Community Life: An Introduction to Local Social Relations*. New York: Harvester Wheatsheaf.

Farr, J. and Osborn, S. (1997) *High Hopes: Concierge Controlled Entry and Similar Schemes for High Rise Blocks*. London: Department of the Environment (cited in Crawford 1998a).

Faulkner, D. (1998) 'A Principled Response', *Criminal Justice Matters*, 31, 4–5.

Foster, J. (1990) *Villains: Crime and Community in the Inner City*. London: Routledge.

Foster, J. (1992) 'Living with the Docklands' Redevelopment: community view from the Isle of Dogs', *London Journal*, 17 (2), 170–82.

Foster, J. (1995) 'Informal Social Control and Community Crime Prevention', *British Journal of Criminology*, 34 (4), 563–84.

Foster, J. (1996) ' "Island Homes for Island People": Competition, Conflict and Racism in the Battle over Public Housing on the Isle of Dogs', in C. Samson and N. South (eds), *The Social Construction of Social Policy: Methodologies, Racism, Citizenship and the Environment*. London: Macmillan pp.148–68.

Foster, J. (1997) 'Challenging perceptions: "community" and neighbourliness on a difficult to let estate", in J. Jewson and S. Macgregor (eds), *Transforming Cities: Contested Governance and New Spatial Divisions*. London: Routledge.

Foster, J. (1999a) *Docklands: Cultures in Conflict, Worlds in Collision*. London: UCL Press.

Foster, J. (1999b) 'Memorandum on Police Recruitment and Training', in the Home Affairs Select Committee evidence to the *Inquiry into Police Training and Recruitment*. London, HMSO, pp.205–15.

Foster, J. (2000) 'Social Exclusion, Crime and Drugs', *Drugs: Education, Prevention and Policy*, 7 (4), 317–30.

Foster, J. and Hope, T. (1993) *Housing, Community and Crime: the Impact of the Priority Estates Project*, Home Office Research Study No. 131. London: HMSO.

Gans, H. (1982) 'The Participant Observer as Human Being: Observations on the

Personal Aspects of Fieldwork', in R. Burgess (ed.), *Field Research: A Sourcebook and Field Manual*. London: Routledge. pp.53–61.

Garland, D. (2001) *The Culture of Control: Crime and Social Order in Contemporary Society*. Oxford: Oxford University Press.

Giddens, A. (1990) *The Consequences of Modernity*. Cambridge: Polity.

Gilling, D. (1997) *Crime Prevention: Theory, Policy and Politics*. London: UCL Press.

Hart, C., Jones, K. and Bains, M. (1997) 'Do the People Want Power? The Social Responsibilities of Empowering Communities', in P. Hoggett (ed.), *Contested Communities: Experiences, Struggles, Policies*. Bristol: Policy Press.

Hill, D. (1994) *Citizens and Cities: Urban Policy in the 1990s*. Hemel Hempstead: Harvester Wheatsheaf.

Hirst, P. (1994) *Associative Democracy: New Forms of Social Governance* Cambridge: Polity.

Hope, T. (1995) 'Community Crime Prevention', in M. Tonry and D.P. Farrington (eds), *Building A Safer Society: Strategic Approaches to Crime Prevention*, Crime and Justice, Vol. 19. Chicago: University of Chicago Press, pp.21–89.

Hope, T. and Foster, J. (1992) 'Conflicting Forces Changing the Dynamics of Crime and Community on "Problem" Estates', *British Journal of Criminology*, 32 (4), 488–503.

Hughes, G. (1998) *Understanding Crime Prevention: Social Control, Risk and Late Modernity*. Buckingham: Open University Press.

Jacobs, J. (1961) *The Death and Life of Great American Cities*. New York: Random House.

Kelling, G. and Coles, C. (1997) *Fixing Broken Windows: Restoring Order and Reducing Crime in Our Communities*. New York: Free Press.

Koch, B. (1998) *The Politics of Crime Prevention*. Aldershot: Ashgate.

Komiya, N. (1999) 'A Cultural Study of the Low Crime Rate in Japan', *British Journal of Criminology*, 39 (3), 369–90.

Lasch, C. (1995) *The Revolt of the Elites and the Betrayal of Democracy*. New York: W.W. Norton.

McAuley, R. (2000) *The Enemy Within: Economic Marginalisation and the Impact of Crime on Young Adults*. PhD thesis, University of Cambridge.

Maffesoli, M. (1995) *The Time of the Tribes*. London: Sage.

Massey, D. (1995) *Spatial Divisions of Labour*. London: Macmillan.

Mirrlees-Black, C., Budd, T., Partridge, S. and Mayhew, P. (1998) *The 1998 British Crime Survey*, Home Office Statistical Bulletin, Issue 21/98. London: HMSO.

Morgan, R. and Newburn, T. (1997) *The Future of Policing*. Oxford: Clarendon Press.

Parker, H., Bury, C. and Eggington, R. (1998) *New Heroin Outbreaks Among Young People in England and Wales*, Police Research Group, Crime Prevention and Detection Series Paper 92. London: HMSO.

Power, A. (1987) *Property Before People*. London: Allen & Unwin.

Power, A. (1997) *Estates on the Edge*. London: Macmillan.

Power, A. and Tunstall, R. (1995) *Swimming Against the Tide: Polarisation or Progress on 20 Unpopular Council Estates, 1980–1995*. York: Joseph Rowntree.

Reiner, R. and Cross, M. (1991) 'Introduction: Beyond Law and Order – Crime and Criminology into the 1990s', in R. Reiner and M. Cross (eds), *Beyond Law and Order*. London: Macmillan.

Sennett, R. (1998) *The Corrosion of Character: The Personal Consequences of Work in the New Capitalism*. New York: W.W. Norton.

Shapland, J. (1996) 'Targeted Crime Reduction: the Needs of Local Groups', in T. Bennett (ed.), *Preventing Crime and Disorder: Targeting Strategies and Responsibilities*. Cambridge: Institute of Criminology Cropwood Series.

Sherman, L. (1998) *Evidence-Based Policing*. Washington, DC: Police Foundation.

Sibley, D. (1995) *Geographies of Exclusion*. London: Routledge.

Smith, D.J. (2000) 'Changing Situations and Changing People', in A. von Hirsch, D. Garland and A. Wakefield (eds), *Ethical and Social Perspectives on Situational Crime Prevention*. Oxford: Hart.

Social Exclusion Unit (1998) *Bringing Britain Together: A National Strategy for Neighbourhood Renewal*. London: Stationery Office.

Tam, H. (1995) 'Enabling Structures', in D. Atkinson (ed.), *Cities of Pride: Rebuilding Community, Refocusing Government*. London: Cassell, pp.129–37.

Taylor, I. (1999) *Crime in Context: A Critical Criminology of Market Societies*. Cambridge: Polity Press.

Walklate, S. (1998) 'Crime and Community: Fear or Trust?', *British Journal of Sociology*, 49 (4), 550–69.

Walzer, M. (1992) 'The New Tribalism: A Difficult Problem', *Dissent*, 39 (2), 164–71.

Williamson, H. (1997) 'Status ZerO Youth and the "Underclass": Some Considerations', in R. MacDonald (ed.), *Youth, the 'Underclass' and Social Exclusion*. London: Routledge, pp.70–82.

Willmott, P. (1986) *Social Networks, Informal Care and Public Policy*. London: Policy Studies Institute.

Wilson, J.Q. (1985) *Thinking about Crime*, 2nd edn. New York: Vintage Books.

Wilson, J.Q. and Kelling, G. (1982) 'Broken Windows', *Atlantic Monthly*, March, 29–38.

Wing, P. (forthcoming) *Disconnected Policing, Policing Disconnected Communities*, Cropwood Occasional Paper. Cambridge: Institute of Criminology.

Young, J. (1998) 'From Inclusive to Exclusive Society: Nightmares in the European Dream', in V. Ruggiero, N. South and I. Taylor (eds), *The New European Criminology*. London: Routledge, pp.64–91.

Young, J. (1999) *The Exclusive Society: Social Exclusion, Crime and Difference in Late Modernity*. London: Sage.

Chapter 9

Representations and realities in local crime prevention: some lessons from London and lessons for criminology

Simon Hallsworth

With multi-agency working characterising how organisations in the field of crime control relate and new criminologies, such as situational crime prevention, establishing what these organisations do, it is evident that the local structures of crime control have changed significantly. In attempting to grapple with the implications of these changes, criminologists have been confronted with an array of difficult questions. Do such changes mark the formation of more benevolent, rational, community-based and concerted attempts to address crime than was evident in police-centred models of the past? Or, from a more critical standpoint, are we witnessing a reconfiguration of state power that is neither benevolent or community-centred but dangerous and repressive?

Given that the world of multi-agency crime prevention partnerships are relatively new, these questions have tended to be answered in ways and that necessarily remain fairly speculative and general in their application. Detailed case studies remain more the exception than the rule in a world that is still attempting to discover whether realities of crime control equate both with political rhetoric and its theoretical representation.

For this reason empirical case studies of crime control remain very important and for the following reasons. First, they provide a vehicle by which the (invariably) positive legitimating political rhetoric can be judged by reference to empirical reality. Second, they provide an empirical test of theoretical conjecture by providing a space in which evidence can be adduced either to support or disconfirm more general claims. Finally, in their focus upon a particular place/space, they provide important insights into the specific ways different crime control systems operate in a world where regional variations remain, as Edwards and Hughes (this volume) note, significantly undertheorised.

This then takes me to the aim of this chapter, which is to use such a case study approach. I will use this study both to investigate the dynamics of crime control as it unfolds in a specific locality and to test a number of propositions that have been formulated about crime control more generally. The case study itself is derived from recent research undertaken in an inner-London borough. The research focus centred around two key issues: examining the rise of street crime in the area and evaluating the current strategies that have been deployed to confront it.

Given the 'local' focus of this book and not least the salience of street crime as a 'hot' political and media issue, the issues raised by this research appear entirely relevant to interpreting how effective current developments in crime control have been in realising their designated aims. It also provides a viable test case through which to investigate how far theoretical representation equates with hard reality. In substance and with this in mind, I will use this case study to address two specific questions:

1. Does the borough's response to street crime reflect the values that are supposed to underpin the local crime prevention effort? Are we, in other words, looking at a world in which crime policy is 'joined-up', 'holistic' and 'integrated and concerted' as specified in current government thinking (see Home Office, 1991, 1998).

2. Or are we witnessing, as more critical approaches to local crime control suggest, the formation of a control apparatus characterised by a dangerous escalation and intensification of state power? (see Coleman et al, this volume; Gordon, 1987; Cohen, 1985).

In seeking to answer these questions I will begin by providing some empirical data about the case study in question looking both at the socio-economic profile of the area and at problems of street crime within it. I will then consider more substantively the organisation of the response that has been directed within the borough to confront street crime. I will conclude by returning to the questions above which I will then examine in relation to this discussion.

The case study: facts and figures

The London borough studied for the purpose of this chapter can be characterised as a multi-ethnic, multiply deprived inner-city area in South-East London. It has a far higher rate of crime in general than the boroughs around it, and a far higher rate of street crime.

Following inner city disturbances in the late 1970s the area has been subject to a significant range of regeneration activity designed to improve the area, support local business and help support indigenous deprived populations. Despite these interventions unemployment still remains high and well above the average level for London. Though exclusion and deprivation are experienced among all ethnic groups, the local black population remains the most seriously disadvantaged.

Though offences such as vehicle crime and burglary have decreased in recent years, street crime has risen as an offence category across London. In the case of the borough studied for the purpose of this project, the rise has been significantly higher than in most other boroughs. In terms of age, perpetrators are predominately male, aged between 14 and 19. According to available statistics the overwhelming majority of perpetrators are also black with this group constituting 82 per cent of the offending population. While the victim population is drawn from across the age range it would appear concentrated among the 16–34 age group. The victim population also appears to be predominantly white, constituting about 65 per cent of this population, though there is also a significant degree of victimisation among younger people in the black population as well.

Given the salience of street crime in British social life (see Hall *et al* 1978), an analysis of the social response designed to address it appears a relevant way of testing the efficacy of current local prevention strategies. In the context of a government committed to 'getting tough on crime and tough on the causes', the area is an ideal laboratory to test how far this rhetoric in fact equates with the reality. In studying the response to street crime in the area, questions about community involvement and the relative 'benevolence' of social control responses can also be legitimately explored.

Responding to street crime

In examining the social response to street crime within the borough I will consider four broad categories of intervention. These collectively embody both reactive as well as more proactive approaches:

- the use of police;
- the judicial response;
- situational crime prevention measures;
- social crime prevention strategies.

In addition to the above I will also examine the way local effort is co-ordinated and integrated.

The use of police and their limits

When the media and politicians debate street crime then typically it is to the police that they turn and it is to the police that they and everyone else tend to look for solutions and not least quick results. An inevitable consequence of this is that it places the police under intolerable pressure to deliver and to deliver solutions quickly. As the performance of the police on street crime indicates, however, their overall impact on the problem remains limited.

To begin with, given inherently finite human resources, the police cannot be everywhere at once and consequently they cannot provide a comprehensive security canopy across the borough. As street crime rises, so too do other calls on police time which reduces the human resources they require to address street crime effectively. They also face the inherently difficult task of trying to be in the right place at the right time in a world in which the people they are doing their best to apprehend are doing their best to avoid them.

While police presence, particularly in high crime areas, can act as a visual deterrent, it also produces a hydraulic effect evident in corresponding rises in street crime elsewhere. This could either be in the form of a spatial or temporal displacement, and both have been regularly observed in the borough. As the police have also found, if effort is subsequently scaled back within a targeted zone, then the problem of street crime also has a habit of returning.

Most crimes that are solved by the police follow from information provided by the public. Though the police do receive useful intelligence from the public that do enable them to detect those involved in street crime, there are a number of factors that clearly limit the quality and quantity of information they receive. First, insensitive policing styles in the past (see Scarman 1981) have created a situation characterised by poor police/community relations, and this legacy, despite changes in policing styles, still lingers in certain sections of the local community.

Second, young people also find themselves socialised into a culture in which the police tend to be negatively perceived. As young people intimated in interviews conducted for the purpose of this research, it was not that they hated the police as individuals, it was rather that they had no language available to consider them in anything other than a negative way. While police tactics such as stop and search certainly reinforced this perception it was also evident that young people in the borough are also aware of and subject to a cultural injunction that holds that no information should or ought to be made available to the police. This culture of silence is also sustained and reproduced by the threat of real violence should anyone choose to transgress this principle.

On situational crime control and its limits

Recent decades have born witness to the creation of a new form of criminology. By nature it is pragmatic. Far from seeking grand solutions to the causes of crime it operates instead by seeking to discover technical solutions to specific problems by effectively attempting to design environments or goods in ways that minimise the threat posed by crime. Championed by the Home Office in the 1980s this form of criminology is often known as situational crime prevention. It is currently one of the most important tools used by local community safety providers in their attempt to reduce problems posed by crime. As a number of commentators have noted (Gilling 1997; Hughes 1998; Hughes *et al* 2002) it is now perhaps the single most important tactic in the armoury of crime control within local partnerships. The borough studied for the purpose of this research was no exception. If we now examine how situational crime prevention measures have impacted upon street crime in the borough, then as we shall see, its results are variable when assessed in terms of their impact. More specifically I would suggest that:

- the forms of situational prevention used to protect fixed targets in the area have helped make street crime more attractive as a crime option for motivated offenders;

- the forms of situational prevention that have been widely deployed to help prevent street crime are largely ineffective;

- forms of situational prevention that might have been applied to 'target harden' consumable goods targeted in street robbery have not been developed or deployed.

If we examine where most community safety effort has been concentrated, then research suggests that most has been concentrated on target hardening the environment (Crawford 1997; Hughes, 1998). The practical results of this policy are evident in a number of developments that have radically reshaped the organisation and design of the built environment. New buildings, for example, are designed in ways that take into account issues of situational defence. They consequently come complete with an array of features that are specifically designed to render them burglar-proof. In the case of commercial premises such as shops, this can include sophisticated alarm systems, burglar-proof locks, camera surveillance and steel shutters that fortify the building when it is closed. The attempt to design out crime also extends much further than single buildings and can include entire built environments such as shopping centres and corporate business districts. The use of this approach also extends into the way products, such as cars, are designed (Johnston, 2001).

Cumulatively, the impact of these initiatives has been to help reduce crime selectively by reducing the availability of lucrative targets. Statistically, the success of this enterprise can be seen both in the falling rate of burglary and car crime and by the relatively low level of crime identified in intensively fortified areas. In the case of Canary Wharf, for example, a heavily defended retail/business area in London, crime rates are minimal.

Paradoxically, an unforeseen circumstance of this strategy, I would suggest, has been to make offences such as street robbery far more likely, particularly in areas such as the borough studied. The reason for this is that street criminals are not stupid. They weigh up the relative costs and benefits associated with crime and many have come to the decision that street crime is less difficult to perpetrate than burglary and there remains little chance of detection. In addition, being young and poor they were unable to accumulate, as they also pointed out in interviews, the necessary resources to initiate more lucrative financial 'scams'.

If we now consider the situational measures that have been adopted to confront street crime in the borough, then this has principally centred around installing an intensive array of CCTV cameras. Though originally located across shopping precincts, current moves are also afoot to extend their deployment into many of the local housing estates. In pursuing this path it should be emphasised that the borough is following a strategy that is not only popular across the county, but a strategy well supported and funded by the government and the Home Office. As a strategy it is also an experiment in crime control that is quite unique to the UK. Other European countries, it could be pointed out, have not embraced the use of situational crime prevention techniques to anything like the same extent. Nor indeed has the US, which might be considered surprising given its otherwise punitive response to crime (Johnston, 2001).

While the use of CCTV installations has been proven to have some impact on crime rates, its utility as a street crime prevention tool in the borough has been mixed. Motivated offenders do consider issues such as where cameras are situated when they plan their crimes and consequently ensure that many of their victims are targeted outside the scan-scapes of the cameras. Cumulatively the hydraulic effect of this is once again to shift street crime elsewhere rather than diminish its prevalence. More disturbingly, it would appear from the testimony of the young offenders interviewed that they had also become well aware of the limits of CCTV as a detection device. This was often tied to their observation that its quality was often so bad and even if a crime was caught on the camera, law enforcement agencies would not be able to recognise anyone from the footage. Street robbers also learned from experience that they were so fleet of foot that they would be long gone before the camera observers could call upon law enforcement agencies to intervene.

Where situational attempts to design out street crime might have worked, these have not been initiated. If mobile phones for example – perhaps the most important object of desire to street robbers – had been designed in ways that made them more difficult to use, then self-evidently they would not be stolen. The corporate producers of this technology, however, did not consider or ignored the criminogenic consequences of the technology they were producing, and this error was compounded in turn by government failure to regulate the industry. And this might be considered odd because the lessons of failing to adequately consider such issues have been well known for a long period of time as the case of car crime well indicates.

The judicial option and its limits

Though the police are often seen as the key institution in the fight against street crime, the role of the judicial system and the organisations that support it must also be considered of fundamental importance. Cumulatively these bodies perform three key functions. First, in the act of punishment dispensed to offenders through the courts, a message is sent out to those convicted that they erred and should desist from further offending. This message is, moreover, also broadcast to other would-be street robbers. To ensure that offenders who have been caught understand the deterrent message they are supposed to receive, they are also subject to a range of other interventions designed to ensure that they are effectively rehabilitated, or at least are not possessed of a desire to re-offend (Garland, 2001).

In terms of the sanctions that the state deploys to deter and punish those guilty of street crime then these range from the benign forms of intervention evident in community sanctions through to what may be regarded as harsh and punitive custodial sentences. With the formation of Youth Offending Teams, steps have been taken to provide an array of interventions that attempt to keep young offenders under 18 from custody, such as supervision orders (though detention is also often used for this age category in the case of street crime). For those over 18 charged with street crime, the sentence is almost always custodial and often lasts for around three years. Whether or not the offence was first time made little difference to the pattern of disposal as we found in our research. Ethnicity did, however, as 96 per cent of young black males received custodial sentences as opposed to a figure of 68 per cent for the white population. The ferocity underpinning this punitive response, it could also be noted, made the tariff for street robbery far higher than that for assault.

With regard to the question of whether this get-tough policy is appropriate and useful, a number of fairly critical observations could be made. First, if the aim of the punitive response was to deter street crime then self-evidently it has failed as the rising tide of street crime offences testify. Second, from research conducted among young offenders, it was evident that far from significantly reducing the will to offend on the part of those receiving custodial sentences, prison appeared to have had the opposite effect. Recidivism rates remain at around 60 per cent, and according to the testimony of young people, far from the experience acting to prevent crime, the experience placed them in a context where they were able to learn a number of new techniques to prosecute it. Testimony from young people also indicated that in the process of learning street crime, primary influences on their criminal careers were those who had already been processed through the penal system. Far from preventing street crime, it could well be argued that the current array of judicial solutions, in their coercive form at least, exacerbate the very problem they are supposed to prevent, in this case by returning young men to their community as fully confirmed career criminals.

On social attempts to prevent street crime and their limits

The responses to street crime considered so far relate to attempts to address the problem either by preventing already motivated offenders from going about their unlawful business or by dealing with them once they have offended and have been caught. In this section I am going to consider various social attempts within the borough to prevent young people from becoming motivated offenders to begin with. The kind of strategies that would fall within the rubric of this form of intervention would include:

- attempts to warn and inform young people about the dangers and moral consequences of rule breaking;
- providing activities so that young people can sublimate their urges in more socially benevolent ways;
- increasing the life chances of young people and their families in ways that reduce the forms of exclusion and deprivation that constitute the structural basis of street crime as an adaptive strategy.

Social attempts to prevent crime can take more ostensibly criminological forms in so far as they are characterised by a conscious attempt to reduce criminal behaviour through a particular policy. They may also be non-criminological in design but nevertheless play a key crime reduction role. Attempts to provide information to young people about crime, for example, would be an instance of the former, while using regeneration funding to support marginal communities might be considered an example of the latter. In what follows, using the three broad character-isations of social crime prevention outlined above, let us consider how each functions to reduce offending behaviour in general and street crime in particular.

Educating and informing young people about crime and the criminal justice system

While young offenders claimed in interviews that they were aware that street crime was a bad thing to do, they nevertheless came to do it anyway and growing numbers of young people appear to be making the same choice – as rising rates of street crime testify. While they had internalised part of the message the wider society would have wanted them to register (that street crime was a bad thing) evidently many young men had not received the message in a way that meant anything substantially to the choices they made. If we now examine why, then we need to attend clearly to a number of problems evident in the content of the messages that are mediated, how crime prevention messages are mediated and those responsible for mediating them.

If we consider precisely what anti-street crime messages are mediated, the first observation that can be made is that those disseminated to young people were not mediated in a clear or consistent way. The reason for this would appear to be that the borough had no clear or coherent policy. To this could be added the observation that the dissemination of such messages was considered the sole business of parents and guardians and, in an uncoordinated and secondary role, teachers in schools. Because there is no clear and coherent agreement between various stakeholders in the area about what such a strategy should be, no consistent message or information has been provided. The upshot of this is that each school adopts a more or less 'go it alone' policy on the issue of crime prevention, and outside of periodic visits by police officers to the schools who would deign to admit them, there is no real consistent crime prevention message. While the free market certainly promulgated the message that consumption was good (which helped provide a motive for street crime) it could be observed that beyond urging people to consume more it has no moral principles attached. As for the pronouncement of moral entrepreneurs such as politicians, these were considered irrelevant to the life worlds of most young people.

The outcome of this is that young people were often left with little understanding of the criminal justice system, how it operates, or what it will do to them if they broke the law and were caught. They also know little about what happens to victims who are victimised, or what happens when weapons are used in events like armed robbery. Though schools certainly have anti-bullying policies, they were not consistent with one another. Evidence from the interviews conducted with young offenders also suggests that young people were not provided with the information that would allow them to access the criminal justice system when they themselves were victimised.

Working with and for young people

While the decision motivated offenders make to target victims will occur independently of whether the local authority provides an array of more gainful activities, the provision of such services still remains important, not least to multiply deprived and disadvantaged young people most at risk of becoming involved in street crime. First, the provision of a wide and comprehensive set of activities for young people can be viewed as part of a process of social investment in young people's lives independently of other reasons that might be used to justify it. They deserve to be able to have designated safe and interesting areas to play and an array of leisure and social activities they can pursue if they so desire. Such spaces also provide opportunities, however, for implicit educational messages about life – including anti-crime messages. By engaging in activities with others, including other young people and adults, positive ties of interdependence can be forged that may act to offset the alienating and anomic tendencies of the wider free-market society.

Like many boroughs in London, the state of the youth service in the borough and, not least, its contribution to community safety effort remains questionable. It is certainly not able in its current form to actively perform the crime prevention role outlined above. There are a number of reasons that may be posited to account for this. First, in common with other boroughs, the idea of a youth service organised around the comprehensive provision of youth clubs has been questioned and abandoned. Second, this questioning has moved hand in hand with a series of sustained budget cuts that have literally decimated the forms of provision the council did operate or support. Third, in the face of financial retrenchment, the local state has responded by effectively offloading responsibility for youth provision onto a voluntary sector, ill-equipped to undertake the infrastructural support role now being foisted upon it. Fourth, given access to inherently limited and precarious funding regimes, those seeking to work productively with young people are forced to engage in what amounts to ugly beauty competitions with each other in order to sustain often minimal funding for their activities.

While by no means decrying the activities of those who do provide services for young people, questions also have to be posed as to whether they meet the needs of all their potential consumers and not least fulfil what may be considered a relevant community safety role. While organisations such as the scouts, guides, army and navy cadets and woodcraft folk are worthy and continue to attract a population of young people, it is by no means evident that their appeal is particularly high to high-risk populations in deprived areas – the populations, in other words, most at risk of becoming engaged in street crime. Though recognising that new spaces in place of old youth clubs need to be constructed, there remain few bold experiments that are orientated at constructing such environments. Many of the kinds of activities that high-risk groups might value, such as gyms and access to studios and electronic music equipment, are either lacking or remain prohibitively expensive – as young offenders themselves pointed out in interviews.

Regenerating communities

If we consider street crime as in part a Mertonian adaptive strategy to thwarted consumption (Young 1999), and thwarted consumption a function of real and rising patterns of relative deprivation in the borough, then self-evidently an important crime reduction strategy must lie in reducing these factors. If we now attend to the social policies that might help achieve this pattern of reduction, then these are embraced within the general rubric of social regeneration measures that have been deployed within the borough for the last two decades. Though the crime reducing aspect of social regeneration measures has never featured as a formally recognised aim of social regeneration, or indeed a principle aim, it is evident that such measures are very important in community safety effort more generally.

While headline figures attest to the inward investment of substantial sums of money in the borough in the last two decades, if we consider how spending priorities have been established and the impact of these regeneration measures, it is by no means evident that a significant crime reduction role can be observed. In fact I will suggest that the uneven and unintended consequences of regeneration have in fact contributed to the street crime problem.

If we consider the scope of regeneration expenditure then it is evidently substantial, as the following figures testify

- SRB £250 million (1994–2007)
- Housing £169 million (1998–2002)
- Health Action Zone £25 million (1998–2005)
- Education Action Zone £3 million (1998–2002)
- New Deal for the Communities £50 million (2001–2011)
- URBAN 2 £16 million (2000–2006)

Regeneration measures have also been implemented with seemingly the best intentions in mind, stressing as they do the importance of 'partnership', 'sustainability', 'people focus', 'work as a route out of poverty', 'connectivity', 'opportunity' and 'influence'. As the local authority and not least the deprived communities have come to recognise, however, the social impact of regeneration schemes has been uneven and not everyone has benefited.

As the regeneration literature provided by the council notes, a considerable slice of the regeneration pie has been spent on improving the environment through physical regeneration projects. Substantial investment in retail has also occurred. To an extent the regeneration pro-gramme has worked to make a once notorious inner-city area attractive both to business and to new professionals who have moved into what is recognised locally as an increasingly desirable place to live. This 'success', however, also comes with significant costs attached. On one hand this renaissance has bought into the area the kind of population which now constitute the majority of the victim population. As new (predominately white) professionals have arrived, they have also pushed up land and property prices. These are now well beyond the reach of poor populations who as a consequence are left with no alternative than to occupy what remains an area characterised by serious pockets of highly deprived and physically denuded estates.

On the downside the regeneration effort has not offset the pattern of existing deprivation in the area to a significant extent, or at least to an extent to which it might impact on rates of crime. Nor has it compensated for economic changes that still act to produce a highly inequitable distribution of life chances in the area. The facts are stark. As regeneration literature points out, the area studied is the only borough in central London to have experienced a net loss of employment over the period 1991–8. The report also states that the area has 'the highest number of unemployed claimants in the central London area across all age groups and for all durations'. Though unemployment and deprivation remains a factor impacting negatively on the health and well-being of all ethnic communities in the borough, its impact has been experienced acutely by the area's indigenous black population, which unsurprisingly make up the vast majority of street crime offenders.

Let us now draw together the unintended consequences of regeneration policy. First, by making the borough more attractive to professionals and business, while secondly doing little to profoundly impact the structural conditions of deprivation experienced by local communities, the cumulative and unintended effect has been to accentuate relative deprivation as opposed to reduce it. As a strategy that might be expected to reduce the social conditions that provoke criminal adaptations, the net effect has been to accentuate the very conditions that provoke it. Hell, as they say, is often built out of the best intentions.

On the integration and coordination of community safety effort

Let me now conclude this analysis of control effort by examining issues pertinent to its coordination and integration. In the era of holistic, joined-up policy and sustained multi-agency working, just how holistic and joined-up has community safety effort in the area proved to be?

At first sight, the borough may be considered to have met most of the terms of the 1998 Crime and Disorder Act in the organisation of its community safety effort. It has a crime unit attached to the local authority, it has constructed a Youth Offending Team and has formalised multi-agency partnership working through the creation of a Crime and Disorder Executive and Community Safety Partnership. It also has a dedicated series of working groups in the field of community safety, not least among which is a street crime strategy group.

If we turn to consider how this edifice of control operates and locates its effort to confront street crime, however, a number of issues could be raised regarding its effectiveness. Cumulatively, as we shall see, they also act to subvert the aim of confronting street crime in an effective and concerted way.

First, while multi-agency working is a feature of the borough, not all relevant agencies are represented. Education and Youth Services have tended to avoid contact with community safety providers, even though their role is of fundamental importance. This absence could be considered a product of three factors: first ignorance of the implications of section 17 of the Crime and Disorder Act 1998; second, a pervasive belief that the council's crime reduction role is solely the responsibility of its crime unit; third, and this is particularly an issue with local schools, the autonomy they have been conceded in order to 'free' them from local authority control, means that they have no obligation to become involved in collective efforts to confront crime if they choose not to do so. Many, it could be observed, have chosen not to.

For that matter, local political elites also, in the face of rising crime figures, appear unwilling to associate themselves with community safety providers, in a context where efforts to confront the spectre of street crime do not appear to be working. In fact political elites in the area have favoured maintaining a complete distance from law enforcement agencies altogether. Practically, this has resolved itself in non-attendance at multi-agency partnership boards and, in the case of the ruling party, an unwillingness to meet with the metropolitan police commander, even when this was requested. Local politics and crime also do not appear to be linked even if high crime in the borough is perceived both locally and nationally as a serious issue.

Though community safety is a term often 'bandied about' in the criminological literature to describe local crime effort, in many respects, if by the term is meant a holistic approach to the problems posed by street crime, then it is hard to suggest that this can be observed in practice. Government established priorities have typically privileged situational prevention, not least through the provision of significant sums of money that local authorities are then obligated to bid for. As for more proactive measures then, as we have seen above, those who might be expected to be involved either absent themselves from the policy-making table, or are so autonomous that they are not obligated to sit at the table at all. The sheer proliferation of funding streams and the orientation towards short-term funding also subvert ideas of collective effort or effort that works towards securing long-term goals. The number of strings typically attached to projects funded by government, working as they do in conjunction with systemic biases that favour situational prevention, also prevent a wider and more holistic agenda being secured, because the necessary autonomy local partnerships require to plan in this way is effectively subverted.

Learning the lessons

If we now consider the implications of this excursion into the politics of street crime, what are the lessons we can derive from this? The first and most obvious point that can be made is that political legitimations and criminological representations do not adequately represent the reality of the world they aspire to describe. For if we attend to reality as I have described it above, then what we find is a world that departs significantly from its theoretical representation.

If we examine issues ranging from the way effort is located, the funding of crime reduction initiatives at the point of practice and the integration and coordination of the crime control system I have described, then what we find is not a particularly holistic integrated or rational response to street crime. On the contrary what we find instead is a disjointed, underfunded, labyrinthine edifice that does little to address the real social forces that propel poor people into crime. In its practice what we have here are control structures that remain far more attuned (as they have always been) to dealing with the symptoms of crime as opposed to its causes.

Let me spell this out and by so doing summarise my findings. Though the problem of street crime in the area has its roots in deprivation and escalating relative deprivation, nothing has meaningfully been undertaken by way of addressing these structural causes. As we have seen, regeneration effort not only made little impact on the extent of inequalities, it actually exacerbated them and by so doing created a highly criminogenic environment in which street crime has thrived. As to the favoured solutions – sanctioned by government and embedded in terms of local practice – then these have not been particularly successful. The role of the police, as I have argued, remains limited in what it can achieve, while situational defences have either provoked more street crime or remain unable to prevent it. As regards the judicial response evident in the visceral sentences now routinely handed out by the local courts, even if we ignore the racial bias, there remains little evidence to suggest that it is working to reduce street crime. At the same time, there is compelling evidence to suggest that they work very well indeed to return confirmed and motivated offenders to the local area. Far then from posing a 'holistic' and 'joined-up' approach to the problem of crime, what we find instead is effort channelled in the direction of a reactive and at times highly oppressive system of control.

If the liberal conceit of an emerging rational and democratic approach to crime is wrong, so too are critical theories who want to see in the emerging configuration of control a system characterised by a progressive widening of what Cohen termed the 'social control net' (Cohen 1985). For while recent changes might intimate the presence of a 'coercive state', the rise of locally-based crime prevention structures do not herald a dramatic extension of state power, or a wider dispersal of discipline we might regard as specifically dangerous or ominous.

If we return to the case study above then the lesson I derive is just how ineffective current expenditures of force actually are. The role of the police, as I have indicated, is limited. In fact from interviews conducted with local offenders it became evident that far from hating the police, they were typically viewed in terms that saw them, less an active enemy so much as a less than credible opposition. While the prisons deal punitively with offenders, very few in fact are actually caught to begin with.

While the eye of the camera has certainly altered the urban landscape, before we journey too far down the road of seeing in such initiatives the formation of a repressive surveillance state, we need to be a little more nuanced in how we interpret such initiatives. First, as a strategy to confront street crime their use has been, as I suggested above, very limited. And while this message has certainly not reached the ear of a government who still wishes to extend their use further, I would argue that what we are witnessing is nothing less than a 'white elephant' in the making. Street criminals simply do their business elsewhere when the cameras hone in upon them. They are also incredibly expensive and time consuming to monitor effectively. As their failure becomes more noted, so the willingness to fund them indefinitely might well diminish. This I grant is conjecture. I wait with anticipation to see how these observations play out in practice.

Far from conceiving what looks like 'soft-edge' developments such as community safety in Cohen's terms as indicative of an ominous dispersal of discipline, I prefer to interpret them in a more benign way.

This would also chime well, I believe, with the benevolent and non-repressive motives of most local crime control practitioners. People like community safety officers, workers in organisations such as Youth Offending Teams and Drug Action Teams as well as outreach workers, youth workers and other support workers do not see themselves as agents of an oppressive state.

The problem lies in the kind of world these control agents occupy. It is not that the forms of power they distribute are of themselves destined to be negative. It is, rather, that the resources, independence and autonomy they require to develop a more humane alternative to what currently endures does not exist given the institutional constraints they confront. Given that they remain relentlessly positioned as little more than peripheral supports in a complex dictated by the unholy trinity of law enforcement, situational prevention and incarceration, it is difficult to see how a more effective distribution of power can be constructed given these constraints, or at least a power complex that is truly democratic, socially just and effective.

If this is accepted, then critical criminology needs to rethink how it views the exercise of power and control as it is mediated at the local level. For while I agree that it remains often coercive, it is not intensive or comprehensive in its remit. In fact, as I have argued, what we have is something that remains too often incoherent, inappropriate and ineffective: an exercise of power of the wrong kind exercised in the wrong way. The problem is not that of there being too much power, but not enough of the right kind of power exercised in the right way.

Conclusion

Far from seeing emergent crime prevention measures as characterised by a coherent and integrated approach to crime, or indeed by an intensive and extensive regulation of social life, I will argue that, in terms of my case study, they represent ineffective and inappropriate investments in social power. They remain ineffective not so much because the ambitions of the control agents who manage the business of crime control are suspect. On the contrary, while many of their intentions are worthy, they are subverted in a crime complex which still persists in addressing problems of crime by reference to a crude repertoire of interventions from which meaningful social solutions exist, if at all, simply as a fringe element.

Ghandi was once asked what he thought of British civilisation. He replied that he thought it was 'a good idea'. For the same reason I also believe that a number of innovations in local crime control are potentially useful and perhaps even just. Provision does need to be comprehensive and an appropriate balance does need to be forged between reactive and proactive approaches to crime. Decision making also needs to be locally-based and service providers ought to be fully accountable to the communities they serve. These principles are general and few beyond the odd authoritarian would have difficulty in accepting them. As this case study indicates, however, there remains a considerable distance to go before brutal reality can be made to equate with professed principles. To bridge this distance certainly requires far greater changes than have currently been attempted. Let us hope that this deficit can be rectified.

References

Cohen, S. (1985) *Visions of Social Control*. Cambridge: Polity.
Coleman, R., Sim, J. and Whyte, D. (2002) Chapter 5 this volume.
Crawford, A. (1994) 'The Partnership Approach to Community Crime Prevention: Corporatism at the Local Level', *Social and Legal Studies*, 3, 497–519.
Crawford, A. (1997) *The Local Governance of Crime*. Oxford: Clarendon Press.
Edwards, A. and Hughes, G. (2002) Chapter 1 this volume.
Garland, D. (2001) *The Culture of Control*. Oxford: Oxford University Press.
Gilling, D. (1994) 'Multi-Agency Crime: Some Barriers to Collaboration', *Howard Journal*, 33 (3), 246–57.
Gilling, D. (1997) *Crime Prevention*. London: UCL Press.
Gordon, P. (1987) 'Community Policing'. in P. Scraton (ed.), *Law, Order and the Authoritarian State*. Milton Keynes: Open University Press.
Hall, S., Critcher, C., Jefferson, T., Clarke, J. and Roberts, B. (1978) *Policing the Crisis*. London: Macmillan.
Home Office (1991) *Safer Communities: The Local Delivery of Crime Prevention through the Partnership Approach*. London: HMSO.
Home Office (1998) *Guidance on Statutory Crime and Disorder Partnerships*. London: HMSO.
Hope, T. and Shaw, M. (1988) *Communities and Crime Reduction*. London: HMSO.
Hughes, G. (1998) *Understanding Crime Prevention: Social Control, Risk and Late Modernity*. Buckingham: Open University Press.
Hughes, G., McLaughlin, E. and Muncie, J. (eds) (2002) *Crime Prevention and Community Safety: New Directions*. London: Sage.
Johnston, L. (2001) *Crime Management and Prevention* Portsmouth: ICJS, University of Portsmouth.
Liddle, M. and Gelsthorpe, L. (1994) *Inter-Agency Crime Prevention: Further Issues*, CPU Paper 52, 53. London: HMSO.

Scarman, Lord (1981) *The Scarman Report: The Brixton Disorders 10–12 April 1981.* Harmondsworth: Penguin Books.

Young, J. (1999) *The Exclusive Society: Social Exclusion, Crime and Difference in Late Modernity.* London: Sage.

Index

philosophies, community crime
prevention, 170–2
piecemeal social engineering, 63, 64,
68, 78–9
Pikies, 126
polarisation, rural villages, 126
police
crisis of public confidence, 190–1
data, crime and disorder
partnerships, 96–7
Merseyside, 98–9, 100
street crime, 200–1
superintendents, 110
Thames Valley, 12, 131–2
Police and Criminal Evidence Act
(1984), 25
policing
city centre, 91
coercive, 11–12
community, 25, 28, 77–8
policy
discourses, 120
experimental evaluation, 71–2
measures, transferability of, 144
realistic evaluation, 74–6
translating, coalitions, 156
see also crime policies; neoliberal
policies
political action
belief systems, 155
understanding possibilities of, 161
political agency, strategic dilemmas,
155–7
political authority, devolution of, 10
political culture, Thames Valley,
129–31
political economic processes,
governmentality narratives, 121
political elites, street crime, 210
political power, 140–1
political trends, crime control and
criminal justice, 169
politics
of community, 37–9
see also local politics
pollution, Mersey basin, 95
poor, perceived as social parasites, 169
Popper, Karl, 63–7
post–Crime and Disorder Act
partnerships, 150–4
postmodern reflections, crime

prevention and community safety,
46–60
postmodernism, political and social
theory, 39
power, reluctance to relinquish, 187
Powers of Freedom, 38
practice, realistic evaluation, 76–8
primary prevention, 24
Priority Estates Project, 183–4, 188–9
private sector, situational crime
prevention, 90–1
private sphere, statization of, 154
problem definition, crime prevention,
172–6
problem–oriented policing, 77
project effect, 148
property crime, 171
pseudo–events, 52
public consultation, 25, 186–7, 189
public information, solving crime, 200
public services, targeting hot–spots of
crime, 12
public space
anti–social use, 159
CCTV, 184
public–private partnerships, 4, 140
punishment, street crime, 203
punitive powers, Merseyside policy,
100
Putnam, Robert, 58

racialised discourse, community
policing, 25
radical communitarianism, 32–3, 39
radical criminologists, community–
based strategies, 28
rational choice theory, 155
rationalities, rediscovery of
community, 54–5
Reading, 127–8
real inventiveness, possibilities of, 34
realistic evaluation, 72–8, 79
reality checks, permanent campaign,
51
recurring ambivalence, liberal
governmentality, 155–6
Reducing Offending, 47
regeneration
of communities, 207–9
Docklands Regeneration
programme, 181–3

state bureaucracies, social contract,
141, 142
status ZerO, 179
strategic alliances, 102
strategic dilemmas
community–based crime control,
145–54
outer–housing estates, 158
political agency, 155–7
street crime
'bestreetsafe' campaign, 93
judicial option, 203–4, 211–12
responding to, 199–200
situational crime prevention, 201–3
social attempts to prevent, 204–9
use of police, 200–1
street justice, 1
Structure of Scientific Revolutions, The, 65

target hardening, 24, 201–2
targeting
competition, 151
crime control, 118–19
policy and resources, 12, 123–4, 133
Taylor, Ian, 97
technology, crime control, 184–5
Thames Valley, 124–5
leverage of resources, 12
liberal enclaves, 131–2
local political culture, 129–31
rural socio–economic change, 125–6
skills gap, 127–9
urban socio–economic change, 126–7
Thames Valley Partnership, 132
Thames Valley Police, 12, 131–2
Third Way, 3, 37, 55, 123
thwarted consumption, 207–8
top–down approach, regeneration, 181–3
Townwatch, 91
transnational corporation, 115
travelling populations, 126
travelling victims, 78
tribalism, 182

unemployment
intergenerational, Bladon, 179
rural, 126
unity of the sciences, 64
urban elites, resources channelled
towards, 94
urban governments, 31
urban regeneration *see* regeneration
urban security, 29, 33
urban socio–economic change, 126–7
utopian social engineering, 63–4

value choice, criminalization, 5
victims
assumptions about, 175
crime and disorder, 78
vigilantism, 1–2, 3
violence, by OSD, 99
violent crime, 171
volunteering, 58
voting apathy, 50

'what works' movement
emphasis on, 23, 46–9
false universality, 13
loosening grip of, 59
white underclass, 26
whitening, of racialised crime and
disorder, 26
workplaces, monitoring by camera, 104

young people
educating about crime and
criminal justice system, 205–6
negative perception of police, 200–1
working with and for, 206–7
youth crime
community–based crime control, 157–60
secure accommodation, 57
withdrawal of funding, 94–5
Youth Offending Teams, 204, 209

zero–tolerance tactics, 57, 118